9

ST. FRANCIS XAVIER

ST. FRANCIS XAVIER

APOSTLE OF THE EAST

BY

MARGARET YEO

NEW YORK

THE MACMILLAN COMPANY

1932

PREFACE

MY most grateful thanks are due to all those who, by great personal help and kindness, have aided me in the making of this book, among them the Most Reverend Alban Goodier, S.J.; Father G. Schurhammer, S.J. (Bonn); Père A. Brou, S.J. (Paris); Padre Francisco Escalada, S.J., and Padre Irala, S.J. (Javier); Padre E. Elordug, S.J. (Loyola); Father G. B. Walkerley, S.J. (Heythrop); and Mr. G. Burns, S.J. (Rome).

To Mr. Gerard Hopkins of the Oxford University Press, for his kind permission to reproduce Fr. Gerard Manley Hopkins's translation of the hymn *O Deus ego amo te;* also to Dorothy Frances Gurney, for her delightful versifications of the Basque songs, and to Charles Vincent Walkerley for reading the proofs.

MARGARET YEO.

November 11, 1931.

CONTENTS

CONTENTS

ST. FRANCIS XAVIER

CHAPTER I

HOME AND FAMILY

ALONG the coast of Guipuzcoa and in the mountains the strata of the brown sandstone rocks sink sharply towards the Bay of Biscay, as if some sudden subsidence of the ocean bed had dislocated their original horizontal lines. Instinctively the fancy turns to the legend found in all the folklore of southern and western Europe of a lost world submerged beneath the sunset sea. The Hesperides, Tir-nan-Og, Avalon—perhaps they are broken fragments of memory of the continent of Atlantis. Perhaps too the Basques are the survivors of that prehistoric cataclysm.

Ethnology declares that they have no racial affinity with any existing European peoples, but the question remains unsolved whether they are remnants of the original Mediterranean race pushed west by successive immigrations of later races or an Atlantean band who escaped the deluge.

The Basque will tell you proudly that his language is the oldest as well as the most difficult in the world, and that a Basque learns Chinese and Japanese more quickly than any other "foreign devil." It is said too that one of the early Jesuit missionaries to Mexico learnt to speak the Aztec tongue in a fortnight because of its likeness to his native Basque.

The "untamable Cantabrians," as Horace calls them, remained unconquered by Hamilcar, Hannibal and Scipio Africanus. Only after fierce and prolonged guerilla war-

1

fare were they subdued under Augustus, and even then a permanent garrison of three legions was needed to keep the peace in northern Spain.

> The legions from Rome
> Would conquer Biscay,
> But the warcry is raised
> Through the length of Biscay.
> All the world may Octavian sway,
> But Lecobidi is lord of Biscay.

So ran the defiant war-song.

When southern Spain had become so Romanised that it had forgotten its own tongue the Basque language, customs, and privileges remained unchanged. Proud, fiercely independent, fearless, practical, yet keenly conscious of the supernatural, the Basque, once converted, treasured his religion as he treasured his freedom. "To say Basque is to say Catholic," declared the proverb. All their folklore, even its pre-Christian beliefs and customs, is tinged with Catholicism. All the old dances and pastorals symbolise the unending struggle between good and evil, light and darkness.

Three of the seven Basque provinces—Soule, Basse Navarre, and Labourde—lay on the northern slopes of the Pyrenees and the south-west coast of France. Of the Spanish provinces Alava, Biscay, and Guipuzcoa were annexed in the twelfth century by the kings of Castile, the kingdom of Navarre alone retaining its independence.

It was overrun in turns by Visigoths, Moors, and Franks. Its first historical King, Sancho Garcia, fixed his capital at Pamplona in 905; and three hundred years later Sancho the Strong, by his defeat and capture of the Caliph En Nasr at Navas de Tolosa, freed north Spain for ever from the infidel. The chains which encircled the Caliph's tent were made into the intricate ironwork which encloses the chapel of the Santa Cruz in the cloisters of Pamplona cathedral, and were immortalised in the arms of Navarre: on a field *gules,* chains *or* charged with an emerald *vert.*

From 1234 the royal family was largely French by blood and sympathy. Charles the Bad, grandson of Louis X and contemporary of the Black Prince, became infamous for his diabolical combination of personal beauty and great mental gifts with the most atrocious crimes and vices.

When Navarre acknowledged the suzerainty of Castile in the fourteenth century she retained all her ancient *fueros* (charters of local rights), all decisions on land, taxation, free trade and the power to conclude treaties with foreign nations. The Junta, a Parliament elected by universal suffrage, continued to sit in the Sala Preciosa of the Pamplona cathedral.

Pamplona—the Roman Pompoelo—stands on the Arga, from whose rushing yellow waters its old grey walls rise like cliffs. On a hill the eleventh-century Gothic cathedral towers above a tangle of narrow streets, little altered, but for its baroque west front, since Francis Xavier was there; the splendid choir-stalls of dark oak were carved by Miguel de Anchueta after young Francis had ridden north to Paris, but he must have known almost everything else in the dark building. Charles III, who restored the cathedral in 1397, lies in the choir beside his wife, Eleanor of Castile, a lion at his feet, two small dogs at hers. Round their alabaster tomb is a long procession which includes two brothers, both cardinals, their hats painted bright red. Over a side-altar is a fifteenth-century painting, like so much early Spanish work oddly reminiscent of the contemporary Flemish school in its intimate detail and sober domesticity.

Near it is a wonderful old crucifix before which Francis is said often to have prayed. The wooden figure is sharply carved, every bone and muscle showing, the rigidity of human agony and death sublimated by divine endurance and dignity. The base of the right foot, worn away by the kisses of the faithful, has been replaced by one of shining silver.

In a corner of the cloisters, with their flamboyant Gothic tracery supporting a typically Spanish flat roof of ridged red tiles, is the chapel of the Santa Cruz and the iron scrolls made from the Moorish tent chains. Beyond it are the Sala Preciosa and the old refectory of the canons, now a chapel dedicated to St. Francis Xavier.

Nothing remains of the citadel defended by Ignatius of Loyola against the French army in which Francis's two elder brothers were fighting; only the name of the great Plaza del Castillo, surrounded by its covered arcade, under which old canons hurry on cold wet days, muffled to the eyes in their circular black cloaks.

Down a little passage from the square is the Calle Zapatería (Street of the Shoemakers), and half-way along it stands a great house of rose-red brick decorated with horizontal bands of blue and white tiles whose geometrical designs are pure Moorish. Over the oak door, iron-barred and studded, is carved a coat of arms, golden diamonds on a scarlet ground. In 1500 the blazon was: on a field *azure,* two bendlets, and two crescents *or,* the arms of the wife of its owner, Arnalt Periz de Jassu, Francis's paternal grandfather.

Here lived Francis's father, Juan de Jassu, alcaide of the Cortes and intimate friend and counsellor of the young Queen Catherine and her husband, Jean d'Albret. Here too lived Francis himself when studying at the university of Pamplona.

The house is let out in tenements, and though much has perished from poverty and neglect it has escaped modernisation. All that remains is as old as Francis's day or older. The ground floor, as in all Basque houses, was devoted to stores and livestock—horses, mules, goats, oxen. Above it a narrow balcony leads to the kitchen. On the other side stairs with steps of brick or stone, wood-edged, mount to the living-rooms. They are large and lofty, the wooden ceilings supported on elaborately-carved beams—all the woodwork is of that Navarrese oak so celebrated that Philip II would allow no other in his buildings. Open fires smoke and flicker on stone hearths backed with heavy hammered-iron plates five hundred years old. Over them jut great projecting chimney-hoods.

It is easy to imagine Francis coming in from the class-rooms on one of those winter days when the wind from the Pyrenees nips with wolf-like tooth, and sitting down to thaw frozen hands and feet on one of the high-backed wooden settles running out each side of the hearth.

The top windows are unglazed and the sleeping quarters are large alcoves with little ventilation and less light. In the one said to have been Francis's is shown the shelf where he kept his books and on which he stood his little oil lamp when working late into the night.

At Sangüesa, twenty-five miles east of Pamplona, was the college in which Francis is supposed to have studied as a boy before coming to Pamplona; and through Sangüesa he would have ridden on his way home from the capital.

From Pamplona the road runs straight as a Roman way

through one of those wide valleys from which Navarre takes her name (*nava,* a hill-ringed vale, *erri,* country). Beyond the fields, over whose brown earth the young corn draws a thin green veil, rise the grey mountains, their rocks like scars showing through a torn covering of low grey scrub and the nut-sweet yellow gorse. The sheep and black-and-white goats grazing beside little milky waterfalls are guarded by lean, wolf-like dogs, while old shepherds, grey and gnarled as the olive-trees below them, lean on long ash-staffs and watch the slow passage of hooded carts drawn by oxen, or riders perched high on scarlet saddle-bags between the heavy panniers of patient little asses.

The road climbs between great woods of pine and beech, oak and chestnut. Below in the valley, among groups of poplars, villages huddle round the square, deeply-buttressed churches with low towers, built, like the houses, of local brown sandstone. Near them black silhouettes of cypresses mark the graveyards, and a convenient angle of the church wall often forms the inevitable pelota court.

Still the road climbs till woods give way to rock splashed with a white foam of blackthorn blossom, and high in the pale blue sky two eagles hang motionless. Suddenly, far below, the Irati appears as if from the bowels of the mountains, and, wide, rushing, yellow-green, it sweeps past the towers and battlements of the walls of Sangüesa.

The little city, which dates back to Roman times, was granted special privileges by Alfonso the Fighter (1132), and in Francis's time had a college whose curriculum ranged from infant-classes to grammar, rhetoric and the humanities.

On the left of the narrow Calle Mayor is the eleventh-century church of Santa Maria la Real with its wonderful carved façade and porch showing the Last Judgement. Inside—it is dark, mouldy, mysterious, like all the Basque country churches—is the ancient statue of our Lady of Sangüesa, carved in wood, dressed in a silver cloak, crowned and holding the Child crowned, a statue before which the boy Francis knelt daily when staying in the house of Pedro Ortiz, his mother's father, just opposite.

Like that of his other grandfather in Pamplona, the house has a Moorish look, in spite of the intricate Gothic tracery of the stone mullions. It is built of huge blocks of stone up to the level of the arched entrance, surmounted by the usual carved blazon. Above that it is of cocoa-coloured bricks. The beams of the wide overhanging eaves rest on magnificent carved wooden supports, and along what remains of the upper storey runs a long line of arches. Even in its present half-ruined state it has an air of rich but sober splendour, an austere dignity as if its crumbling brick and stone remembered that they had protected the childhood of Doña Maria de Azpilcueta, mother of the saint, and of the schoolboy Francis himself.

At the end of the long Calle Mayor the road to Javier climbs the hill. In Francis's day it was only a rough bridle-path. Even to-day, when covered at breakneck speed in a dilapidated car, it is not exactly a bed of roses. Up and down it sweeps for five miles, the valley on the left rich with olive-orchards and vines whose young leaves, the colour of long-buried Mycenean gold, shine sharply against the bare earth. The brown sandstone hills, clothed here and there with yellow gorse and broom, squat bilberry-bushes and patches of Virgin-blue veronica, have an air of aloof and brooding severity. Then, over the last spur, the castle of Javier is seen below, tawny as the hills on whose lower slopes it crouches like a lion guardant.

Finely restored, it is now—but for the basilica which occupies the west wing where Francis was born—structurally the same as in 1506.

At least a thousand years old, this little royal castle is a perfect example of a medieval Spanish fortress. Built when the Moors were still a menace to north Spain, it guarded the frontier of Navarre against the aggressions of Aragon till it was dismantled by order of Cardinal Ximenes in 1517. In old days a moat surrounded the enclosure, which could be entered only over a drawbridge and under a portcullis'd gate. The arched doorway of the interior entrance is unchanged, crowned by the crescents and golden bars. Over the door, and on the three towers are the openings between projecting stones for throwing down missiles or boiling oil on the besiegers. Inside, the castle is completely circled, but for the end occupied by the basilica, by a fosse-way, commanded on the outer side by the walls manned by the garrison, on the other by the castle itself, with its loopholes used for arrows or later for the tiny toy cannon of the twelfth century and the heavy ordnance of a later date. These stand inside, with their piles of stone and iron munitions beside them. A low, narrow door, with iron grille, finally admits to the tortuous, dark passages of the interior. Up worn circular steps six hundred years old is reached the little stone arch which is the entrance to the tiny oratory of San Miguel, dimly lit by one loophole in the immense thickness of the walls, with the rock on which the castle is built projecting here and there in walls and floor.

Here hangs, where it hung in Francis's day, the greatest treasure of his home, the miraculous Christ of Javier. The figure, detached from the cross, was found in a hole in the wall (1320) where, tradition said, it had been hidden during the Moorish occupation. It is really probably not older than early eleventh century. Formerly supposed to be of leather, like the famous crucifix of Burgos, it is now known to be of nutwood to which the stuff of the loin-cloth was tightly stuck before the whole was painted over —a curious technique, not unknown in Spanish work of that date. As on the Pamplona crucifix, the figure is lean, the skin tight over bone and muscle. The head, crowned with a narrow twist of thorns, eyes closed, has sunk in death towards the right shoulder. This crucifix, venerated by his mother's family for generations before Francis's birth, by himself, his father, mother, brothers and sisters, was seen by the survivors to be covered with a bloody sweat on Fridays during the last year of his life in the east.

His own room is a lofty, spacious one, with a splendid view from the oriel window. On the plain dark-oak tables and stools lie priceless examples of Spanish printing of the fifteenth century. Above the archway to the kitchen can be seen remains of the destruction ordered by Ximenes. The ironwork over the open fire holds a resin torch, and by it is the huge spit, long enough to roast lamb or kid whole. The primitive drinking-cups are of cowhorn. The glazed plates, dishes and bowls show a Moorish design in blue and white.

From the great central tower of San Miguel is a glorious view. To the north rise the snowclad Sierra Leyre, with the famous monastery of San Salvador, burial place of the kings of Navarre. The river Aragon, frontier of Aragon and Navarre, winds through a wide valley, variegated with the vivid yellow-green of maize and the darker green of corn, brown vineyards and the cold grey of olive-orchards. In one place a bare stretch of sandy soil is thickly dotted with queer conical-shaped hillocks like miniature volcanoes or giant ant-heaps. To the west the sandstone rocks show dull umber above the gold of gorse. South a spur of the hills hides the little town of Sos, birthplace of Ferdinand of Aragon, and on the nearer slope is the parish church of Santa Maria de Javier, where stands the six-sided twelfth-century font of grey stone in which Francis was baptised.

In winter bitter winds and snow sweep down from the Pyrenean passes. In summer the sun blazes with a torrid fierceness which has won the valley the nickname of "the frying-pan of Spain." The country, like the old crucifixes, has an air of aloof yet passionate austerity, of stark heroism and stern endurance that is of the essence of the Spanish spirit.

As evening draws near snow mountains and low brown hills glow a warm rose-gold, with pools of clear cobalt shadow; then, while the sun sets, the nearer mountains harden to steel, while in the far distance snowy peaks, shining dim through a haze of rose and mauve, seem to hang in heaven, unsubstantial as a dream.

In mid fifteenth century Maria de Aznarez and her young husband Martin de Azpilcueta lived in the *palacio* in the Calle Mayor at Sangüesa. Descended from Adam de Sada, first alcaide of Javier in 1236, Doña Maria had inherited the little royal castle and its domain with all their feudal rights; she was related to all the oldest nobility of Navarre, and came from the same ancestry as the royal families of Navarre and Aragon. Her husband, owner of a castle on the French frontier, was richer in courage than worldly goods, but his family proudly boasted that it had kept the Faith untarnished since before the defeat of Charlemagne's invading army at Roncesvalles.

Maria, the elder of their two daughters, born about 1463, married before her mother's death Don Juan de Jassu, a rising young lawyer and politician of Pamplona, who had taken his doctor's degree at the university of Bologna. He was already an important Court official. In 1476 he had been made alcaide of the Cortes; three years later he was regulating an important frontier question between Navarre and Aragon, and, as reward, his hereditary estate was raised to the first rank of nobility.

His ancestors had come originally from near St. Jean Pied-de-Port on the French side of the Pyrenees, and about 1350 Pedro de Jassu, by his financial abilities, had founded the fortunes of the family. Juan's father, Arnalt Periz, lived now in the house in the Calle Zapatería at Pamplona, where he was auditor of the Court finances, and had married Guillerma de Atondo, daughter of one of his colleagues.

Juan was the eldest and most successful of their six children and became the most trusted adviser of the young Queen Catherine and her French husband, Jean d'Albret. It was between Juan's hands that the three Estates of Navarre placed their oath of fealty to the newly-crowned king and queen in 1484.

National and Court business made Juan's visits to the home at Javier rare and hurried, but his young wife remained there, busied with the cares of household and estate and her growing family. Three daughters were born, Maria, Magdalena, and Ana, and later (about 1495 and 1497) two sons, Miguel and Juan. Soon after the birth of the second boy Doña Maria left Javier for some

time to look after her aged and widowed father, and on
his death she brought back with her her sister, Violante,
thirteen years younger than herself.

In the summer of 1505 Don Juan spent some time at
home, rejoicing in the almost monastic quiet and severity
which were such a contrast to the Court at Pamplona,
which was largely French in manners and culture, as its
sovereigns were by blood and sympathy.

The household at Javier now consisted of Doña Maria,
already growing old, her sister, Violante, a nun in all but
vows, the eldest girl, Maria, waiting to enter the novitiate
at Santa Gracia in Pamplona, and her youngest sister and
brother—for Magdalena, a favourite lady-in-waiting to
Queen Isabella, had left the Castilean Court before her
death (1504) to enter the convent of Poor Clares at
Gandia. Miguel, the elder boy, was probably already page
to Jean and Catherine.

Since 1500 Doña Maria's cousin, Martin de Azpilcueta,
had lived in the castle as alcaide, for the management of
the estate, with its complicated rights and privileges, had
proved too much for its chatelaine.

The lords of Javier, by old royal grants, had absolute
jurisdiction over their own vassals and tenants. They
could and did imprison malefactors in the dungeon, where
long rows of wooden stocks and piles of rusty chains are
still dimly seen in the gloom. The lords themselves could
not be imprisoned save by written order from the king
himself, to whom they paid no tribute and owed no alle-
giance save in case of war. The castle had rights of sanctuary, and refugees from Castile or Aragon could claim
asylum there. Flour-mills and salt-works supplemented
the income from fields, orchards, and vineyards, and toll
was claimed from passengers and livestock using the road

below the castle and from boats going down the Aragon river.

The old parish church had been enlarged and restored by Doña Maria and her husband, and an adjoining presbytery built, the regulations and endowment having been completed in 1504. Don Miguel de Azpilcueta, a relative of Doña Maria, was now vicar, and lived in the *abbadia* with two prebendaries, a servant, and a scholar, on the proceeds of the tithes, vineyards and portion of land bequeathed to the church. The life was carefully ordered by the terms of endowment. Women under sixty were forbidden the house; meals were taken in silence, or to the reading aloud of religious books; gardening and fishing were allowed as recreations, hunting and games of chance forbidden, while the singing and saying of the Divine Office was minutely regulated.

In the castle itself there was the same regular life: morning and evening prayers and rosary in the tiny oratory before the old crucifix, all other service and loyalty giving way to that of God and His Mother.

The long summer days of 1505 slipped by in peace and serenity. Outside, brown rocks flung back the torrid heat of the July sun; the harvest was cut and carried; grapes ripened, heavy under their reddening leaves. Within the thick walls of the castle, lit by the narrow, unglazed loopholes, was a cool, still dimness, a family life moulded by the love and service of the Divine Majesty.

In August, less than nine months after the death of the great Isabella, Ferdinand of Aragon—then fifty-four—married the beautiful Germaine de Foix, thirty-six years his junior, niece of Louis XII of France and cousin of Catherine of Navarre. With his clear sight and diplomatic experience Don Juan probably foresaw some of the ill results likely to ensue from such an alliance; for Navarre, a small state, had depended largely on the quarrels of its more powerful neighbours to maintain its independence.

In the autumn, however, came surprising news, which for the moment effaced from his thoughts international complications. His wife, now well over forty, was expecting the birth of another child about Easter.

CHAPTER II

CHILDHOOD AND YOUTH

On Tuesday in Holy Week, April 7, 1506, as Divine Office was being chanted in the parish church, there was born in the great room in the west wing of the castle of Javier the sixth and youngest child of Don Juan de Jassu and his wife Doña Maria de Azpilcueta. The boy was baptised without delay by the vicar, Don Miguel, in the church of Santa Maria. Over the roughly-carved font, already four hundred years old, hung the christening-robes of the children, and among the dusty and yellowing *tuniquellas* of his brothers and sisters, all so much older than himself, was placed that of Francis.

Why this name was chosen by his parents is not known, for it appears in no records of their families. Only a short time before the baby's birth they had written that to every good Christian Lent brings Christ's Passion to mind in a very special way, so possibly they could think of no more appropriate name for the child born in the week of our Lord's Passion than that of the seraphic devotee of the Cross, the saint of Assisi.

After the fashion of the day, the child was given to a wet-nurse, but he was kept in the castle under his mother's eye and care.

Sound is possibly the first thing outside itself of which a child's dawning intelligence becomes conscious. As the walnut-wood cradle, carved with rude geometrical pat-

15

terns, rocked on the beeswaxed floor of the stone-walled nursery, the lullabies croned over it held not only the universal language of nurse to child but also that whimsical twist which is the essence of Basque humour.

> Grant, God on high,
> To this babe I keep
> To still its cry
> Four hours of sleep!
> Then, baby, sleep, have a little sleep!

> And I will give you a sweet,
> Your father will give you more,
> Your mother give two to eat,
> But the Lord God will give you a score!
> Then baby have a little sleep!

The Basque is said to be born and to die with a song on his lips, and at Javier the clear hill air was full of song. There was the daily, nightly chant of Office from the nearby church of our Lady of Javier. Through the night came the songs of the shepherds as they guarded their flocks, sitting by the great fires that pierced the darkness of the hilltops like fallen stars. The farmer sang as he goaded the slow oxen ploughing the rocky slopes. In the castle songs were accompanied by the clatter of horses' hoofs on the stones of the court, the baying of hounds, the noise of pots and pans. The basis of all the tunes was the rhythm of the Church's chant, with an echo of marching feet as the pilgrims of the world passed on their way to Compostela. But these were but the embroidery on a theme as changeless and old as the hills, a melody vague, elusive, melancholy as drifting mist across an evening landscape.

Song and bells—the two keynotes of Basque life—
these memories of Francis's childhood were to follow him
through life, to echo through the streets of Portuguese
forts in the Indies, across the sun-scorched rocks of Cochin,
the volcanic slopes of the Moluccas. There were the great
bells pealing or tolling from the churches, the silver sound
of the sacring bell (said to be an omen of death if it
sounded as the clock struck the hour), the little brass bells
blessed by the priest and hung round the necks of cows
and rams and goats, the tiny bells that jingled merrily on
the falcons' hoods and on the twinkling feet of dancers.

The first words Francis stammered after his nurse, the
first prayers he learnt on his mother's knee, were in
Basque, the language he was afterwards so proudly to pro-
claim as his own, in which his dying lips were to gasp as
he lay delirious in the ruined hut on Sanchian. The strange
old crucifix in the castle chapel fostered his devotion to
the Passion which grew deeper with the years. The dedica-
tion of the chapel and of the great tower of the castle to
the Captain of the Hosts of the Lord marked St. Michael
as the patron whose protection he invoked during earthquake and tempest. In the parish church, dedicated to
Santa Maria de Javier, he acquired that passionate and
particularly Spanish devotion to our Lady, to whom he
was heard to cry for help in that midnight struggle against
the powers of darkness in the church at Meliapor.

From his mother he may have learnt the old rhyme
which says so much in so few words:

> "Vera vergena María,
> Vera vida, vera fes,
> Vera vertatz, vera vía!"

From Doña Maria he passed to lessons with Don

Miguel, began to read and write, learnt the first words of Latin, began his first understanding of the Church's ritual, which moves through the year splendid and majestic as the unchanging cycle of the changing seasons. From retainers, farmers and peasants, he heard the folk-tales, as quaint as those as of the Italian peasant whose humorous, affectionate familiarity with sacred things is so alien to the modern northern mind. Over the snow of the Pyrenean passes, through the pines of the Navarrese forests, along the yellow sands of Guipuzcoa and the rocky shores of Vizcaya St. Peter wandered with his Master, often a kind-hearted buffoon, sometimes a common-sense Sancho to the divine Don Quixote.

The *Bertsulariak*—professional entertainers, generally old women who wandered from house to house with gossip, new poems and old tales—told of the *lamiñak,* who, like English brownies, did house and farm work for those providing fire, food and drink for them at night. There were others like leprechauns guarding crocks of fairy gold, or Moorish magicians whose spells raised fairy bridges or palaces in a night. And darker tales, whispered fearfully, of witches' Sabbaths on nearby hilltops where *Jaun Gorri,* red lord and prince of evil, received the homage of lost souls.

Everywhere was the consciousness of non-material powers, the interpenetration of the natural plane by the supernatural, of the unending struggle between the powers of good and evil. This struggle had had its material expression in those eight centuries of warfare with Islam which have stamped on Spanish Christianity a stark heroism, a burning chivalry possessed by no other race. It was only fifteen years before Francis's birth that Granada had fallen, only five years before that Alonso de Aguilar had

perished at the hands of the victorious Moors in the rising
in the Red Sierra. It was not till eighteen years after
Francis's death that the last Moorish rebellion in the Al-
puxerras was finally stamped out by Don John of Austria.
In travellers' songs, in the rude *pastorales* of the countryside, Turks or Moors, dressed in red, represented the evil
principle, while blue, the colour of heaven and our Lady,
was the livery of right and truth.

Every stone of the castle walls, every sombre brown
hill, spoke of war—over the valley had swept so many
invading armies, Roman legionaries, Visigoth barbarians,
Frankish knights, Moorish caliphs. The blast of dying
Roland's horn, which Charlemagne heard at Fuentarrabia,
must have echoed too from Roncesvalles to the nearer
frontier at Javier.

So passed uneventfully the first five years of Francis's
life, with its dual inspiration of religion and war. Mass
was said daily in the church, on Saturday in honour of our
Lady, on Monday for the Holy Souls. Vespers were
chanted every evening. On great feasts Terce was sung
before Mass. On solemn feasts, vigils, Saturdays, and
Sundays, Compline, and about ten times a year Matins as
well, were sung. Every evening the *Salve Regina* finished
the day. There were processions on Good Friday and
Corpus Christi, and doubtless the national dance figured
in them, as it still does at Seville. "San Miguel" danced
along the Via Dolorosa on Good Friday, and outside the
church at Corpus Christi the intricate steps and entrechats
of the sword dance were performed by the *dantza tchikiak*.

There was military discipline in the border castle, with
the drawbridge raised and the portcullis lowered at sunset,
with sentinels on walls and towers, and all the feudal
régime so minutely regulated in *Las Siete Partidas,* the

laws of Castile imposed by Alfonso X in the thirteenth century.

The father whose visits from the Court at Pamplona were so rare and brief can have been little more than a shadow to the child. It was Martin de Azpilcueta who was such a devoted foster-father that he won the title of St. Joseph of Javier. Francis can scarcely have seen his second sister Magdalena, since it was before his birth that she had entered the convent at Gandia. The other two girls were grown up; Maria was about to go to Santa Engracia, and the youngest, Ana, was betrothed to Don Diego de Ezpeleta. An offer of King Ferdinand to take Miguel as page had not materialised, and he and his younger brother Juan seem both to have been at the Court of Jean and Catherine of Navarre. Doña Maria, now about fifty, divided her time between her duties as chatelaine and prayer. Wool and flax were carded, spun, and woven into cloth and linen by the maids. Cider and wine were made from the home orchards and vineyards. In the autumn enough meat had to be smoked and salted, and butter salted, to last till spring. Cheese was made from goats' milk, and bread was baked from the flour ground at the mill on the Aragon. There were sick to be visited, fed, and physicked, poor beggars and travellers to be fed and clothed—among these only too often crippled wrecks from the continual wars in Italy.

During the six years when Francis was acquiring the first principles of religion and chivalry the tide of war abroad ebbed and flowed. The blunt old Italian Pope, Julius II, changed from side to side as he strove to keep the balance of power between France, Spain, Venice, and the Empire. The favour of England was not yet worth bidding for. The papal determination to rid Italy of the barbarians entailed a game of diplomacy and deceit as tortuous as that played between Ferdinand of Aragon and Louis XII of France, each of whom openly boasted of the number of times he had cheated the other. In 1508 that great patriot and churchman, Cardinal Ximenes, opened the new university of Alcalá, and the next year himself led the Spanish troops against the Moors at the capture of Oran, where he declared that in war against the infidel the smell of gunpowder was sweeter than incense.

In the spring of 1512 Don Juan came home for the marriage of his daughter Ana, which was celebrated with great pomp and state. The fortunes of the family seemed at the zenith, but this splendour, like the dazzling beauty of a summer landscape against the blackness of an advancing storm, was to prove only a memory of the last happy reunion. Not long after Easter news had come of the battle of Ravenna and the death in the moment of victory over the Spaniards of the brilliant young French genius, Gaston de Foix, "the thunderbolt of Italy," who had been brother to Ferdinand's young queen and cousin of the Queen of Navarre.

The Spanish defeat in the distant Romagnan marshes was to bring ruin to Javier. Broken by the death of their leader the French fell back to the Alps, and the wily Ferdinand determined to carry the war into the enemies' country by an attack on the south-east frontier. Ten thousand English, under the Marquis of Dorset, were landed in Guipuzcoa (June, 1512) to support the Spanish army massed at Vitoria under the old Duke of Alba. Juan de Jassu, who had hurriedly returned to Pamplona, found Catherine and her husband determined on concluding an alliance with the French. Ferdinand's demand for a passage for his army through Navarre and a temporary occupation of its six strongest fortresses brought matters to a head. Plenipotentiaries were hurried to sign the treaty with Louis XII at Blois. An embassy, headed by Juan de Jassu, was sent to gain time by negotiations with Ferdinand. By an ironic freak of fate, however, the terms of the treaty were revealed to Ferdinand before it was signed: one of Jean d'Albret's secretaries was murdered by his mistress; the draft of the treaty was found by her among his papers and betrayed by a Pamplonan priest to the Spaniards.

Ferdinand struck at once. The Duke of Alba advanced on Pamplona (July 23); it surrendered the next day. The king and queen fled to Lumbier, only a few miles from Javier, then to France, where they died in exile five years later. By the end of the month Navarre was in the enemies' hands; her independence, which had been preserved for seven centuries, was lost for ever in little more than seven days. The glory had departed. The proud little kingdom became a province of Castile.

Don Juan, faithful in ruin as in prosperity, joined his exiled master and mistress. Not for two years did he manage to return to Javier, then only to die (October 16, 1515), his last days darkened not alone by his country's misfortunes but by worry for the future of his wife and children—for under the new *régime* he found it impossible to obtain the rents, moneys due for tolls, and other rights.

Francis was nine and a half, and the old customs of the countryside were calculated to stamp indelibly on a child's mind his first experience of death. A tile was taken from the roof to give the soul free passage; the smoke from hay burnt on the threshold symbolised the upward flight of the soul, the falling ashes showed the crumbling of the body. The beehives were draped with black cloth cut in shape of a cross; the bees were ceremoniously informed of the death of the *Etcheko Jauna* (head of the house) and requested to "make light for him," by supplying wax for the candles that burnt round the bier. Friends and neighbours, on their way to the Requiem Mass, in mourning-cloaks and hoods, made a sombre procession along the sun-baked hillside and against the glory of the autumn woods.

As the days of that winter drew in the fortunes of Doña Maria and her three sons darkened. She appealed in vain to Ferdinand for her rights at Javier and Pamplona. No restitution had been made when he died in the new year (1516), and the town of Sangüesa obtained from the Spanish authorities the profits of pasturage, water, and mills which had always belonged to the lords of Javier.

Miguel, now twenty-one, and Juan, two years younger, did their best to persuade the ten-year-old Francis to follow a career of arms like them. By the sword their ancestors had won fame and glory, they argued; by arms in the service of their rightful king and queen they themselves would do the same. Francis, intelligent, quick-witted, greedy of knowledge, had already a wider vision than his soldier brothers, and a will as firm. He declared that he would follow in his father's footsteps, and by learning, not fighting, would restore the ruined fortunes of the family.

In a few weeks the two elder brothers were gone to join in the attempt to bring back Jean and Catherine (March, 1516). That stern old Franciscan, Cardinal Ximenes, regent for the absent King Charles, was not one to allow such revolts to succeed or repeat themselves. Though he was eighty-one, and worn in body by penance and austerity, his genius burned as fiercely, his severity was as ruthless as ever. His fiat went forth that every dangerous fortress in Navarre should be razed to the ground. That of Azpilcueta was entirely destroyed. There seemed little hope for Javier, stronghold of keen nationalists, but the Duke of Najera, Spanish viceroy at Pamplona, ventured to mitigate the worst severity.

Opinions differ as to the extent of the destruction in his home witnessed by Francis. Padre Escalada, S.J., author of several books and the great local authority on the saint, holds that it was not so bad as is generally imagined, while Père Cros, S.J., after work on contemporary documents, came to the conclusion that the surrounding walls, with a large part of the towers, battlements and stairs were destroyed. The great tower of San Miguel was certainly pulled down to half its height, and considerable damage was done to the inside of the dwelling—witness the broken arch over the kitchen entrance. At any rate, Javier was no longer a sentinel on the frontier of a free people but a shelter for the few old men, women, and children who were now its only garrison. As a last humiliation a Castilian agent was installed to keep an eye on suspected nationalists, and when Charles V fortified Pamplona the Jassu house was one of those pillaged for wood and building-materials (November, 1517). Such things must have bitten deep into Francis's young mind and, as a result of war, have strengthened his resolve to devote his talents to learning rather than to arms.

On November 8, 1517, died Ximenes de Cisneros. With him passed the generation that had seen the union of Spain, the conquest of the Moors, the discoveries of the New World by Columbus and of the sea passage to the

East by da Gama. Even in Spain feudalism had crumbled before the new humanism. The heroic romances of chivalry, the epics of Amadis of Gaul, Roland, the Cid Campeador, were to be superseded by the satire of Don Quixote, the naturalism of Lope de Vega. But the death of an age, the birth of a new, brought no change to the little party among the ruins of Javier. Miguel and Juan had vanished into the swirl of guerilla warfare among the mountains. Doña Maria's one comfort was that Francis was too young to join them even if he wished; but her daily cry of anguish remained unanswered: "God send us the angel of peace!"

In 1518 there rode from the Court of Spain to Pamplona a young Guipuzcoan nobleman whose possessions consisted of five hundred scudi, two horses and his sword. Left unprovided by the death of his patron, officer of the royal treasure, he was led naturally by his adventurous spirit to the centre of danger, and the Duke of Najera, who knew a good fighter when he saw one, appointed Iñigo de Loyola a gentleman in his suite.

In early 1521, when the revolt of the Communeros against Charles V had spread like wildfire through Spain, all available troops were withdrawn from Navarre. The adherents of young Henry II at once seized the opportunity, and among the troops of Francis I rode Miguel and Juan. Pamplona surrendered, and Herrara, who commanded the small garrison of the castle, was about to do so when Iñigo de Loyola refused, took command, and led the heroic defence. So impressed were the French with his courage that when he fell and the castle was taken they sent him home to his brother's castle near Azpeitia. The story of his convalescence and conversion needs no retelling, but it is strange to think that the cannon-ball which fractured his leg may have been directed by one of Francis's brothers.

For the next two years the brothers were fighting, being captured, and escaping. All Miguel's goods were confiscated. He was condemned to death and specially excluded from the general pardon of Charles V, December 15, 1523.

Francis, now nearly eighteen, had reached his full height, rather above medium. His thick hair was dark, his black eyes full of life and expression, his gay mouth always laughing. The clear, bright skin of his face flushed easily at any sudden emotion or excitement. Strong and healthy in body, he was a trained athlete, the best runner and jumper among all the youths of the neighbourhood. He loved to excel in all games and sports, among them no doubt the javelin-throwing which is still practised by the Basques, and the *jeu de paume* from which evolved modern tennis and the famous Basque *pelota*. To-day the threefold centre of the typical Basque village is the church, the cemetery, and the pelota-court. Even in 1528 Andrea Navagero, the Venetian ambassador, remarked in his travels through north Spain that every gentleman's house had, adjoining it, a court, with thatched roof and levelled earthen floor where the men spent "all day" playing ball-games.

The country round Javier abounded with game. Wild boars, deer, hares, rabbits, partridges, flocks of pigeons which migrated south in autumn and north again in spring, afforded sport with horse, hawk and hound, as well as providing a welcome addition to the larder. In the winter the wolves which roamed in the forests of oak, beech, pine, and chestnut grew bold, and it was necessary to protect sheep and goats in guarded enclosures. Occasional raids were made too from the castle to chase off robbers who were cutting down trees in the home woods, or to demand toll from the shepherds, who now tried to evade payment when they passed with their huge nomadic flocks whose passage raised a smoke of white dust like the march of an invading army.

First in sport and games, Francis carried his desire to excel into his studies too. Educated at first, as we have seen, in the castle, he probably attended classes at the college in Sangüesa, and is said to have completed his studies at Pamplona, from spring 1524 till summer of the following year. On his return in 1525 he found both his brothers at home. The long struggle for Navarrese independence had failed, and Charles V had granted an amnesty and, in name at least, had restored to Miguel, now lord of Javier, his property and ancient rights.

The old argument about Francis's future began, but he saw no reason to alter his decision. His brothers, by their career of arms, had brought to their home ruin, defeat, poverty, misery. He was conscious of his own powers, ambitions, as all healthy, intelligent youth must be. But his ambition was deeper than the mere desire to excel personally. He had all the hidalgo's pride of birth and race added to the reserve and determination of the Basque-Navarrese. No degree at a Spanish university would satisfy him. Paris, "the university not of a town but of the whole world," was his goal. Yet this strength of will, ambition and pride, usually such unlovable qualities, were transfigured by his irresistible charm. The rare but priceless gift of personal magnetism eludes analysis and depends neither on intellect nor moral character. Francis had this gift in a supreme degree from the beginning to the end of his life. His was a fascination which won the hearts of all from the first moment they knew him. It was, as his cousin the famous Doctor Navarro shrewdly remarks, "a grave danger which he would never have escaped without the gift of a natural reserve and a virginal modesty which everyone admired in him."

He won his way now and, in spite of poverty, his mother agreed that he should finish his studies and take his degree at Paris. The profits of a mill at Burguete were legally made over to him, and in September, 1525, ended the nineteen years of his childhood and youth in the old border castle, the only home he was ever to know, to which he was never to return.

CHAPTER III

PARIS: STUDENT DAYS (1525-1530)

IT was early September when Francis looked his last on Javier. In the morning sunshine battle-scarred castle and long slope of sun-scorched rocks had the austere unearthliness of those primitive paintings of northern Spain where stiff, gold-halo'd saints and angels seem the natural outgrowth of rose-gold hills and cobalt-shadowed valleys.

Down from the bare heights, through Sangüesa, into the stone-paved streets of Pamplona rode Francis to join the little band of Navarrese students on the long journey to Paris. Under beech, oak, and chestnut, gilt by autumn, and pines whose needles made a fragrant, springy carpet underfoot, past Fuentarrabia, where nationalists had made their last stand, over the border into France, yet still in their own country with the familiar Basque sounding round them. Bayonne lay behind them and the Landes stretched interminably on their right, purple with heather, dun with rushes, and on the left the sea, sparkling in the sunshine or heaving sullenly under white fog.

> Over the sea a grey mist is lying
> Towards the bar of Bayonne;
> And I love you, my own,
> More than loves her young the bird
> round me flying.

So the gay young voices sang; then, with talk and laughter, they would tell of love—dreams, ideals, experience, bitterness—while Francis rode silent, his cloak close-muffled against the wind that blew from the New World, dreaming not of love but of fame and glory to be won.

Bordeaux, Poitiers, Tours, Orleans—names blazoned in French history—were passed, while the days drew in and the night air nipped more sharply. Then, about Michaelmas, the travel-worn band saw the gleam of the Seine and, beyond the towering splendour of Notre Dame, the northern heights of Montmartre.

There could be no greater contrast to the lonely upland spaces and the devout, well-ordered household of Javier than the Latin Quarter, which was to be Francis's home for the next eleven years. In the narrow semicircle between the sweep of the Seine on the north and the walls of Philip Augustus on the south three or four thousand students were crowded in the welter of churches, monasteries, hospitals, colleges, lecture-halls, taverns and lodgings. In many places the narrow, winding streets were little better than open sewers. The college buildings were old, dark, damp, entirely lacking in sanitation and cleanliness. "I carried nothing away from Paris," grumbled Erasmus about a visit to the University a few years before: "but a body infected with disease and a plentiful supply of vermin."

The College of Ste. Barbe, where Francis was entered as a *camériste-portioniste,* was comparatively modern. Founded by Lenormant, Master of Grammarians at the College of Navarre in 1460 (eight years after the reform of the University by Cardinal Estouteville), it prided itself on its progressive outlook and its brilliant staff of professors. The Principal, de Gouvea, a Portuguese, seeing the immense growth of the Portuguese empire in the east, had persuaded John III to found fifteen bursaries for missionary students, from whom Francis would hear of the wonders and riches of the East Indies. On the teaching staff were the Spanish Aristotelian Gelida, the French Latinist Louis d'Estrebay, Fernel, whose encyclopædic knowledge of mathematics, astronomy, philosophy and philology recalled the days of Albertus Magnus and Thomas of Aquin, and Mathurin Cordier, whose manuscript notes show the fervour of the best professional educationalist: "Begin with principles, begin with speaking of God and the things of heaven." Such crowds of students, indeed, flocked to the lectures at Ste. Barbe that often the great hall would not hold them and the chair had to be carried out for the professor to lecture in the open.

Francis, dressed now in the long black gown with the leather belt, paid for board and lodging in the college. The bare room which he shared with the principal and two or three other students had little furniture beside the straw mattresses on the floor. At four o'clock in the bitter blackness of winter mornings, as in summer dawn, a bell was rung by one of the senior students, who came round to see all were awake and when necessary to light a few dim candles. An hour later all collected in hall for the first lecture, the students seated on the stone floor on straw in winter, hay in summer—"to encourage humility," says Estouteville edifyingly, in reality for economic reasons. Mass was followed by breakfast of a roll hot from the oven, then between eight and ten came the main lecture of the day, afterwards an hour's "exercise." At eleven masters and students dined together in the great hall, the students' table being waited on by the server for the week, with a napkin knotted round his neck. While meat and vegetables were being eaten the Bible or lives of the saints

were read aloud, and after grace the principal gave out
notices for the day, and distributed punishments or repri-
mands. Questions on the morning's lectures preceded
recreation and the afternoon class from three to five.
Supper at six was followed by a *résumé* of the day's work,
night prayers and Benediction. Curfew rang at nine for
lights out, though it was possible to obtain special permission to study till eleven.

Tuesdays and Thursdays were the weekly recreation-
days, and on summer evenings games and sports took
place and walks were taken on the *Pré aux Clercs* on the
left bank of the Seine below the city. Francis excelled
athletically as he had done at home, and was enormously
proud of his fame as a runner and jumper. There were
other and less peaceful outlets for exuberant spirits.
"Whipping and brawling abounded, both of tormented
youths and of masters besotted with anger and irritation,"
says Montaigne, while Ribadeneira, in his life of St.
Ignatius, tells of less bloody arguments. "One discusses
before dinner, during dinner, after dinner, in public, in
private, everywhere. One ends by discussing whether the
pig is led to market by the man who takes it or the string
he holds!" The same keen conflicts were waged over
academic distinctions as in the days when Abelard's fame
had brought students from all over the known world or
when Thomas of Aquin, a century after, was laying the
foundations of the world's greatest system of philosophy.

A new spirit was stirring the old atmosphere. The neo-
paganism which was so widespread in Italy was bringing
to Paris the Greek values, tending to put intellectual
ability before moral character, to set mind above soul.
And, under cover of this new thought, crept in a still
newer spirit of revolt and denial, the spirit which had first

come into the open when Luther had affixed his theses against indulgences to the church door at Wittenburg in 1517.

One far greater intellectually than the renegade Augustinian was now a fellow-student of Francis's at Ste. Barbe. Calvin had come there to work under Cordier, after a brief stay at the adjacent College Montaigu, scorned by the Barbistes as a home of reactionaries and obscurantists. Calvin, deeply indebted to the brilliant grammarian, repaid him by so infecting him with heresy that in 1528 he definitely joined the "Reformers." George Buchanan was another stormy petrel, later to be imprisoned by the Inquisition when teaching at Coimbra, to become John Knox's friend, and the infamous traducer of Mary Stuart. Born in the same year as Francis, the young Scot had already studied two years in Paris, fought in the siege of Werk, taken his B.A. at St. Andrews and returned in 1526 to take his M.A. and teach grammar at Ste. Barbe. So cleverly indeed was humanism used as a mask by heresy that Bobadilla coined the aphorism: "To humanise is to Lutheranise."

The whole University course lasted nearly twelve years —one of humanism, three and a half of philosophy, three of teaching as "regent," the final four of theology, law or medicine. We have seen that, during his first years (1525-1529), Francis was brought into contact with those holding heretical views. This was not his only danger. Keen on intellectual and athletic achievement, he had too all the natural desire of youth to gain its own experience and knowledge of the world. Nominally strict as were the college rules, they were in fact continually evaded and defied. One master in particular used to lead bands of students at night to the houses of ill-fame hidden away in the back streets, and Francis went too. We learn from his own lips, in one of those precious and all too rare moments of self-revelation, that through this time he was wonderfully preserved from evil. "About the life of the students, he said they and the masters were very immoral, that they often left the college at night with one of the professors and took him [Francis] with them. . . . Yet never till the day he confided these details to me had his chastity suffered the slightest harm," wrote Gaspard Coelho, vicar at Meliapor, soon after Francis's death.

Fear, he said, had been the human element in his preservation during those two years in which he had seen minds and bodies rot from the results of vice, had seen his master die in misery and disease from his sin. To that master succeeded Juan de Peña, whose good influence completely freed Francis from the sensual dangers which fear and fastidiousness alone would have been powerless to avert.

In 1528 financial difficulties at home, and perhaps rumours of the bad company he had been keeping, made Francis's family practically decide to recall him before he had taken his degree, and it was only a letter from his sister Magdalena, now Abbess of the Poor Clares at Gandia, that decided the question in his favour. "Do all you can to help the studies of my brother Francis," she wrote home: "for I have a firm conviction that he will become a great servant of God and pillar of the Church."

So Francis began the last five months of study before his baccalaureate exam., still keeping horse and servant, the state he considered his right. "He wished to keep up appearances," Torsellini tells us: "and to be noticed by those who were his equals in birth; hence his unnecessary extravagance." There was nothing strange about that. It was of a piece with his pride of birth, his varied ambitions. But it was indeed strange that, between him and one of his room-mates there should have sprung up what Père Brou describes as "one of those strong yet tender friendships which only the saints know." Son of humble Savoyard peasants and born in the same year as Francis, Peter Faber, while watching his father's flocks on the Alpine slopes, at the age of twelve had bound himself by a vow of chastity, with difficulty obtained his parents consent to finishing his studies at Paris, and was assigned to the same room as Francis when the two arrived at Ste. Barbe in 1525. Between the haughty, ambitious young Basque nobleman and the shepherd-boy there seemed at first little affinity. Francis had all the proud, reserved dignity of the Spanish hidalgo, Peter a simplicity as pure and limpid as one of his mountain streams. Yet both were burning with the same passionate desire for knowledge, both had that irresistible personal fascination which is so rare a gift. "Faber," wrote Simon Rodriguez: "among his other virtues had a rare and delightful sweetness and charm which I have known in no one else to the same degree. . . . His amiability, his charm of talk, inclined all those in his company to the love of God."

Together the two did their four-and-a-half years' humanity and philosophy, passed their B.A. exam. in the spring of 1529, and a year later took their Masters' degree, which enabled them, while continuing their own theological studies, to lecture as "regents" to the younger students. "May the Divine goodness be for ever blessed for having given me a master like Juan de Peña and society such as I enjoyed with him. I speak specially of Master Father Francis," wrote Peter in his "Memorial."

Francis had now finished the first period of university

life. He had successfully passed the magisterial test for which barely half the students even entered and which only a small fraction of the rest survived. He had now the "bonnet" which gave him the right to teach. The congratulations, the banquets, the celebrations were over, the crowds dispersed. He was free to look back on the past five years, forward to his six years of theology. The last year had brought one great sorrow, for in July, 1529, his mother had died at Javier. His brothers were both married. He was alone and independent.

From the tower of Notre Dame he may have looked down on the university and city he now knew so well, beyond the old walls to the winding Seine; the cornfields and vineyards were still in their winter brown, but on the wooded heights a purple bloom told of rising sap and swelling bud. Beyond the Pont St. Michel rose the roofs of the Palais Royal, where Francis I had been deliriously welcomed back in 1526 after the disaster of Pavia and the disgrace of a Spanish prison. And further than eye could reach the mind's vision saw "the kingdoms of this world and the glory of them." In England the fallen Wolsey was sick to death, while the king, gilding brute lust with hypocritical scruples, chased the calculating coyness of Ann Boleyn. In Italy Clement VII, the second Medici Pope, nicknamed "Willy-Nilly" from the uncertain pendulum of his diplomacy, had returned from captivity to Rome, whose sack by Imperial troops in 1527 had seemed to the horrified peoples a destruction "not of the city but of the world." The "Ladies' Treaty" of Cambrai in 1529 had at last brought peace to a world sickened with war, and Francis saw now more clearly than ever before that the greatness he strove for and knew himself capable of lay not under damascened cuirass and plumed helmet but under soutane and tonsure. He saw Cardinal Ximenes with Spain and the young Charles V in the grip of his thin brown fingers, the fabulous splendour of Wolsey as Papal Legate—there were worthy models for young ambition; the red hat, and beyond that perhaps even the triple tiara. Almost there seemed a whisper from the leering stone lips at his shoulder: "All these will I give thee if . . ."

CHAPTER IV

PARIS: PROFESSOR AND CONVERT (1530-1535)

In the spring and summer of 1528 and 1529 Francis must often have passed, in the filthy Rue du Chien between Ste. Barbe and Montaigu, an elderly student, bearded, shabby, with a pronounced limp. Tales had gathered round "the Pilgrim," as he was nicknamed, since his arrival from Alcalá early in 1528. He gained disciples, persuaded them to accompany him to weekly confession and Communion at the Carthusians and Franciscans—an extraordinary proceeding in the university, where it was considered pretentious and hypocritical to frequent the Sacraments oftener than once a year, in Lent.

In October, 1529, the Pilgrim began his philosophical studies at Ste. Barbe, where he shared a room with de Peña, Francis and Peter. To Francis was assigned the work of helping the backward pupil of thirty-seven, an uncongenial job which he handed on to Peter. He was surprised to learn that this eccentric character, who spent his summer vacations in England and Flanders begging for alms to cover the expenses of the year's study, was a Guipuzcoan nobleman, of birth equal to his own, that he had been wounded at the siege of Pamplona and had spent the seven years since then at the monastery of Montserrat, in a cave at Manresa, on a pilgrimage to the Holy Land and studying at Salamanca and Alcalá. Between Ignatius of Loyola and Francis there sprang up none of

38

that instinctive sympathy which had so quickly united
Francis and Peter, but when the young "regent," in
October, 1530, began to lecture on Aristotle at the Dor-
mans-Beauvais College, he found that his own evasion of
help was being repaid by his room-mate's quietly persuad-
ing all he could to attend the lectures and so augment
Francis's scanty income.

Francis had already received the tonsure, and in 1531
obtained the document attesting his noble birth and iden-
tifying him as "the right noble Don Francisco de Yasu y
Javier, Master of Arts, a cleric of the diocese of Pamplona." He forwarded this to his brothers, asking them
to obtain for him the stall of a canon in the Pamplonan
chapter so that this benefice would enable him to finish
his theological studies without further financial worries.
This first step accomplished, he felt he could press on to
the goal of his ambitions.

These dreams and ambitions he painted in glowing
colours on winter nights in their room or on long summer
evenings by the river. Peter, ambitious too, but in the
service of his Master, not for self, was silent, but, in a
moment's pause of the eager talk, Ignatius's quiet voice
would be heard: "What doth it profit a man, Master
Francis, if he gain the whole world and suffer the loss of
his own soul?" It was annoying, this continually repeated
question, and Francis's only answer was laughter and a
jest as he went on rearing his dream palaces. "The
Father Master Francis was a little difficult and obstinate,"
says Texeira discreetly: "for, though he enjoyed greatly
the conversation and friendship of Ignatius, yet he did not
dare to change altogether the estate of his life, as he was
naturally inclined to the honour and pomp of the world."
The struggle was long, but Ignatius persisted; he had

already seen in Francis the makings of a unique saint. "I have heard our great sculptor of men, Ignatius, say that the hardest block he ever had to handle was, at first, the young Francis Xavier" (Polanco).

In the spring of 1533 came news of Magdalena's death. It had been revealed to her that the end of one of her nuns would be terrible, her own easy. Her prayer was answered. The nun died gently as falling asleep. On the heroic Abbess was laid an agony of soul and body so awful that after her death her Poor Clares found she had torn her tongue to pieces in her determination to still her cries. Little wonder that she was revered as a saint, that miracles were said to have been worked at her tomb.

In the summer vacation of that year Peter Faber went home to bid his last farewell to his parents, for he had promised to leave all and follow Ignatius. During the seven months of his absence his two friends were thrown still more together. Already Ignatius had persuaded Francis to accompany him every week to confession and Communion at the Carthusian church by the Porte St. Jacques. Daily, nightly he prayed for the young man whom he loved as our Lord loved St. John. Prayer, long intimate talks and always, breaking the bright spell of worldly dreams, those warning words: "What shall it profit a man?"

The true history of any conversion is known only to God. The preparation is a thing slow, hidden and secret as the growth of the seed in the soil, the babe in the womb, till suddenly this gradual maturing breaks forth into flower and conscious life. We know no details of Francis's final capitulation, nor when he at last decided to place his life in Ignatius's hands. By the time Peter returned, at the beginning of 1534, Francis had been entirely won. He was willing to sacrifice his professorship, the end of his studies, as he had already sacrificed his worldly ambitions. His was one of those generous natures which know no half-measures, a heroic soul that feared nothing but its own limitations. "To give and not count the cost, to fight and not heed the wounds, to labour and ask for no reward"—Ignatius's words were indeed applicable to the greatest of his children.

Among the few books which had been all Ignatius had brought to Paris on his ass was a manuscript on which he had been engaged since 1522—the first draft of the "Spiritual Exercises," which have been one of the most potent spiritual and psychological forces of the last four centuries. Peter Faber on his return from Savoy spent forty days in retreat under the direction of Ignatius, the first to do the "Exercises." By the beginning of August, 1534, the other disciples, with the exception of Francis, had done the same. They were four in number—Lainez and Salmeron, two youths who had followed "the Pilgrim" from Alcalá, Bobadilla, a fiery little Spaniard of twenty-seven, and Simon Rodriguez, a Portuguese, rather younger.

For master and followers the future was to be left entirely in the hands of God. They resolved, after much prayer and discussion, to bind themselves by a triple vow to poverty, chastity and a pilgrimage to Jerusalem. There they should ask the divine guidance whether they should devote themselves to missionary work among the heathen, there and further afield, or return to Europe. If prevented from starting to the Holy Land, they were to place themselves unreservedly under the Pope's orders. Meantime for the next three years all should continue their present life and their studies. It took the united persuasions of all to persuade Francis to retain his professorship. "He was already burning with such ardour," says Rodriguez, "that he was almost broken by the effort to force himself to teach Aristotelian philosophy in public for another three and a half years."

Peter Faber, who had been ordained priest and said his first Mass on July 22, 1534, tells of the taking of the vows: "The same year, 1534, on the day of the Assumption of the Holy Virgin, all those of us who at that time shared in the designs of Loyola and who had undergone the Spiritual Exercises (except Master Xavier, who had not yet received them) rendered ourselves at Notre Dame de Montmartre, and there we made a vow to serve God and to depart on a certain day for Jerusalem, to give up relatives and all the rest, taking with us only the viaticum. Besides we resolved to go after our return from the Holy Land and put ourselves at the disposal of the Pope. Now those who were present at this first reunion at Notre Dame were Ignatius, Master Francis Xavier, I Faber, Master Bobadilla, Master Lainez, Master Salmeron, Master Simon Rodriguez" (Memorial). Faber, as the only priest, celebrated Mass, and before he distributed Communion each one, kneeling, said aloud the vow of poverty, chastity and a pilgrimage to the Holy Land. The seven then broke their fast on bread and water, and, seated by the little spring said to have been dyed with the blood of the martyred Denis, they spent the rest of the day in "loving conversation."

At the end of the month Francis withdrew for forty days into a lonely house, where Ignatius visited and directed him. Universal as is the appeal of the Exercises, to Francis it must have been a special one. Through them runs the Spanish tradition of stark heroism, burning chivalry, of military discipline and ceaseless yet unweary-

ing battle with the enemies of God. "Let us not leave
the battle for the wounds we have; those we shall receive
will make us forget the old ones"—the words from *El
Conde Lucanor* strike the keynote to this dauntless
night-errantry. "It is necessary to make ourselves detached
in regard to all created things . . . so that we on our
part should not wish for health rather than sickness, for
riches rather than poverty, for honour rather than ig-
nominy, for a long life rather than a short one." Such
was to be the inspiration of Francis's life from now on,
the "Principal and Foundation" that, in its sublime and
supernatural self-abnegation, is the rule of all religious
life, the logical, inevitable outcome of the realisation that
"man is created to praise, reverence and serve God our
Lord, and thereby to save his soul."

Knowing Francis's noble generosity, his tremendous
capacity for love and sacrifice, we cannot wonder that
during his retreat his zeal broke all bounds, that he re-
venged himself on the finely-trained body for his old
pride in its achievements. "Binding his body very hard
with a small cord which caused him intolerable pain he
went some days together in that manner. . . . He was
carried something too far in abstaining four whole days
from eating anything. A rash attempt indeed but yet
faultless, being excused by the fervour of his new beginning and youthful years" (Torsellini).

According to Rodriguez, an eye-witness, it was now
that occurred the incident which later biographers rele-
gated to the journey to Venice. These same bonds, tied
so tightly and for so long round arms and legs, caused
such acute inflammation that the cords entirely disappeared
in the swollen and ulcerated flesh. It was impossible to
cut them out, and after two days and nights of agony

amputation of one arm seemed inevitable. Having described the ceaseless prayers of Francis's friends, Rodriguez concludes cautiously: "By a singular mercy of God he was completely cured, and I am entirely ignorant how this sudden cure was effected." "Francis came out of the Exercises a changed man," says Père Brou: "From now on it is the life of a saint that we are writing."

Early in the new term Paris awoke one morning (October 18) to find the streets placarded with a call to religious revolt containing the most terrible blasphemies against the Church and the Holy Eucharist. Calvin, after leaving Paris to study law at Orleans, had declared himself a "reformer" and, under the protection of the king's sister, Queen Margaret of Navarre, had now secretly returned. The king, for all his instability and unscrupulous diplomacy a faithful son of the Church, declared: "Were my right hand heretic I would cut it off." He organised a great procession of reparation through the city, and on January 25, 1535, sent a royal herald to ride through the University and cite to court seventy-three indicted heretics, among them five monks, six masters and the principal of Tournay College.

January 25, the conversion of St. Paul, 1537, had been the date decided on at Montmartre for the departure from Venice to the Holy Land, but now an unforeseen trial was to fall on the "companions." Ignatius, who for some time had been suffering from severe internal trouble, was ordered by his doctor to leave Paris and return to Spain in search of health. It was the harder for him to leave his children and for them to be left because, as was inevitable, their unusual mode of life had attracted inimical attention. Heresy, which seemed to be creeping in everywhere, was suspected in this little band of enthusiasts, and Ignatius was actually denounced to the Inquisitors, who knew him well enough to shrug their shoulders.

Gossip was rife—spread, then as now, by fools who spend their leisure like dogs wallowing in filth, by knaves who, afraid to attack a man to his face, stab him from behind with a woman's weapon, the tongue. Rumour had penetrated even to Navarre, and when Ignatius set out he took with him a letter from Francis to his brother, Don Juan, then living at Obanos, nine miles from Pamplona. Dated March 25, 1535, it is the first extant of that wonderful series of letters which fill seven volumes in the edition of 1667 (Poussines); the final, authoritative collection was published in the *Monumenta Xaveriana,* 1899-1900.

We know nothing of Francis's parting with the master he called "my true and only father, my father in the bowels of Christ." It was the first of those farewells which from now were to be the milestones of Francis's life, but in his letter to his brother is the burning love, burning indignation too against the traducers of Ignatius, which show Francis so intensely human:

"In all his business what has distressed me most has been the thought of the deep grief caused you by the statements of some wicked and perverted men, whom I should much like to know to pay them their deserts. That however is impossible since they pretend to be my friends. God knows the anger I feel at not being able to reward them according to their deeds. My only consolation is that *quod differtur non aufertur!*" (The anger of these lines was considered so unedifying by the early editors that they suppressed them.) "And that you may know the great favour which our Lord has bestowed on me when He acquainted me with Master Iñigo I give you my

word of honour that in all my life I could never repay him
the great debt I owe him. For he has not only frequently
supported me in my needs through money and friends but
he has also influenced me to give up the society of bad
companions whom, on account of my inexperience, I did
not recognise as such. . . . I most fervently beg you to
welcome Master Iñigo, to confer with him and believe all
he says, for I am sure that his advice will be most profitable
to you, since he is in a special degree a man of God. And
all that he tells you from me, believe as if I myself were
speaking to you."

CHAPTER V

VENICE AND ORDINATION (APRIL, 1535–JUNE 24, 1537)

THE months passed slowly and uneventfully. News came from England that the Chancellor and Cardinal Fisher had been executed for denying the spiritual supremacy of the king. On the Feasts of the Assumption, 1535 and 1536, the vows were renewed at Montmartre by the companions, who now numbered nine, and were under the authority of Peter Faber. Ignatius was already waiting for them in Venice, for after a few months' convalescence in Spain an attempt to resume his studies at Bologna had brought on a recurrence of his old illness.

Then, in the summer of 1536, war broke out again. The French king poured his troops into Spain. The Emperor retaliated by an invasion of Provence, which was devastated by its defenders. It was obviously unwise for Spanish enemy aliens to remain longer than necessary in France. Travelling was impossible through the smoking ruins of south France and the north-west of Italy, seething with the remains of the broken Imperial forces. It was accordingly decided by the nine that instead of waiting for the end of term an immediate start should be made on November 16.

Their few preparations were complete and all was ready when a courier arrived from Navarre with a letter for Francis announcing that he had been unanimously elected to a vacant canon's stall in Pamplona cathedral. The stipend was rich, the position an important one. The way stood open to power and success. The prize that he had so long striven for and dreamed of was in his grasp, and, as so often in life, he desired it no longer. It was the world's last temptation, his family's final attempt to turn him from the wild enterprise on which he was embarking.

Memory was indelibly stamped by those words of Ignatius: "What shall it profit a man?" Mind and spirit were irrevocably moulded to the heroic ideal of the Exercises. Francis had never been one of those niggardly souls content to plead: "I have done that which was my duty to do." If his namesake of Assisi had called himself the troubadour of God, Francesco de Javier was indeed God's knight-errant, setting out gaily, generously, courageously on a quest which for the remaining sixteen years of his life would lead him without pause or rest through hardships and dangers, shipwrecks and savages to failure and a lonely death.

"Their manner of travelling was this:" Torsellini tells us of the winter journey, "they were clothed in coarse and old habits, everyone with a staff in his hand and a short leather mantle on his shoulders, like poor pilgrims. About their necks they hung their beads, thereby to be known for Catholics as they travelled among heretics, and their writings they carried at the back in a little bag." Their daily routine was Mass said by the three priests when possible, the others receiving Communion from them. Before leaving the inn or lodging they knelt publicly in prayer, as they did on arrival in the evening. The hours of the long day's tramp were beguiled by prayer and meditation, song and talk.

Even the northern route on which they had decided was

full of disbanded soldiers on their homeward way, pillaging, burning, murdering. About three days after leaving Meaux came a thunder of pursuing hoofs. All were relieved when it proved to be Rodriguez's brother, who having only just heard of Simon's secret departure had galloped after him to dissuade him from this mad scheme. He returned alone to Paris.

Eastward tramped the companions, along those interminable straight roads bordered with desolate poplars and brimming ditches; and always it rained, till it seemed that there was no dry spot anywhere—certainly not in their sodden gowns and frozen feet. Metz was reached, with its steep narrow streets and white drifts of pigeons against the cathedral façade. Three days were spent at Nancy to visit the shrine of St. Nicolas, then on again into Switzerland, through Basle to Constance.

The forests of Alsace, oaks and beeches still clad in dun leaves, pines dark as the nave of Notre Dame, must have reminded Francis of the autumn eleven years ago when, an ambitious youth of nineteen, he had ridden through the Navarrese woods on his way north to conquer the world. The ceaseless murmur of mountain streams gave way to the silence of Alpine snows and, if the Basque song did not rise to Francis's lips, it surely lingered in his mind:

"All the passes are full of snow . . .
I am not afraid of the snow or the darkness.
My beloved, for you I would pass through night and day.
Through night and day and through deserted forests."

"My Beloved!"—there indeed was the inspiration of the whole adventure, which changed hardships and misery to gladness and joy because endured for love's sake. So

Simon Rodriguez tells us when he writes long after about this very journey: "His grace and love filled them with intense joy and incredible gladness, so that they cheerfully endured all difficulties and even danger of death, for these sufferings indeed were as nothing compared to what they were ready to suffer."

In Switzerland to the hardships of snow and bitter cold was added an ignorance of the language which continually caused the travellers to lose their way. This was the country of heresy, and no sooner did they reach their lodging at night, cold, wet, famished, than their rosaries would be noticed and word go round that here were Catholics. The village or town would be scoured for anyone with a smattering of Latin or divinity, and instead of warmth, rest and food, a fierce theological argument would be the bill of fare.

The last stages led through Catholic country again, through Feldkirch, Bozen and Trent—where sixteen years later Lainez and Salmeron were to win world fame at the Council—past Verona, and so at last (January 8, 1537) to their journey's end and the joyful reunion with Ignatius.

After the jostling noisy crowds, the clatter of hoofs and wheels on the cobbles of the Paris streets, the waterways of Venice held the strange remote silence of a dream. The city itself was compact of the shifting, mingling contrasts of a dream—east and west, barbarism and voluptuous luxury, with, in theory, the government of a Hellenic city republic, actually an oriental tyranny under the Doge and the Council of Ten.

The capture of Constantinople, the discovery of America and the opening of the sea passage to the East round the Cape of Good Hope had sounded the first notes of the death knell of Venetian supremacy as the world's great market, but still the Bride of the Adriatic lay among her lagoons, splendid as a bedizened courtesan, unconscious of decay. Titian was painting those gorgeous canvasses which hold all the beauty of earthly form and colour. The Aldine Press was printing the classics which made it world-famous. The façades of exotic Gothic palaces glowed with decorations as fantastic as a fairy-tale. In the harbour lay over three thousand ships, in the arsenal the fifty fighting galleys of the fleet and the monster Bucentaur, from which on Ascension Day the Doge cast the gold wedding-ring into the sea. Above the porch of St. Mark's, Byzantine in architecture and mosaics, pranced the gilded horses of Nero, brought back from Constantinople in 1204 by the great Doge Enrico Dandolo. In the slums and the Giudecca were huddled human beings in a state of indescribable filth and misery. In the piazza of St. Mark, up and down the palace steps to waiting gondolas, drifted gilded youths in silken hose and doublets and feathered caps, elegant and effete as the yellow-haired angels of Carpaccio and Crivelli. And women, pearls threaded in their dark red hair, their pearl-pale or painted faces framed in lace, their bodies in huge farthingales of satin or velvet. In the churches the murmur of the celebrating priest was drowned by talk and laughter, the scuffles of rowdy students from Padua. Clergy, lounging in their stalls, gazed round and greeted friends. Choirmen substituted obscene songs more in tune with the lascivious music than were the words of the Office. Even at the moment of the Elevation all but a few remained standing. To the companions with their burning zeal, to Francis with his "angelic purity," what sights and scenes of horror!—the darker because behind them, black as a thunder-cloud behind the ethereal loveliness of the Campanile, loomed the menace of Islam.

Under Suleyman, the Magnificent (1520-1566), the greatest of all the Sultans, Turkish power reached its zenith. Belgrade and Rhodes had fallen to him; his victorious armies swept over eastern Europe. But for the heroic defence of Vienna the whole of central Europe might have been lost to Christianity. Here, as in his youth, Francis was faced with the eternal struggle between opposing ideals, the Cross and the Crescent, self-denial and self-indulgence, charity and the sword—the Two Standards of the Exercises: "Christ calls and wishes for all men under His standard, and Lucifer contrariwise under his. . . . There are three stages, the first poverty against riches, the second reproach or affront against worldly honour, the third humility against pride." The choice had already been made in Paris, but as the spiritual life deepens and strengthens the soldier of Christ asks to serve in harder battles, to suffer more grievous wounds and privations. Already, probably, Francis's thoughts and desires were reaching out, past Jerusalem, dominated externally by the mosque of Omar and the Crescent, to those countless millions of souls beyond, of whom he had heard in Paris from de Gouvea and his missionary students. Meantime no pilgrim-ships were sailing till June, and instead of the rest and quiet that ordinary men would have demanded the companions at once on their arrival set to work on the hardest and most trying job to be found. Appalling as were the conditions of the poor, those in the hospitals were far worse. Every necessity, hygiene, money, helpers, all seem to have been lacking, and Ignatius took up his quarters with four of his children at the hospital of SS. John and Paul, sending Francis, Peter Faber and four others to the hospital for incurables, started fourteen years before by Cajetan of Vicenza, one of the founders of the Theatines. The companions devoted themselves to the menial work of the hospital. They swept and scrubbed floors, washed and cleansed the miserable patients and their filthy rags, emptied accumulations of foulness, prayed with the dying, laid out the dead and carried the corpses to the graves which they had dug for them.

Gossip sprang up. Curiosity was rife. Who were these young men, dressed in travel-worn, faded black gowns, hardly able to stammer a few words of Italian, yet obviously men of breeding and education, who did not shrink from the most revolting tasks? Merchants and senators, members of the Supreme Council, came, saw and were conquered, but still the work went on undisturbed by visitors or talk.

Francis, with his keen imagination, his personal fastidiousness, the aloof reserve of the hidalgo, and his natural admiration for healthy bodies, perhaps found the work more difficult than any of the others, and for that very reason threw himself into it with keener enthusiasm. It is in work for others that man finds his surest content and in the nearness and sympathy of those he loves the greatest earthly happiness. Such content and happiness were Francis's during those two months of early spring, 1537. He worked with his beloved Peter in the Incurables' Hospital. There were the daily meetings, the long talks and plannings with his yet more loved "father in Christ."

One wonders if the two Basques talked the language of their youth. One can be sure that Ignatius described his own pilgrimage to the Holy Places fourteen years ago, its perils and difficulties, its joys and spiritual consolations. Certainly Ignatius himself retained an indelible memory of these weeks in the hospitals for he decreed that every Jesuit should spend part of his novitiate in the care of the sick and dying. Francis's radiant face was noticed by all. In each broken body he and his fellow-workers saw not physical horror and the wages of sin but the likeness of the Master Who had promised: "Inasmuch as ye shall do it to the least of these my brethren ye shall do it unto Me."

It was the custom for those about to set out for Jerusalem to obtain the papal blessing before they started, and in mid-March the companions left Venice to do this. Ignatius did not accompany them. He was afraid that his presence might be prejudicial to their reception, for at the moment two men were in Rome with whom he had had difficulties—Pedro Ortiz, lecturer at the Sorbonne and now delegate from Charles V to oppose the divorce of Henry VIII of England from the Emperor's aunt, and Cardinal Caraffa, who had hoped to persuade Ignatius to join the Theatines. Once again the band set out on foot, this time without money or provisions. Once again it rained and rained. The network of rivers overflowed their dykes. The low-lying meadows of the Romagna were in many places flooded so deep that only the tops of the pollard willows and the vines trained against them were visible. Walking barefoot, sometimes as much as thirty miles a day, in places wading through water shoulder-high, the travellers had for food at best a piece of the peasants' black bread, at worst the fir-cones they were reduced to picking up as they reached the long avenues of pines beside the canals near Ravenna. Rodriguez gives a vivid little picture of "one of them"—Francis again— barefooted, his shabby gown kilted to his knees, as he wandered through the market of a town they passed, begging for alms, gratefully and humbly taking gifts from stall

holders, a fruit here, a vegetable there. His charm of
manner, his unfailing and smiling good humour, must have
made him the most successful beggar of the lot. For the
rest it was their last experience of such hard journeys, for
Francis the beginning. "God was to allow him only fifteen
years of work," says Père Brou: "but fifteen years of
ceaseless travel, without rest—hardest of all, without the
comforting companionship of his beloved brothers."

Ravenna, Ancona, Loreto—at last the three-hundred-
mile journey drew to its end. Rome was reached in Holy
Week, and Francis with his compatriots found welcome
hospitality in the Spanish hostel. Ortiz, the man whose
opposition Ignatius had feared, not only arranged an audience soon after Easter but himself conducted the pilgrims
to the great new palace of the Popes. St. Peter's, as they
approached it, was hidden in a forest of scaffolding and
mountains of stone and marble for use in the rebuilding
which had been going on since 1506.

Titian has painted Paul III as Francis and his brothers
saw him—an old man of seventy-one, his long face deeply
lined, an aquiline nose, high forehead, thick white hair
and beard spread over the white fur and purple velvet of
his mozetta, a great square ring on one of the beautiful
hands. The piercing dark eyes, deep-set under black
brows, saw a little group of a dozen young men of various
nationalities, in shrunk and faded students' gowns; but,
clear sighted as he was, the Pope can hardly have realised
that this audience was to have more far-reaching results
than any he had ever given.

Like Janus, Paul looked backward and forward. His
youth, like Alexander Farnese, had been spent in the
meridian of the Renaissance. His culture was as wide, his
tastes as splendid, his possessions as great as his ambitions.

During the reign of the second Medici pope, Clement VII, with his irresolute and feeble diplomacy, Cardinal Farnese had maintained a strict neutrality between opposing French and Imperial factions, and now that he sat on the chair of Peter he was still unwilling to commit himself without extreme caution. "He would not refuse what was asked . . . nor yet definitely consent" (Dandolo). Accordingly, having listened to all the Imperial ambassador had to say, his Holiness summoned some of his own theologians, and a discussion in philosophy and divinity took place between them and the strangers, in which, Torsellini tells us, all did well, but Francis best.

The Pope professed himself satisfied with the result, as he well might be, since many of the Italian clergy could hardly read, and more had the greatest difficulty in mustering enough Latin to say Mass or even to learn the form of absolution. He gave the companions his blessing, with leave to be ordained by any bishop, their learning to stand in lieu of patrimony. Having given them alms for their pilgrimage he concluded with the ominous words: "I fear that, after all, you will not succeed in going to Jerusalem." They did not know, as he did, that war was on the point of breaking out again between Venice and the Turks, so they made the return journey with light hearts, and rejoined Ignatius in Venice in mid-May.

On June 24, feast of St. John the Baptist, Ignatius, Francis, Bobadilla, Lainez, Salmeron, Codure and Rodriguez were ordained priests by the bishop of Arba, who declared that no other ordination had ever given him such spiritual consolation, such was the fervour of the new priests—two of whom, Ignatius and Xavier, were to be elevated to the altar.

CHAPTER VI

BOLOGNA AND ROME (JULY, 1537–MARCH 16, 1540)

By the end of July, 1537, it was evident that no pilgrim ships would be able to evade the Turkish blockade of the Adriatic, so the new priests, a month after their ordination, left Venice to prepare themselves in solititude for their first Mass. Francis and Salmeron chose for their quarters a ruined hut near Monselice, perched on a volcanic hillside that looked east across the plains to the River Brenta and the Gulf of Venice.

"Having found in a private place a desolate and ruined cottage," Torsellino tells us in his Life of Francis: "he thatched the roof thereof with straw and so made himself a little sorry habitation. Then, that experience might make a deeper impression on his mind of the poverty of Christ whilst He was a child, and of His solitude when He was a man, he tasked himself to this kind of life. He ate very sparingly of such meat only as he got by begging. If perchance he got a little oil or other meat, he thought he had made a dainty meal indeed. He lay on the bare ground with straw under him in the foresaid hovel, exposed to rain, wind, and weather." When, fifteen years later, he lay dying on Sanchian in just such a ruined hut, he must have remembered the penances and ecstasies of those August days on the Italian hill, and the

57

gold of harvest-fields, the green and purple grapes, the silver of olives and willows, bathed in luminous gold till, with sunset, the deadly malarial mists came creeping up from the marshes.

"Remembering that God leadeth a soul into solitude and there speaketh to her heart, he gave more attentive ear to what his Lord God should speak within him. He prayed therefore very much and often. . . . What discommodities and painful labours he endureth in that place, and what true and perfect consolation he received through converse with the Heavenly Spouse we may easier imagine than by words express" (Torsellini).

In that remote and silent solitude, where the soul, free from human activities and distractions, could lose itself in divine contemplation perhaps his thoughts turned again with longing to the complete silence and solitude of the Carthusian life. It had drawn him so strongly in the first days of his conversion that Ignatius had had as much difficulty in keeping him from the cloister as he had had in winning him from the world. Now too, in the light and troubled sleep on the ground, came again those vivid dreams which revealed the deep and hidden desire that was to grow stronger as its fulfilment seemed to recede. Lainez has told us how often, when he and Francis were sharing sleeping-quarters, Francis would wake suddenly with the cry: "Jesus! I am crushed! I dreamed that I was carrying on my back an Indian so heavy that I could not lift him."

By his long talks with de Gouvea—of the Portuguese empire in the Indies and the millions of heathen beyond its frontiers, or of the hopes or fears of the missionary students being trained for work in the East—the seed of his future apostleship had already been sown at Ste. Barbe.

In the piazzas of Venice he had seen in the gigantic negroes who followed rich senators and merchants not slaves bought in the world's market but souls for whom Christ had died. And the pilgrimage, so often deferred—its ultimate goal for him was not Jerusalem, but beyond, the unknown lands whence had come the Wise Men to worship at Bethlehem.

The forty days of their retreat over, the two men went out to preach and teach in the surrounding villages. Francis would borrow a stool, mount on it in the street, and waving hat and hands call to the people. Idlers and loafers would collect, thinking that this half-starved pair in tattered black gowns were strolling mountebanks or jugglers. Laughter and coarse jests punctuated the uncouth Italian, plentifully sprinkled with French and Spanish words. Others came to join in the joke. Gradually laughter was silenced, the audience caught and held. Ardent love, whether for God or man, speaks a universal language which needs no interpreter.

During September the eleven reassembled at Vicenza in the deserted convent of San Pietro in Vanello. Sitting on a little straw among the ruins while the rain drove through gaping doors and windows, they discussed the future, and the new order was christened. "Considering that they wished to serve no other leader but Jesus it seemed to them that they should take His Name and call themselves the Company of Jesus" (Polanco).

When and in what church in Vicenza Francis celebrated his first Mass we are not told, though one would like to imagine, knowing his devotion to our Lady, that it was in the little old pilgrimage church of the Madonna de Monte, with its wide view over the fertile plain to the little town circled by its two rivers.

Torsellini has tried to express something of his fervour. "You would say that he did not so much *believe* That which is contained under these sacred mysteries as he *saw* it and *beheld* it with his eyes. And such indeed was the ardent fire that inflamed both his soul and body that they who beheld the tears streaming so sweetly from his eyes could not themselves abstain from weeping. And this singular feeling of devotion he from thenceforward retained throughout his whole life in such sort as if coming every day like a new priest to the altar he had tasted that first sweetness of those sacred mysteries."

But human strength had reached its limits of endurance. Semi-starvation, exposure to cold and wet and malarial mists, nights of prayer and continual penance at last broke the body of whose strength and swiftness Francis had been so proud. He and Rodriguez collapsed with fever and had to be carried back to the hospital for incurables where they had worked so hard. The two were laid on a narrow bed in an annexe open to wind and rain. While one, burning with fever, flung off the one poor blanket, the other, shivering with cold, tried to huddle it round him. Their recovery was rather an answer to prayer than the result of human care.

It was now seen that the pilgrimage to Jerusalem must be abandoned. Ignatius, himself bound for Rome with Lainez and Salmeron, sent out the rest, like the Apostles, by two and two through the towns. Francis and Bobadilla were assigned to Bologna, Francis because of his university training and degree, also probably because his winning charm and the courtesy of a great gentleman would counteract the bluntness and occasionally tactless ardour of Bobadilla.

It had been at Bologna—with Paris, Salerno and Oxford the oldest of the great universities—that Juan de Jassu had taken his doctor's degree, and his son must now have felt thoroughly at home in the familiar academic atmosphere. The streets which rayed out from the central cathedral of San Pietro were full of students and professors, in hoods or swathed, turban-like caps, full-skirted caped black gowns, and boots of soft leather. The air rang with the same arguments as at Paris, with the quick staccato of the Italians, the slower, heavier Latin of English, Germans, Swiss.

The scholastic year had just begun when Francis arrived with Bobadilla early in October. It was not to the lecture-halls that he hurried, though, but to the tomb of St. Dominic. As he knelt before it, guarded by the angel of the young Michael Angelo and its kneeling fellow, his fervour was noticed, and when, after taking up his quarters at the hospital, he used to say Mass at the altar before the tomb, a Spanish lady, a Dominican tertiary, was so impressed by his devotion that at last, with a friend, she ventured to speak to him. Both were convinced that they had spoken with a saint, and one persuaded her uncle, a Canon of San Petronio and rector of Santa Lucia, to offer Francis the hospitality of his house and altar. Francis could not well refuse lodging, but insisted on continuing to beg his bread.

His days were filled not with academic arguments but with the care of the sick, prisoners, miserable and outcasts. His sermons were of the simplest, without rhetorical flourish; their directness and zeal cut, like a flaming sword, straight to the essentials of religion. The oft-repeated motive was the necessity of frequenting the sacraments;

and soon the primitive custom, so long fallen into disuse, of frequent confession and Communion spread through town and university.

His host was so deeply impressed by his holiness that ultimately he gave his house to become the first Jesuit college in Bologna. Meantime he tried in vain to induce his guest to take more sleep and food, not to pass whole nights in penance and sorrow for the sufferings of Christ. His mother's prayers and meditations during Passion Week, those few days immediately before his birth, seem to have stamped indelibly on Francis's heart the seal of the Cross. When he celebrated the Mass of the Passion it was always with tears, often with such ecstasy that his wearied and impatient server would try to recall him to himself by repeated pulls at his chasuble.

Christmas was over. The winter was cold and unhealthy. Bitter winds swept down from the Apennines. Fogs from the Romagnan marshes enveloped the city in a wet white shroud. Day after day Francis's thin cloak and gown, his thinner body, were drenched with icy rain. Another breakdown was inevitable. Burning with fever, his teeth chattering with ague, he tried to struggle on—for Bobadilla, who might have controlled this rash excess of zeal, had been summoned to Ferrara on the death of Hozes. When he and Codure arrived in Bologna in March, 1538, it was to find Francis only just able to crawl from his sickbed, and when the three reached Rome at Easter all were aghast at the invalid's appearance. "He was pale, thin, unrecognisable, no longer a living man but a corpse," wrote Rodriguez. No one dreamed that he would survive the Roman summer or ever again be capable of work, and his name was omitted from the lists of preachers and organisers. For Francis of Xavier, only thirty-two, exterior activity was apparently over, life drawing swiftly to its close.

"The strange priests," as Ignatius and his nine companions were nicknamed, were already well-known figures in Rome. They lived in a small house below the Ara Coeli, near the Torre del Angelo, which was lent by a friendly citizen and had the reputation of being haunted. Seven churches in the centre of the city were filled by their preaching. Orphanages and asylums were founded, the sick and prisoners visited, sinners pursued and reclaimed.

The blazing heat of the Roman summer drove all who could escape to the coolness of the Apennines or the Lake of Albano. The Jesuits, still at work in the airless and fetid slums, were suddenly attacked. An Augustinian friar, a brilliant and popular preacher whose heresy they had exposed, stirred up calumnies. With the aid of a Navarrese to whom Ignatius had refused admittance to his band, he declared that the companions had been chased by the Inquisition from Spain, France and northern Italy. Not content with a verbal retraction, Ignatius followed the Pope to his villa at Frascati with the result that, in November, 1538, the Governor of Rome, by order of Paul III, pronounced official sentence proclaiming the innocence of Ignatius and his sons.

The winter then beginning was one of the worst ever known in Rome. Cold, rain and snow, lasting till the end of May, 1539, resulted in a terrible famine. The Jesuits worked day and night, feeding three or four hundred at their house, carrying to shelter those dying of starvation in the streets, burying the corpses of those lying in the gutters. At the beginning of Lent, when their work of

charity was at its height, the Pope ordered Rodriguez and
Broet to Siena. This precipitated the decision as to the
future. The pilgrimage to Jerusalem was now impossible,
and the Pope had pertinently inquired: "Why are you
so desirous of going to Jerusalem? Italy is a good and
true Jerusalem, if you wish to gather fruit for the Church
of God."

Ignatius put before his nine companions the question:
Should the union begun at Montmartre four and a half
years before be now ended by a general separation to different fields of work, or should a permanent society be
established which should survive the death of its founder
and first members? At the close of the evening a unanimous resolution was passed that a permanent society be
founded. After a month of further prayer and deliberation
Codure, acting as secretary, recorded: "We decided, not
by a majority of votes but with complete unanimity, that
it was convenient and indeed necessary to live under
obedience" to a superior elected from among themselves.

On September 3, 1539, the five "chapters" of the suggested outline for the constitution of the Company were
laid before the Pope, who at once expressed his verbal
approval. Rome, as always, moved slowly, and it was
not till over a year later that the Papal Bull *Regimini
militantis Ecclesiæ* was promulgated with the final approval and confirmation of the Society of Jesus. By that
time Francis was eleven hundred miles away, preparing in
Lisbon for his departure to India.

During these two years (April, 1538–March, 1540) we
hear little of Francis. Only rarely incidents relating to him
flash out like the gleam of spearheads in the night. In
spite of the fears of his friends he regained his health
little by little. By Lent, 1539, he was preaching in the

French church of San Luigi, and hearing confessions. He too had to endure his share of calumnies, and one specially wounding to his sensitive nature. Believing one of his penitents to be as innocent as himself, he became involved in a scandal stirred up by her; and this was probably the reason for an incident related by Rodriguez. Rodriguez, ill, lay awake one night watching his infirmarian, Francis, asleep on a mat by his bed and was suddenly startled to see him leap up with a cry of horror, flinging out his hands as if to beat off an attack, while blood poured from nose and mouth. "What is it?" "Nothing." Then the invalid, pardonably irritated by such an answer, exclaimed: "What, *nothing*, when you are streaming with blood?" He could get no explanation, however, and it was not till months later that Francis, about to embark at Lisbon, drew Simon aside and told him how he had dreamed vividly that, during a journey, a woman had forced her way into his room in the inn, and the violence with which he had repulsed her had broken a blood-vessel in his chest.

Sometimes Francis acted as porter, as on the occasion when Araoz, a nephew of Ignatius, came to call on his uncle; but the greater part of the time he was Ignatius's private secretary, and helped him to deal with the correspondence, which was already beginning to assume heroic proportions. It is refreshing to find that his efficiency was not always equal to his enthusiasm. Father Estrada, young and cheerful, enjoyed teasing his senior over the lack of answer to several of his communications. "Whose fault? Lord Master Francis's, of course! His hands are numbed with cold and it does not dawn on him that fire was made to warm oneself at!"

Ignatius, with that Napoleonic genius which saw so far and so clearly and had the same grasp of the minutest details as of world-wide combinations realised the immense importance of correspondence in the work of an order controlled from Rome while its members were scattered through the world. At Easter, 1538, there were ten companions in Rome. At the death of Ignatius eighteen years later the Society numbered thirteen provinces, and its chain of missions circled the world from Brazil to Japan.

During these two years, perhaps the happiest of his life, Francis's character hardened into a stronger mould. He and Ignatius were alike in so much, in race, in nobility of birth, in heroic courage, in burning enthusiasm. It was not strange that in every case needing careful consideration they should, invariably and independently, reach the same conclusion. Two people living together and united by deepest love and sympathy tend to speak and think alike, though it is difficult or impossible to tell how much the stronger influences the decision of the weaker.

Of these two Ignatius of Loyola was the stronger. With less intellectual training than Francis he had a supreme genius for organisation and for training men. He had too that other attribute of genius which makes it so often incomprehensible and unsympathetic to the commonplace mind—the vision beyond present difficulties to the ultimate goal, and an apparent ruthlessness which knows that a great end cannot be achieved without the sacrifice of lesser things and affections.

Francis had not this power naturally. Highly strung, sensitive, sympathetic, he had some of the failing, as all the virtues of the artist. To the end of his life he kept the qualities of youth—burning zeal and enthusiasm, dauntless courage, unbounded generosity, the spirit of gay adventure, consuming love.

Ignatius, who had bought his own experience so dearly, knew the folly of excessive fasting, penances, and castigation of the body, knew that in this world soul and mind cannot function adequately through the instrument of a broken and worn-out body. "The spirited steed needs curb, not spur. No man can fight successfully if he is overladen with weapons." The golden mean of Aristotle, the moderation which is virtue between its two excesses which are vices—its acceptance did not come easily to Francis, but from the hands of Ignatius he took and kept it.

Then came the moment when Ignatius had to make what was one of the hardest decisions of his life. In August, 1539, Don Pedro Mascarenhas, Portuguese ambassador to the Pope, received a letter from his king asking for Jesuit missionaries for the East. The Pope referred the matter to the Society, whose acceptance was immediate. Simon Rodriguez, Portuguese by birth, one of the students who had been sent by the king to Ste. Barbe, was the obvious choice for one of the two who were all that could be spared, and he was accordingly recalled from Siena early in 1540. Bobadilla, working at Naples, was the other to be chosen. His fierce ardour, his dominance, his quick decisions, seemed likely to be suitable to work among the heathen. Obstinacy and impetuosity, which were a disadvantage at home, might prove invaluable half a world from headquarters. He also was recalled to Rome to start with Rodriguez and the ambassador.

He arrived, barely convalescent from an attack of fever and paralysed with sciatica. Rodriguez, also weak with fever, had been sent on to Lisbon by sea. The ambassador, ready to start, unable to wait for Bobadilla's recovery, clamoured for another to replace him. The only possible candidate for the mission was Francis.

How many reasons against such a decision, apart from the cry of Ignatius's own heart! The loss to himself of his secretary, his *alter ego,* the final separation in this world from his best beloved son—knowing Ignatius we know that this would weigh nothing in the balance. But Francis had not fully recovered from his illnesses. He was still liable to violent attacks of fever. Was it not madness to send him to a climate still more deadly? He had not yet held a position of authority and responsibility. Had not the Holy Father himself pointed out the supreme need of Italy for the companions? Francis's fine mind, trained intellect, and charm of person and manner would be lost to Rome and Italy, wasted in work among untaught savages whom a man of coarser grain would surely handle more successfully. If Francis was to go Ignatius knew that he would send him to lifelong exile, to almost certain martyrdom, while his gifts would be finally lost to Europe. As for Francis, his heart too was torn in opposing ways. To go—it had been his dream and desire for so long to carry the tidings of Christ into the darkness beyond the sunrise—yet to go meant not only to leave for ever in this world his "father in the bowels of Christ" and his beloved brethren and friends, but also to assume such a position of authority and responsibility as the sensitive soul always fears. Easier for him, though, since not with him rested the final decision. He had only to hear and obey.

Ribadeneira compresses the climax of the interior drama into a few words: "Suddenly Ignatius, who was ill in bed, called Master Father Francis Xavier and said to him: 'Master Francis, you know that by order of His Holiness two of us are to go to the Indies and that we have chosen Master Bobadilla for this mission. Illness prevents his departure. The ambassador cannot wait for his recovery. The work is yours.' At once the blessed Father gladly and quickly replied: 'Good! I am here and ready.' " (*Pues, sus! Heme aqui!*)

Francis had twenty-four hours to make his preparations. They were soon finished. He mended his torn soutane and put together the few possessions he was to take with him—crucifix, breviary and Marcus Marulus's *Institution of the Religious Life*. All three are still extant, the breviary at Nantes, the other two at Madrid. The crucifix is the famous one known as that of the crab, from its miraculous rescue from the sea. Both cross and figure are of wood, with metal rings at the end of the cross-bar; the figure, which is nailed to the cross, is beautifully carved and about four inches in height. The book, a thick octavo volume of 680 pages, printed at Cologne, in 1531, though worn by use, has its page margins empty of notes. Already Francis observed the future rule that a Jesuit should write nothing in a printed book.

He made out three papers—his approval in advance of all that should be ruled in the Constitution of the Order, his form of profession, and his vote for the superior to be elected. He then went to receive the Papal commission and blessing. Among the Ciceronian periods of the speeches with which Torsellini's imagination has adorned this interview one sentence seems to have the true Xavierian ring. In answer to the Pope's question why he had been chosen to go Francis answers: "It belongeth not to him that obeyeth to judge what he can do but to them that command."

The next morning he was riding north across the Campagna with the ambassador and his suite on the way to Lisbon (March 16, 1540).

CHAPTER VII

LISBON (MARCH 16, 1540–APRIL 7, 1541)

ONCE again Francis rode north into the unknown. Once again, after so many weary journeys poor and on foot, he travelled as befitted his birth, with a good horse between his knees, the ambassador's suite at his service, with an official riding ahead to prepare lodgings and food in wayside inns. By the time they reached Loreto (Palm Sunday, March 21) the conquest of Pedro Mascarenhas was already complete, and his kindnesses such that Francis wrote to Ignatius: "I do not know how I could resign myself to them except to think that in the Indies I shall be able to repay them, perhaps by the sacrifice of my life."

They rode along the Adriatic coast to Ancona and on to Bologna in time for Easter. Francis, the ideal travelling-companion, first up in the morning, smoothing difficulties and ruffled tempers, helping grooms with recalcitrant horses, ready to exchange his picked mount with another dissatisfied with his, was as popular with the ambassador and Don Francisco de Lima, a young Portuguese nobleman on his way home from the grand tour of France, Germany and Italy, as he was with grooms, servants and secretaries.

Bologna, which had not forgotten him during his two years' absence, gave him a royal welcome. The house where he stayed was besieged. The church of Sta. Lucia was packed hours before his Mass begun. He was mobbed

70

in the streets, spent most of the night as well as the day in the confessional.

On Easter Day came letters from Rome, and somehow he managed to find time to answer them. His to Ignatius was the first of that wonderful series which ended only with his death, and through it rings the cry of the heart for the anguish of bodily separation which was to echo again and again across half the world: "God knows what consolation and joy they gave me. I think that in this life we shall meet again only in letters, but in the next world we shall see each other face to face—and with how many embraces! While the rest of this life lasts let us visit each other often by letter. I will do so. I shall write often, as you bade me." (March 31, 1540.)

The departure from Bologna was to the accompaniment of cries, lamentations and tears, but Francis's heart was leaping forward to his reunion with Peter Faber, who had gone to Parma with Lainez eight months before. Parma was reached. God asked another sacrifice. That very day Peter had left to visit a sick novice at Brescia fifty miles away. "He deliberated whether or no he should go after me to see me, but his companions and the ambassador also advised him to remain. It was the better part and the better advice." (Faber.)

It is likely that during the stay at Parma Francis met a young Italian student, Antonio Criminale, who had made the Exercises under Faber. This pure and ardent youth was to be received into the Society the next year by Ignatius, to follow Francis to India where he was to be the first Jesuit martyr (1549).

The long journey across the Lombardy plains, over the Alps to Lyons and through southern France to Bayonne, was full of adventure—men nearly drowned in flooded rivers, overwhelmed by snow, crushed by the fall of their horses; and always Francis, by prayer or fearless attempts at rescue, was the means of saving them. To his Portuguese namesake Francis devoted himself specially, soon won his confidence, and heard the story of his travels, his gay careless life in the great towns he had visited, his long neglect of the sacraments. The young fidalgo tells us how Francis "showed me great friendship, sought out my company, lightened my heart by his natural gaiety as we rode side by side." The end was inevitable. The two turned aside into a church they were passing. Don Francisco de Lima made his general confession: "Then, for the first time I understood what it is to be a Christian." (Cros.)

Once more Francis thrilled to the familiar sound of Basque as they left Bayonne and, as far as Fuentarrabia, retraced the steps of his journey of fourteen years ago. Away beyond the Pyrenees to the east lay Pamplona, Sangüesa and Javier, now the property of his eldest brother, Miguel. They passed San Sebastian, huddled round Monte Urgull while the Atlantic breakers, thundering day and night, flung white spray into the soft air; then the company turned inland up the valley of the Urola, for Francis carried a letter from Ignatius to his elder brother, Don Beltran de Loyola, who was to offer hospitality to the ambassador and his suite.

Here every sound and sight reminded Francis—if he had needed reminder—of his beloved father in God, whom in this life he should meet no more in the flesh.

The river, dull jade green, writhed snake-like between the hills, clothed here and there with oaks still wearing their russet of last year's leaves, and beeches vivid with new leaves. Pastures and fields of young corn gleamed emerald. The dull purple of judas-trees made sombre patches amid the snow of pear- and cherry-blossom, the rose of almond and apple. High on the mountains the grey rocks were streaked with yellow standstone, like steel damascened with gold. Heavy white clouds drifted slowly by before the breeze that silvered the copper aspen leaves, and where their shadows passed the hills turned to dull bronze against the sky. A country with the clean hardness of metal, the brilliance of enamel, a people with lean hard bodies and olive faces that might have been hewn in wood—this was the country, this the people of Ignatius, and no man can be fully known till the country that nurtured him, the people that bred him, open their hearts.

The valley widened. The Urumea came leaping over its rocks, strong with heavy rain and melting snow. Through the narrow streets of Azpeitia, huddled below towering pyramids of gaunt grey rock, rode the weary company, and in the evening glow saw the little square fortress-house of Loyola where Don Beltran waited to welcome them. In the time of Ignatius's grandfather the house had been demolished to half its height as a penalty for continuous fighting. It had been rebuilt, and the huge stone blocks of the original thirteenth-century stronghold were surmounted by two storeys of pinky brown brick ornamented with horizontal bands of an intricate diamond pattern, and little round towers at each corner.

So many things reminded Francis of his own home. Over the arched door here, as at Javier, the family arms were carved in stone, the two wolves of Loyola. In the tiny chapel, as at Javier, was an object of special veneration. Like Francis's sister Magdalena, the bride of Ignatius's eldest brother, Doña Magdalena de Aroaz, had been a favourite maid of honour of Isabella, who had given her as a wedding-present a painting of the Annun-

ciation. Like the miraculous crucifix at Javier, it was said
to have been seen to sweat on several occasions. In this
little chapel Ignatius had worshipped as child, boy and
youth. Here, as soon as his wounded leg could bear him,
he had come during his convalescence, and after his conversion in 1521. Here, eleven years later (1551), Francis
Borgia, now Duke of Gandia and viceroy of Catalonia,
was to say his first Mass,—Loyola then belonging to his
younger brother, Juan, who had married Lorenza de
Loyola, Ignatius's great-niece. Here, too, Francisco de
Javier must have said daily Mass during the ambassador's
stay, and spent hours in prayer before the Madonna—like
the paintings in Pamplona cathedral, quiet and homely
with downcast eyes, under the long rippling hair the
brooding face of unawakened innocence. As, having knelt
here for the last time, he turned in his saddle for a last
look back at the rose-grey house set in the rose and snow
of its spring orchards, Francis surely felt that yet another
link was severed, one more farewell completed. It is a
matter of deep regret that the letter which he wrote to
Ignatius from Loyola is no longer extant.

On they went, through Burgos, with its old leather
crucifix that men said was moulded of human skin,
through Valladolid, where Ferdinand and Isabella had
been secretly married and where, a few weeks after
Francis's birth, Christopher Columbus had died in want
and misery, through Salamanca, with its Roman bridge
below the hill-perched town, and the cavalcade entered
Portugal.

South they rode as the early June sun beat down fiercely
on pines and maples and junipers, cork-trees and ilexes.
In the Tagus valley white magnolias, honeysuckle and
roses filled the evening air with heavy sweetness. On the

uplands sheets of yellow and white cistus were mingled with the clean fragrance of wild rosemary. Almeirim, the royal winter palace, was passed, and the old Moorish fortress of Santarem with its minaretted church of St. João, then the widening river was spired with masts of ships from every nation, and there, regal on her seven hills, lay Lisbon. Round her the fertile country poured its riches, orange- and lemon-orchards, olive- and mulberry-trees, figs and vines, wheat and rye and oats, but in the plains towards the sea the trees bent south-east as if they hunched their shoulders against the wind that blows in from the Atlantic eleven months in the year.

Francis's first thought on arrival was to rejoin Rodriguez in the Hospital of All Saints, where he had been since his arrival by sea two months before. Far from having been cured by his voyage Simon was still a prey to fever. "The day I arrived in Lisbon" (mid-June), wrote Francis to Ignatius, "I found Master Simon expecting his bout of quartan fever. My coming caused him so much joy, and mine was so great, that the two joys combined effectively banished the fever, and since that day a whole month has passed without his having suffered from it again."

Along the banks of the Tagus rose the great houses of nobles and merchant princes, built of dazzling white limestone from Alcantara in the *Arto Manoelino,* called after the present king's father. They were a strange mixture of flamboyant Gothic, Italian renaissance, Moorish and Indian. As in Venice, everywhere east and west mingled. The men who brought home giant fortunes from India brought, too, an Oriental voluptuousness and love of display which showed itself in the gorgeousness of their houses and dress, the splendour of their retinues. In the

narrow, winding streets climbing to the cathedral of São
Jorge that had been the Moorish citadel for three hundred
years, along quays crowded with ships loading and un-
loading till the air was laden with the smell of spices,
came and went a throng from every part of the world,
fidalgoes and merchants, wild soldiers and sailors burnt
to the red of mahogany, huge negro slaves from East
Africa, turban'd Hindus, slim brown Cingalese and
Malayans.

And behind all this gay pageant and wealth, as Francis
soon found, was the appalling misery of the poor,
huddled in foul slums beyond the splendid façades of the
river palaces. Most miserable and furtive of all were the
Marranos or New Christians, the survivors or descendants
of the Jews forcibly baptised by Manuel I in 1497. In the
month of Francis's birth two thousand wretched Jews had
been massacred in a riot in Lisbon alone. Those who had
managed to escape and had settled in Holland by their
money and brains were already preparing a Dutch com-
merce which was ultimately to ruin Portuguese power in
the East. Four years before Francis's arrival (1536) King
John had established the Inquisition, in imitation of Ferdinand and Isabella, whose grand-daughter Catherine he
had married. Pope Paul III for some time refused to sanction the institution and still withheld his approval of the
appointment of the king's brother, the Infante Enrique,
as Grand Inquisitor.

A few days after Don Pedro had reached Lisbon he
fetched Francis and Simon to an audience in the royal
palace, which was near the hospital, looking south across
the Tagus to Almada. The king, four years older than
Francis, was alone with the queen when the ambassador
introduced the two Jesuits and for an hour he questioned

them closely about the Company, its constitution, objects, rules, and methods of silencing calumny.

The keen interest that he displayed at this first interview was to persist. He showed himself a generous benefactor of the Society of Jesus, amongst other benefits putting them in charge of the great university of Coimbra, their first college. Pious and well-meaning, he was inspired by Francis to great schemes for the evangelisation of the East and for the moral improvement of his own Court and capital, but a fatal weakness undermined his character, made him incapable of measures strong enough to purge the Augaean stables of his eastern administration, and brought on him the well-deserved reproaches and warnings which Francis did not hesitate to write from India. Now, however, all was serene and hopeful. The king commended to the two the young men of his Court for whom he felt himself responsible, then he summoned the survivors of his nine children, the Infanta Maria, aged thirteen, and Prince John, a baby of three. They received a Jesuit blessing, and as the audience ended the king exclaimed enthusiastically to the ambassador: "Whatever it cost me I should like to have all the members of the Company here in my kingdom!"

It was with the greatest difficulty that Francis and Rodriguez escaped from the board and lodging arranged for them in the palace of Paços de Ribeira and remained at the hospital near by. Soon, however, pressure of work made it impossible for them to beg their bread. The entire Court was under their direction. Simon Rodriguez, Portuguese by birth and originally one of the students sent to Ste. Barbe at royal expense to be educated for mission-work in the East, was at home, among his own people, speaking his own language. Had Francis learnt Portu-

guese from fellow-students in Paris, on journeys with
Simon or during the three months on the way to Lisbon?
At any rate his success with the pages and young courtiers
was complete and instantaneous. With him youth was
always at its ease, because he retained to the end all the
best qualities of youth. His quick humour, his smiling
mouth, his shining, uplifted eyes, his sympathy and laughter were lures which drew—and, once drawn to him, all
were caught and held. Young nobles and courtiers, boyish
pages—he saw again in them his own ambitions, his love
of splendour and display, his dreams of fame and glory.
Then, as Ignatius had done with him, he gave them the
Exercises, set before them the Two Standards, the
"amendation and reform of life and estate," "how we
ought to dispose ourselves to come to perfection in that
state of life whatever it be which God our Lord shall grant
us to choose." Perfection, not the bare minimum necessary
to salvation, but the highest of which each soul is capable
when emptied of self and filled with the grace of God.
Crowds made the Exercises. Francis and Simon were so
busy in the confessional that no time was left for the
sermons which, at royal command, they had begun to
preach. In Francis's first letter to Ignatius (July 13, 1540)
he describes the changed aspect of the Court, and the
attempts already being made to prevent their departure
for the Indies.

A few weeks after Francis's arrival in Lisbon he had
witnessed the return of the East Indian fleet, its battered
galleons coming to anchor under the beautiful Torre de
Belem, west of the city, and the splendid Hieronomite
Monastery, built on the site of the sailors' home of Henry
the Navigator where Vasco da Gama had stayed before
he sailed in 1497 round the Cape to India. On one of

these ships returned a man who could have told Francis
more than any other about the Moluccas, which he had
governed with such justice and success that he had been
offered by the natives the crown of Ternate. It is unlikely
that the two men met, for a grateful country rewarded
Antonio Galvão for his heroic services by leaving him to
die, penniless and alone, in a hospital.

Another work, more difficult and more heart-breaking
than that at Court, was now assigned to the two Jesuits.
In the prisons of the Inquisition, established four years
before, were fifty "New Christians"—Jews and Moors
who, forcibly baptised, had been discovered practising the
religion of their fathers in secret. The king's brother,
Cardinal Anrique, appointed Francis and Simon chaplains
to these prisoners. Catechising, instruction, and in some
case the first week of the Exercises (the meditations on sin
and hell, leading to examen of conscience), were given,
and not always in vain. A learned Rabbi from Africa was
converted and others softened. "God has bestowed a
great grace upon us," said some of the exercitants, "because He has granted us grace to know so many things
necessary for our souls' salvation." Doubtless, after
knowing Francis, many would have echoed de Lima's
cry: "Then, for the first time in my life I understood
what it is to be a Christian." Two, recalcitrant to the end,
were accompanied to the stake by Simon and Francis (the
first executions under the Portuguese inquisition), and the
sight of that fiery death agony can hardly have left finely-
strung nerves intact.

There was other work too, among the sick in hospital,
the poor and miserable in the stinking, airless slums. The
summer passed, with its enervating, life-draining heat, and
it is scarcely surprising that when Simon writes to Ignatius

on October 8 Francis, exhausted by heat and overwork, has been sent for a few days' holiday at Pedro Mascarenhas's country house at Palma. "Master Francis and I are worried about the Indies," says Rodriguez, "not because the voyage is impossible but because the king will not consent to it. From what we hear he says that we are absolutely necessary at his Court. . . . Let us know your feelings in the matter."

Early in November the two Jesuits accompanied the Court to its winter quarters at Almeirin, on the left bank of the Tagus about forty-five miles from Lisbon. Francis was corresponding with his cousin on the maternal side, Martin de Azpilcueta, generally known as the Navarrese doctor, who had been sent by Charles V at his brother-in-law's request to lecture at Coimbra. Martin wrote three times to try to arrange a meeting, and Francis declares that his letter of October 22 "filled my soul with such joy and consolation that nothing could give me greater pleasure except the sight of you" (November 4, 1540). But Francis was not to visit the "Portuguese Athens," where he might have met a poor but well-born young student, Luiz de Camoens, who, a year after Francis's death, was to go to India and by the publication of his great epic the "Lusiads" to become Portugal's national poet. Martin caught fire from Francis's missionary enthusiasm. "I should have ended my life long ago," he wrote afterwards, "if, before his departure, he had not considered that at my advanced age (forty-eight) I was not capable of such missionary work. He wrote telling me to bear our separation on earth patiently, in hopes of meeting in heaven." Here is a glimpse of the new Francis, born during those two years in Rome with Ignatius, wise, far-seeing, prudent—for others, never for himself.

It was already more than a year since the Pope's verbal approval of the Company, but strong opposition in the Sacred College delayed its official confirmation. John of Portugal brought pressure to bear through his agents in Rome. Ignatius promised three thousand Masses. His nine "children" joined their prayers to his. Before Christmas, 1540, news came to Almeirin from Rome, with a copy of the Bull of September finally approving and confirming the foundation of the Society of Jesus.

Still the future of Francis and Rodriguez remained uncertain. The king, Court, and people demanded that they should stay in Portugal, where they had already worked such wonders. Cardinal Enrique added his persuasions to those who claimed them for the East. "It was impossible to detain these fathers without opposing the decree of Providence, which had brought them to Portugal only to go on the foreign mission." Before the new year John talked of founding a Jesuit house at Lisbon or Evora; then, increasing the bribe, he wrote to Ignatius of a Jesuit university, of confiding Coimbra to Jesuit direction. Francis, too, wrote for a plan of study and discipline for students. "If a college is built for us here we foresee no difficulty. Everyone is ready to build houses for us if there is someone to fill them." A letter came from Ignatius in answer to that of Rodriguez, bidding him and Francis submit to the king's decision, but adding that he himself thought the best solution of the difficulty was that Simon should stay, Francis go. The king agreed. The Court returned to Lisbon, and preparations began for the sailing of the fleet, which generally took place in mid-March.

With Francis were to go Micer Paul de Camerino, an Italian secular priest who had been admitted to the Society and returned to Rome with Rodriguez in the spring of

1540 as a volunteer for the Indian mission, and Francis Mansilhas. The latter was the only recruit for the voyage secured in Lisbon in nine months of unwearying effort. In spite of studying in Paris he had not been able to muster enough Latin to be ordained priest, but Francis hoped that the scarcity of priests in the Indies would enable him to be ordained.

Don Martin de Souza, the new governor, was going out to India with the fleet this spring, and the king commanded the Count of Castanheira, who was in charge of the naval equipment, to arrange for the priests to be on board the governor's ship and to have everything of the best. It was the custom for passengers travelling at State expense to be supplied with all necessaries, so Castanheira asked Francis for a list of all he would need for himself and his two companions. All Francis asked for was a warm soutane apiece to protect them against the cold of the Cape and a few books of devotion which would be unobtainable in India. He refused all provisions and the servant offered him. "You must take him for the sake of your position," argued the count. "You cannot wash your own linen and stir your own stew." "Señor," answered Francis gravely, "this jealous assertion of a pretended dignity, this zeal to keep up pretensions, is what has brought Christianity to its present deplorable state. As for me I intend to wash my linen and cook my own meals as well as attending to those of others. By doing this I do not expect to lose any respect."

On March 18, 1541, Francis wrote his letters of farewell to Rome, where Ignatius, Lainez, Salmeron, le Jay, Broet and Codure were gathered to elect a general for the Society. Francis had left behind him his written choice: "I, Francis, am of this opinion: the general of our Society . . . should be our true father Don Ignatius; for, as he has united us with no little effort, so he will certainly know how to sustain, rule, and increase us . . . for he knows us best." By unanimous votes Ignatius was elected general; but on April 22, when he and his five companions made their solemn profession in San Paolo Fuori, Francis was a fortnight south from Lisbon on the way to Goa.

In his letter to Ignatius Francis, who expected to sail at once, begs for a long letter of advice by the fleet of next year. "For, while admitting that experience will teach us to a certain degree what line to take, yet we trust in God our Saviour that it will please His divine Majesty to reveal the rest to us through you, how we can best serve Him, as He has done up till now. . . . And, beside your customary remembrance of us in your prayers, we beg you to give us a more particular one, for the long voyage and the new relations with the heathen for us who have so little knowledge, gives us the right to greater help than usual. . . . From here there is no more to tell you than that we are on the point of sailing. We end by begging Christ our Lord that He will grant us to see each other again and be reunited bodily in the next life, for in this I do not know if we shall meet again, so great is the distance that separates Rome from India and the harvest that will be found there without seeking elsewhere." Here again is the pain of farewell, the realisation of how utterly he was to be cut off from Ignatius and his companions, the shrinking, too, of the sensitive but eager soul from the appalling responsibility which was to rest on him alone, without help from any other human being.

Everything was ready for departure. Francis was armed with the papal brief appointing "our dear son, Francis

Xavier, member of the said Company of Jesus, professor of Theology," as Apostolic Nuncio to the East, and a second brief giving special powers of absolution, indulgences, and so forth. With these were two letters from the Pope, one adressed "to David King of Ethiopia," the other "to all princes and lords of the islands of the Red, Persian and Indian Oceans and of all countries on this side of the Ganges and beyond it." The king, in his final interview with Francis, asked to be supplied with full details on the state of religion in the East and the best means of spreading the Faith. "He begged him to visit every crown dependency and to take all measures necessary for the progress of religion," Texeira tells us, and the words are important, for they are the best answer to those critics who complain of Francis's incessant journeyings after his short stay at Goa.

Everything was ready, but day after day the wind remained contrary and the fleet lay idle at anchor. Then, after three weeks of waiting, the weather changed, all were ordered on board.

One of the most brilliant passages in the *Lusiads* describes the departure of the fleet for the East. The church of the Hieronomites at Belem was crowded. The shore was crowded too with those left behind—mothers, wives, lovers who never expected to see their dear ones again. The Mass of the Angels was sung, as it was through the year for those in peril at sea—the Mass so familiar to every Lourdes pilgrim, for all the music except that of the Credo is as old as the time of Francis or older.

On this seventh of April, 1541, the monks carried out a pulpit and Francis preached from it to the multitudes assembled on the shore. It was told too how as he was making his thanksgiving after his Mass in the monastery church he was fetched hurriedly to a young noble who had just been mortally wounded in a duel. Kneeling beside the bleeding form Francis heard the dying man's confession, but could not induce him to forgive the enemy who had wounded him. "Would you not pardon him if God granted you to live?" The man, who was already almost dead, gasped an assent. "Then you will recover," answered Francis, who gave him absolution. His promise was fulfilled.

Before he stepped on to the boat, Francis drew Simon Rodriguez aside and explained the dream which had caused him to break a blood-vessel, as well as the cry, "More! More!", with which he had wakened Simon in the Spanish hospice at Rome. In that dream had been revealed what great hardships were in store for him, and with his fearless generosity he had asked for more. "I hope that the hour is come," he added, "when what God revealed to me at that time will be fulfilled."

The shore of Restella, where embarkations took place, should have been called the place of tears, men said. It was wet with tears, the air heavy with sobs of women, the crying of children. For Francis the last farewell was said. The strip of sea widened till he could no longer distinguish the face of Rodriguez, separate his black clad figure from the crowd. The white houses of Lisbon, the Tower of Belem slipped from sight. The point of Trafaria was rounded. Before them lay the open sea, the unknown. It was Francis's birthday; he was thirty-five.

CHAPTER VIII

LISBON–GOA (APRIL 7, 1541–MAY 6, 1542)

"BEFORE my departure I wrote you all the news from Lisbon. We left on April 7, 1541. I was sea-sick for two months, suffering badly for forty days along the Guinea coast, partly on account of the great heat, partly from bad weather. At last God our Lord has been pleased to allow us to reach an island where we have stayed till now."

In a letter to Rome written from Mozambique on New Year's Day, 1542, Francis dismisses the five-months' voyage in these few bald words. Of his own sufferings he had never much to say, but here Torsellini lifts the veil a little: "Although he was ready to languish away also through intolerable heat, yet such was his courage of mind, such the force of the Holy Ghost (Who is ever a most sweet refreshment in heat)," that he managed to continue. . . . "Sea-sick and full of loathsomeness in his stomach, he did at the same time perform all those heroical exercises of charity. The divine virtue which was in him overcame the weakness of his nature, and his noble and constant courage held in the troublesome vomiting of his stomach."

The last, perhaps, may be regarded as not the least of his many miracles! The account of these physical miseries may stand for all the future voyages—always sea-sickness, always, on land or sea, physical prostration from the heat, which even in Lisbon had utterly exhausted him. But it was not only bodily wretchedness that weighed him down, but a sickness of the soul at his surroundings, an inferno both of body and spirit.

The Indian fleet that year consisted of five ships; the three missionaries were on the flagship, the Santiago, with Don Martin de Souza, the new governor. Don Martin, handsome, courteous, with black hair and beard, had spent twenty years in the East Indies as admiral of the fleet and in Brazil. He drew a glowing picture for Francis of nations waiting for the Gospel, of "a certain island of India, inhabited by heathen unmixed by Moors or Jews, assuredly a bountiful harvest, and without doubt the king and all his subjects would become Christians."

Meantime Francis had little time for roseate visions of the future. The caraques, with their three masts, their high bows and sterns, were so little sea-worthy that an average of one in ten was lost on every voyage. The state-rooms in the stern were comparatively large and airy; one of these was assigned to Francis. He was never in it except for the few minutes he managed to snatch alone with God; his berth was occupied by some sick or dying wretch he carried there from the main body of the ship. In the hold, without light or air, were jammed the "steerage" passengers, a strange and godless mixture of adventurers and ne'er-do-wells, small merchants, navvies, soldiers of fortune, negroes, half-castes, paupers, criminals, out-of-works—united only in one thing, the hope of making a fortune in those fabulous colonies of the eastern empire. Many, when they embarked, had no luggage but a spare shirt, a couple of loaves, and some dried fruit.

Once in the open Atlantic the horrors of the voyage began. The top-heavy vessels rolled and staggered under the blows of the waves. Everyone was sick. Ill, dying, and comparatively well were herded together, without sanitary arrangements, ventilation, or berths. The hold, with its seething mass of men and vermin, was a hell whose stench and din beggared description. Worse was to come when for forty days the ships lay becalmed off the coast of Guinea, rolling slowly on an oily swell or shuddering under a cat's-paw of wind hot as the breath of hell. Sometimes, from a low lid of cloud, came torrents of hot rain. Generally the brazen sea flung back the blaze of copper sky with blinding glare till, as one voyager says, "the flames entering the nostrils penetrated the brain and made it boil inside."

In this stifling, heavy atmosphere, torrid day and night alike, little wonder that men's worst passions were forced to unnatural growth. They fought for a mouldering crust of bread, for an extra mouthful of water which was an almost solid mass of worms, for a square foot of shade. They gambled away their last morsel of food, their last rag of clothing. Sweating, naked, mad, they fought with hands and knives. Blasphemies, moans, shrieks of the wounded, gasps of the dying filled the hold. Life was so vile, yet so dear and short, that men snatched at vice, like brutes satisfied every lust.

Into this inferno, like the angels of the Lord into Sodom and Gomorrah, came Francis, and with him Micer Paul and Mansilhas. Continually sick, wasted by heat and racked by fever, yet his spirit still rising above the poor, worn body, he preached on Sundays, catechised and instructed, made peace, silenced oaths, blasphemy, obscene songs. How often the familiar words of the Exercises must have come to his memory: "My soul imprisoned in this corruptible body and my whole self . . . in banishment among brute animals." That he daily gave away his portion of good food from the governor's table can scarcely be counted an act of heroic sanctity, for he can have had little stomach for food what with sea-sickness and the fetid air of the hold where he spent his days. At evening, a few precious moments were spent in his cabin alone with God, recharging the exhausted forces of soul and body. Then some dying wretch, cleansed from filth of body and spirit, would be laid in the cabin and Francis climbed on deck.

At last the Gulf of Guinea lay astern and the five ships forged south along the coast of Angola. The great orange sun sank below the horizon which hid the rocky peak of St. Helena. The phosphorescent waves glowed and sparkled with a strange, unearthly beauty. Round the ship dolphins leapt and dived, as they had round the pirate ship which, bearing Dionysos prisoner, had blossomed magically into vine and grape. The sudden darkness of the tropics fell. The Southern Cross swung up into the sky. Francis laid his aching bones on a coil of rope, the anchor which was his pillow hot under his thin cheek. He was in one of those light, dream-laden sleeps which were all that exhausted nature could snatch.

He was a child, nestled in the voluminous folds of his mother's skirt, sleepy yet wide-eyed as he gazed at the yellow candle-flames that lit the Aurora Mass in the tiny chapel of San Miguel. Above hung the miraculous Christ on the Cross, worn, wounded, dying. Below lay the Babe in the Manger worshipped by wondering Navarrese shepherds. Outside a white silent world was mantled in snow that had driven south through the Pass of Roncesvalles.

He was a boy, riding home under the autumn sunset. He drew his cloak closer, for the frosty air struck chill, and the falcon on his wrist jingled its bells as it eyed the feathery bundle of partridges and pigeons at the saddle-bow. The mist that crept up from the Aragon clung about the brown towers of Javier as softly as a bride is veiled. Was that Doña Maria calling? No, it was Micer Paul, in the dark hour before the dawn, come to tell him that the sick man, in his agony, was crying for Father Francis.

The Cape of Good Hope was rounded. Bitter winter gales blew straight from the Antarctic, but if Paul and Mansilhas were bidden to put on their warm woollen sou-tanes Francis's was more likely to be covering some shiver-ing sinner in the hold. It was September. By now India should have been reached, but so long had been the delays in starting and off Guinea that the monsoon sea-son was at hand, and it would be necessary to winter in Mozambique.

The Santiago that dropped anchor in the shadow of the palm trees on the south coast of the island was a very different ship from that which had left the Tagus. Her gaily-carved and gilded prow and stern were battered and tarnished; her sails torn and stained, yet, like the ship of the captive god, she had suffered a strange transformation. Instead of oaths, fights and vice there was peace and order, instead of bawdy songs hymns. For a century and more those same hymns sounded on every Portuguese caraque eastward bound. For longer still the dying at sea invoked Father Francis in their last agony, the highest praise of any missionary growled by rough soldiers or sailors was: "He's another Xavier."

"The cemetery of the Portuguese," as the island was called from its unhealthiness, had been captured forty years before from the Arabs, who had overrun the coast of East Africa in the tenth century. It was a great trading-centre for slaves and gold, brought down from the chief of Mocaranga. The Portuguese settlement was in the southern part of the island. To the north lay the native quarter of mud-walled, palm-thatched huts. Everywhere was colour and varied life. The Portuguese, lords of all they surveyed, strutted about with negro slaves holding parasols over their heads. In the market were bearded Arabs in turbans, belted tunics and baggy trousers, Hindus with red caste marks on their foreheads, their slim bodies and narrow feet in flowing white garments and scarlet slippers, natives from the hinterland, their naked bodies gleaming like polished bronze. On the mainland, a few miles away, crocodiles lay in the malarial swamps of the Zambesi. Flocks of flamingoes rose with the beauty of dawn-clouds into the sky. Elephants, buffaloes, rhinoceroses came crashing through waving plumes of bamboo. On still nights the roar of lions, the weird cries of hyenas and jackals, floated across the straits, and little green parrots greeted daybreak with shrill chattering.

The ships unloaded their human cargo. The governor and officials took up their quarters in the fortress. From the San Pedro landed one Don Alvaro de Ataide, son of the great Vasco da Gama, brother of the present governor, whom Souza was to supersede; this Alvaro in ten years' time, as governor of Malacca, was to prevent the entrance of the Cross to China and to send Francis to his lonely death on Sanchian. The healthy found accommodation where they could, in poor houses or mud huts. The sick filled the hospital to overflowing, and with them, as always, was Francis, refusing the invitation of Don Martin.

The hospital was a large square building, surrounded by a verandah and houses for the doctors. It was staffed by negroes and seems to have been run with comparative efficiency—necessary indeed when the arrival of a ship outward or homeward bound meant a flood of fever and plague-stricken patients. The eighty deaths reported by Farncis during his five-months' stay were apparently below the average. It was the worst time of the year in the island, only fifteen degrees south of the Equator. In November the temperature sometimes reaches over a hundred in the shade. In December begin the rains which last with little intermission till March, making the air like steam. Malara is rife, sleepy sickness common.

The story of Francis's work in the hospital need not be repeated. It was to be the same always and everywhere. Neglecting the commonest precautions, he worked ceaselessly, bringing hope instead of despair, his smile softening the hardest hearts, his magic personality snatching souls from the very gates of hell. Two instances stand out. On hearing, soon after their arrival, of the death of a young man who had been on the Santiago, Francis asked if he "had known Christ." "No," answered de Souza, who then inquired the reason for Francis's deep depression. "You did not even know him." "That is what grieves me. If I had known him I should have taught him. To think that I had been with him on the same ship all those months and not spoken to him of Christ!"

About Christmas the doctor found Francis, teeth chattering and body shaking with fever, at the bedside of a patient, and ordered him, under obedience, to his own bed. Francis pleaded for a few hours' grace because a "brother" had sore need of him. The "brother" was a young sailor who was dying in delirium unrepentant and unshriven. The next morning the doctor found the man laid on Francis's "bed," a rough wooden frame with interlaced cords and a tattered cover while Francis sat by him on a broken gun-carriage—delightfully inappropriate seat! The sailor regained his senses, made his confession, received the last Sacraments, and died at sunset. Francis then obeyed the doctor, lay for three days delirious, in danger of death, yet managed to pull round in spite of being bled seven times in a few days. It is not surprising that his letter to Ignatius ends somewhat abruptly: "Much as I should like to write more my illness prevents me from doing so at the moment. I was bled to-day for the seventh time and do not feel too well. God be praised!"

His sufferings were not only bodily. He was an idealist, judging others by his own high standard, seeking and expecting only the best. He had left Lisbon with a roseate dream of countries and peoples waiting to be converted, of the Portuguese eastern empire as a forerunner of the kingdom of Christ, with governors, officials and king only desirous of garnering the harvest of souls. Ultimately disappointment and disillusion with the human material he found useless or definitely hostile was to darken this dream. Already, as one can read between the lines of his letter, there was rising on the horizon the cloud "the size of a man's hand."

"One of our consolations, and not the least, is that the lord governor and the nobles of the fleet have discovered that our desires are very far removed from the ambition of human favour, but that they are only for God; for the sufferings were such that I should not dare to face them a single day for anything in this world."

Already were beginning the intrigues which were to weave a devil's dance in Francis's Portuguese environment for the rest of his life. Early in the new year two small vessels arrived from India commanded by a certain de Mello. This man, condemned to death for piracy by the old governor, da Gama, had escaped and came to win favour in de Souza's eyes by vile accusations against da Gama and his administration. As Bellesort cynically but truly says: "The satisfaction of a Viceroy in assuming office was incomplete if he had not succeeded in destroying the reputation of his predecessor." Don Martin, no better than most, leant a willing ear to de Mello's calumnies. On the arrival of the Coulam, a galleon sent from Goa by da Gama, he arrested the captain and, to make assurance doubly sure, Alvaro de Ataide (da Gama's brother) as well. He determined to sail himself in February on the Coulam and thwart any plots in Goa by an unexpected appearance. Micer Paul and Mansilhas were to be left behind. Francis, in spite of prayers and protests, was ordered on board, and the Coulam set sail accompanied by an escort of two small boats.

During his free moments—few as ever—on the voyage north, Francis must have looked west across a sea smooth and transparent as the Apocalyptic sea of glass to the palm-fringed coast, and thought of the millions beyond it waiting in darkness for the coming of Christ. Not till nineteen years later did the first Jesuit missionaries penetrate inland from the Portuguese possessions on the east coast. A few months after Father Gonçalo de Silveira reached Zimbabwe he and all his converts were martyred by order of the Great Chief (March 16, 1561).

They were to put in at Melinda (a little north of Mombasa) for water, fruit and poultry, a welcome change of diet after weevily biscuits and maggotty salt meat. As they sighted the promontory which sheltered the town, Francis's eyes were rejoiced by the towering cross, one of the six *padraos* erected by Vasco da Gama—stone columns carved with the Portuguese arms and topped by a cross.

It was to remain in his memory. "God knows what consolation we received," he wrote in his account of the last part of the voyage, "when we saw it standing alone and triumphant in the midst of all the Mohammedanism."

For the first time he had an opportunity for sight-seeing and learning something of the inhabitants. Bellesort asserts of him that "his spirit, occupied with the soul-world, rarely catches a reflection of the beauties of nature." True, perhaps, but surely only a half-truth. Before starting on a missionary journey to some new country or island he will fill his letters home with descriptions of their features and peoples which show keen and careful study.

At Melinda he probably had his first inkling that those he had come to convert were not naked barbarians but in many cases highly civilised and luxurious men. The local sultan, a faithful vassal of Portugal for forty years, came out to pay his respects to the new governor. Camoens's description of da Gama's reception at Melinda equally fits de Souza's. It glows with colour, glitters with gold—the great royal barge, manned by naked rowers and trumpeters blowing deafening blasts on horns; silk banners aflutter; under the many-coloured umbrella the king, in gold and purple, gold crown, neck-chain and belt, high velvet boots studded with gems.

One of the Sultan's companions, seeing Francis was the only priest on board, entered into conversation. What was the state of religion and the Church in Europe? "Here," he continued—and the words have a strangely modern ring—"there are seventeen mosques, only three still in use and but few worshippers in those. Can you explain such decay?" "I wonder more that your religion has been so long successful," answered Francis with unusual bluntness, "than I wonder at its present decay." Another Arab declared impatiently that he should cease to believe if the Mahdi, whose coming Mahomet had promised before the end of the world, did not appear within the next two years. "It is the misfortune of infidels and great sinners always to be restless and dissatisfied," was Francis's comment later on this conversation.

There was to be one more port of call on the way to Goa—Socotra, a barren island at the entrance to the Red Sea, two hundred and twenty miles from the Arabian coast. Its granite peaks towered four thousand feet into the scorching sky, and since neither wheat nor rice would grow on its rocky soil the chief food was a kind of bread made from dates. The Apostle Thomas was said to have evangelised the island on his way to India. There had certainly been churches here in the fourth century, and travellers had reported a Nestorian population during the Middle Ages, when it had been a meeting-place for Arabian and Indian trade in aloes, ambergris and dragons' blood. A small Franciscan mission had been founded after the Portuguese capture of the island in 1507, but the friars were compelled to leave when the garrison was evacuated by order of Albuquerque four years later.

Francis, eager to begin his labours at once, landed, inquired into local manners and customs, and entered the hut in which the people performed their devotions. This was a mud hovel whose walls were lavishly smeared with butter before the services, several times daily. On a rude altar was a cross, also well greased and regarded with almost idolatrous reverence. Before it incense and candles were burnt and the mingled odour of incense, rancid butter, and crowded, sweating humanity must have been reminiscent of the Santiago hold. Hymns were chanted by the *caciz,* who understood nothing of them. Somehow

Francis managed to note the words of some of the hymns and prayers in Chaldean. Somehow—probably helped by an Arab interpreter and gestures—he made them understand the necessity of baptism rather than circumcision (which had replaced it), the evil of Islam and moon-worship. As in Italy, at Monselice, personal magnetism, burning love and desire captured his audience. Smiles, tears, beckoning hands and open arms, the sign of the Cross bridged the gulf between him and the poor, cowed natives. They crowded round him, clung to him, begging him to stay, brought their children for him to baptise, date bread for him to eat.

Twice he landed. The second day he went from house to house baptising. Crowds pressed about him. He picked up two brown, naked boys to baptise. Their angry Arab mother swooped like a hawk and snatched them away. There was a furious outcry from the onlookers: "Do not baptise them even if they wish it! The Moors are not worthy to be Christians. We will never allow it!" Francis returned to the Coulam exhausted but soul aflame. There was so much to do here, so many souls to save. Like St. Thomas, he would tarry here on the way to India, remain when the Coulam set sail for Goa. Da Souza smiled drily but gave sensible if cynical advice. "Be not over greedy to set upon the first feast, for fear you should lose one that is better."

Regretfully Francis watched the peaks of Socotra sink below the western horizon. But a little longer and a great work might have been done, Christianity reared on a sure foundation, but de Souza had smiled and given orders for anchor to be weighed and sail set. It was Francis's first taste of the cup of bitterness whose dregs were on his dead lips in the lime on Sanchian. Only ten years of life remained to him, and all the while his enthusiasm, his endeavours, his noblest impulses and dreams were to be checked and thwarted by the men of his own continent and creed. "A man's foes shall be they of his own household."

He never forgot Socotra. When the expedition of 1546 failed he wrote indignantly: "The Moorish chief . . . persecutes the natives, carries off their daughters for his harem, forces the Koran on them, ill-treats them in every way." He implored Rodriguez: "For God's sake, do something for these poor wretches." (January, 1549.) He chose two Jesuits from his scanty workers to leave Goa for Socotra at the beginning of 1549. But the King of Portugal had stipulated that Portuguese interference in Socotra "should not exasperate the Mohammedans" and Garcia de Sa (then Viceroy), had concluded peace with Islam. So the mission was cancelled. After Francis's death the attempt of two other Jesuits to carry out his wishes was again frustrated. The last traces of native Christianity in Socotra have long vanished.

Easter was spent in mid-ocean. The favourable south-west monsoon had set in. The voyage was uneventful. The monotony of the lengthening spring days was not even broken by sight of an Arab felucca laden with spice and pilgrims for Mecca. It was May 6, 1542, thirteen months after leaving Lisbon, that the smoothness of the eastern horizon was broken by the Quemada Islands south of Goa. Astern a long wake of glittering gold stretched to the setting sun. The palms of the Indian coast were silhouetted black against the clearness of the evening sky.

It was midnight when the Coulam dropped anchor in deep water under the fortress of Pangim, half-way up the river to the town of Goa. Etiquette demanded that the outgoing viceroy or governor should have left the town before his successor entered it. De Souza had no intention of making things pleasant for his predecessor. He had come with a strong force and a cargo of calumny supplied by the escaped pirate. Now he sent an offensive message to warn da Gama of his arrival and waited to make his own entry next day.

For the last time Francis lay on the deck of the Coulam. The air was full of strange eastern perfumes, cries, and the distant throb of drums. Yet over him shone no longer the unknown southern stars, but the friends of childhood, the belt of Orion, the homely tilt of the Wain, and above it, the fixed centre round which all others moved, the pole-star, symbol of Him in Whom is no change nor shadow of variation.

CHAPTER IX

GOA (MAY 6, 1542–SEPTEMBER 20, 1542)

THE rise of the Portuguese power in the East under the great Alfonso d'Albuquerque had been amazing, but even now, forty-four years since Vasco da Gama had first reached the Calicut coast, the conquered territory was nowhere more than a narrow fringe along the seaboard, and in many places, such as Mozambique and Malacca, only trading-posts protected by strongly garrisoned forts.

The crusading spirit, symbolised by the red crosses on da Gama's sails, soon gave place to something ignoble. His reception by the Zamorim reads like a tale from the *Arabian Nights*. Gold, jewels, silks, velvets, marbles, sandalwood in the palace of Pandarene recalled the fabled wealth of Solomon, suggested that here lay the Ophir from which he drew his endless treasures of gold.

Through the gaping crowds of Rome (1514) wound a cavalcade such as had never been seen even in the days of Imperial triumphs. Three hundred mules laden with silk, brocades, cloth of gold, an Arab horse to whose saddle clung a Persian panther, trained for hunting, the ambassador mounted on a stallion whose harness was stiff with gold and gems—such was the show provided by Manoel the Fortunate in token of gratitude to His Holiness for spiritual favours granted to the Eastern empire.

It is a strange paradox that gold, the devil's best bait in his fishing for souls, inspires heroic deeds and epics worthy of them. The El Dorado of the western world, the Ophir of the east, hold a romance which has still power to thrill, and in Camoens's *Lusiad* have achieved an immortality second only to that of Greek and Trojan wanderers.

The sixteenth century was an age of piracy. Drake and his fellow freebooters put up no pretence that they sailed westward-ho to bring the glad tidings of the Reformers' gospel to Spanish conquistadors and Indian chiefs. It mattered little to them that the gold of El Dorado was red with the blood of Spanish women or Indian squaws so long as it reached Plymouth or Tilbury safe in the holds of their battered little ships. It was left to Whig historians and Victorian clergymen to create the roseate, auric legend of the Elizabethan age.

With the Portuguese it was otherwise. Human motives are impossible to disentangle fully, and no doubt at first anyhow the crusading spirit was genuine with some. The crosses on his caravels' sails, the standard of the cross which the king placed between his hands on the tear-wet strand of Belem, the crosses erected wherever he landed in the east, these were a symbol of an inspiration which enabled that indomitable, terrifying hero da Gama to carry through an enterprise which none other would have brought to a successful end.

In Portugal, as in Spain, the memory of centuries of struggle with the Moors had bitten deep into the national consciousness. Everywhere, as the first explorers pushed north up the coast of Africa, rounded Cape Comorin and Ceylon, sailed on to Malacca and even to the south of China, everywhere they encountered the old enemy, heard from the minarets of a thousand mosques the old lie: "Great is Allah and Mohammed is his prophet!"

Here was the ancient war, pushed to the remotest confines of the earth. The Pope, inspired, granted countless spiritual privileges to all: "who go to the Indies, stay and return or die in fighting for the propagation of the Faith." John III endowed scholarships at the Paris university, fostered vocations to mission-work in the East, begged Rome for Jesuits to send out, waxed eloquent in his farewell to Francis Xavier over the countries and continents waiting his advent.

All these fine dreams and ideals were in startling contrast with the reality.

Women were forbidden on the ships sailing to India from Lisbon. The first three white women who reached Goa as stowaways in 1524 were publicly whipped through the streets by order of Vasco da Gama who had just come out as governor. Even in 1549 it was considered as shocking and amazing that the new governor, Jorge Cabral, should bring with him his wife, a well-bred Portuguese lady.

Practically every Portuguese in the Indies kept one concubine (most many more), whose children, like the majority of half-castes, inherited the worst qualities of both races. To this day, in many parts of the Malay Archipelago, innumerable descendants of these unions bear some of the noblest names in Portuguese history and, in spite of being as dark as or darker than the pure-blooded Malay, look down on him with infinite scorn.

Sins of physical passion, though, rot mind and spirit less than the almost ubiquitous vices of avarice and corruption. It was commonly said of the Portuguese judges and officials in the East that for money they were willing to contrive any miscarriage of justice, while to justify themselves no libel was too vile. Barros, the sixteenth-century author of *Decadas da Asia,* wrote of his own people: "The Portuguese prefer their own deeds to be forgotten rather than that their neighbours' should be praised." When the great Alfonso d'Albuquerque (governor, 1509-1515) erected a war-memorial at Malacca engraved with the names of its captors, such a storm of jealousy was roused that he had the stone turned face to the wall and its back carved: "The stone which the builders rejected." "We rejoice at the mistakes and misfortunes of others," he said bitterly; "we even try to make them commit errors so that we can bring an accusation against them." A continual stream of slander flowed from Goa to Lisbon. De Souza, as we saw, was in the fashion by his behaviour to his predecessor; but in this case he had his trouble for nothing, for none of his charges against Stephen da Gama could be proved. "The lust of the flesh, the lust of the eyes and the pride of life" flourished like weeds on a dung-heap, and the few priests scattered through the Eastern empire might well despair in their apparently hopeless struggle.

The first Franciscan mission, founded in Calicut in 1500, was soon destroyed by the Mohammedans. D'Albuquerque preferred Dominicans, who appeared in 1503 but in a few years had vanished. Secular priests and Franciscans were stationed from Mozambique to Malacca, but, as Père Brou points out, before the coming of Francis Xavier the records of the Eastern missions are fragmentary and unchronological. In 1510 Goa, finally recaptured, was declared the capital of the Portuguese possessions in the East, and the earliest mud chapel was soon replaced by the cathedral. The converted mosque which became the Franciscan friary in 1517 still stands, and its porch of carved black stone is almost the only surviving relic of

Portuguese early sixteenth-century architecture in India. The majority of churches, palaces, and large houses were built of the local red porous stone, heavily carved and gilt. Unlimited gold and unskilled labour combined with ambitious ideas in a result more remarkable for opulence than beauty.

The end of Alfonso d'Albuquerque's governorship saw Portuguese power well established in India. "Peace was universal from Ormuz to Ceylon. . . . And from the Cape of Comorin eastward Alfonso d'Albuquerque left the kings of those countries in perfect peace and friendship with the King of Portugal." (Commentaries of Albuquerque.)

In 1521 it was decided to make Goa a bishopric, but the first bishop did not arrive till seventeen years later. John d'Albuquerque, former Franciscan provincial in Portugal and the king's confessor, was chosen by him. Though of Castilian blood, he was already old, and his selection caused some surprise at Rome. One of the Cardinals remarked rather cynically that perhaps one reason was that a religious, who had already renounced everything, should not find it so hard to be buried in India.

D'Albuquerque reached Goa too ill for the official reception prepared for him, but as soon as he recovered started bravely on a work which demanded the strength of Hercules and the perseverance of Sisiphus. His diocese, like the Viceregal powers, extended from Mozambique to the Moluccas. A few Franciscan missions survived in southern India and Ceylon. Elsewhere a handful of secular priests struggled with Portuguese garrison and merchants and some hundreds of native converts. The Jesuit Father Valignano, who, from work out there knew what he was writing about, says: "There was such a deficiency

of clerics, religious and other workers to help the bishop
in his labours that they were not enough for the needs of
the Portuguese. In the whole of India the only religious
were a few Franciscan fathers. . . . Few and isolated,
they could not supply all needs, so little attempt was made
to convert the heathen. The Portuguese, specially those
far from Goa, were hardly looked after. In the whole of
India there were barely two or three preachers. Almost
everywhere the Portuguese remained for years without
hearing the word of God. Often they had neither clergy
nor any to administer the Sacraments or say Mass." (History of the Company of Jesus in the East Indies, 1574.)

Such was the state of Portuguese India when the Coulam anchored in the river and, to the thunder of cannon
and blare of trumpets, the new Governor was received.
The old bishop probably regretted the late governor more
than he welcomed his successor. Stephen da Gama had
proved a worthy son of his great father. Instead of amass-
ing wealth he had paid Treasury deficits from his own
purse, had boldly rebuked the avarice and corruption of
officials and fidalgoes and, most astonishing of all, had
openly and regularly frequented the Sacraments.

Local tradition points to the shore at Marmugoa as the
spot where Francis Xavier first set foot on Asian soil. He
at once presented himself to the bishop and kneeling before him handed over the brief appointing himself Papal
Nuncio in the East. "I will use it only when and how it
pleases your Excellency." "Make use of all the powers
given you by His Holiness," answered the Franciscan,
delighted and charmed by such humility. Holiness recog-
nises holiness at first sight, and no doubt the old man felt
instinctively that at last his prayers for ardent and spiritual
helpers had been answered. That moment laid the founda-

tion of a warm friendship which remained unbroken till his death.

Francis, as usual, took up his quarters at the hospital, which was conveniently near the landing-place. The cassock in which he had gone on board the Santiago thirteen months before was little more than a rag. It would indeed have been a miracle if it had been otherwise, and Francis, who was to win such fame as a thaumaturge, had as yet shown no sign of his gift. The hospital steward brought from his store the usual black gown supplied to poor priests. It was of coarse silk, the ordinary wear, for wool, which had to be brought all the way from Lisbon, was an expensive luxury. Francis, horrified, refused to wear silk and after some search, a black *loba* (a gown of rough cotton without sleeves or belt) was found, and met with his approval. The suggestion that a new pair of shoes would be an improvement on the broken ones he was wearing was met with a smiling refusal: they were good enough, and would do for a while longer.

He slept on a mat on the hospital floor, so that the slightest moan or cry would break his light slumber and bring him at once to the bedside of suffering or dying. By dawn he was up, hearing confessions, giving Communion before he said his Mass; and after it he set out for the prisons. There were three, the Tronco or Governor's, near the ramparts, the bishop's, and a third. Pyrard de Laval, himself imprisoned in one half a century later, gives a revolting and vivid description of hundreds of the lowest and vilest criminals herded "in the foulest and most stinking hole in the world." The Brothers of the Misericord, who also tended the hospital, kept the prisoners supplied with the bare necessaries of life. Francis instructed and prepared them for a general confession in the mornings before he trudged off to the lazar-house beyond the south-west suburb. There, on Sundays, he said Mass and communicated the lepers. "I preached to them once, and they have become my friends, my great friends."

Begging from door to door for his sick, his lepers, his prisoners and his poor, he grew familiar with Goa under the blazing sun of May, the thunder and lightning of June, torrential rain and water-spouts that made streets and squares into running rivers and wide lakes. "It is a beautiful city," he wrote home: "There is a large Franciscan monastery and a very fine *Séo* (cathedral) with an important chapter, as well as many other churches. Our Lord God is deeply to be thanked that the Name of Christ flourishes thus in these distant lands and amid the multitudes of heathen." No further description of the beauties of Goa, not one word about the corruption masked by these outward decencies. That large friary, that fine cathedral, those numerous churches, can hardly have blinded him to evil. Perhaps, appalled, he turned for comfort to the houses of God; also it was never his way to write or talk of evils unless by doing so he could correct them.

"He who has not seen Lisbon has not seen beauty" was a favourite saying on the Tagus. Here local patriotism went one better in the boast: "He who has seen Goa need not trouble to visit Lisbon." The climax of its splendour (1575-1625) described by de Laval, Mocquet and Linscot, was yet in the future, but already, as well as the cathedral, churches, and viceregal palace, there were splendid private houses, show and luxury everywhere.

The first of the Asiatic possessions of Portugal, Goa lay on an island surrounded by two rivers and an arm of the sea. The apex of the triangle divided the harbour into two anchorages. By turns Hindu and Moslem, it had been the starting-place of Indian pilgrimages to Mecca, the centre of export for Arab horses. D'Albuquerque had allowed the natives to retain all their customs except suttee and on the island there were still about forty thousand heathen who openly worshipped their idols with heads of elephants, apes, and cows, and kept festival in temples where nautch-girls danced all night bearing lighted lamps in their slim brown hands.

The main street of the city, the *Rua Drecha* (Straight Street), ran from the viceregal palace to the church of the Misericord, and was lined with jewellers' and goldsmiths' shops and banks. The air was filled with a babel of Hindu, Persian, Arab, Portuguese, Chinese, the cries of mahouts perched on elephants, the shouts of brown porters sweating under loads of fruit, coconuts, spices, fish, salt, rice. The smells were as varied. The odour of frying fish cooked by native women at street corners, the sweat of naked bodies, the strange perfume of musk and clove and cinnamon, mingled with that strong yet indefinable smell of the Indian bazaar.

Through the motley crowds strutted the Portuguese, dressed in silks, satins, and brocades, superciliously conscious of the ineffable superiority conferred by the possession of a white skin. "Cape nobility" was the nickname for those nobodies who were said to have cast manners and Christian modesty into the sea off the Cape of Good Hope before they blossomed into fictitious splendour in the East.

Goanese society consisted of a scale of social values as complicated as those of the modern London suburb. At the top were Viceroy or Governor, Bishops, fidalgoes and officials. Fidalgoes, mounted on Arab horses, with large parasols carried over their heads, rode abroad surrounded by pages and followed by a train of slaves. "Every man who thinks himself a little above the vulgar sort will have his *ombrello* carried over his head, another servant to carry his cloak, another to carry his sword," an English traveller notes. If rain came on, a slave rushed to put a scarlet cloak round my lord's shoulders; generally one carried his hat to save him the fatigue of taking it off to a friend. *Casados* (married men) wore cloaks and affected a standard of decency in speech and behaviour not expected of *zoldados* (single men). Soldiers banded together to buy a slave and a smart suit so that they might take it in turns to go out and play the gentleman. The *castico* (Portuguese born in India) despised a *mestico* (child of a Portuguese father and native mother) almost as much as he did the *canoreinos* (native converts). The latter had to stand aside, cringe and salute when they met a white; omission was rewarded by a rapier-thrust. All important posts were debarred to them, though as a rule they were much better educated and more intelligent than the Portuguese.

If, on his way back from saying his Mass at the lazarhouse on Sunday, Francis turned in to the cathedral, the scene there was reminiscent of those he had seen at Venice. Though it was the rarest thing for anyone to frequent the Sacraments, attendance at Sunday Mass was a favourite social function. On great festivals, when the Viceroy attended in state, drums were beaten through the streets the day before to summon the three or four hundred men of position to attend at the palace the next morning dressed in their best and mounted on richly caparisoned horses. On ordinary Sundays these gentlemen were carried to church in palanquins, followed by slaves leading their horses, carrying hats, chairs, cushions, embroidered stools.

The few Portuguese ladies, dressed in extravagant and
jewelled gowns, appeared only at great feasts, when their
litters were set down in the church so that their pages
could support them as they tottered a few yards on their
high-soled Spanish shoes, surrounded by their children
and slaves with carpets, cushions, fans, gilt Chinese chairs,
velvet bags and perfumes. At the Elevation a momentary
attention was paid, all beat their breasts and cried: *"Deos
de misericordia!"* before resuming interrupted talk or
ogling.

A thin figure in the coarse black loba, red with dust or
coated with mud, the old shoes so clumsily patched by
himself, Francis became a familiar sight as he trudged
through the city on his daily begging. Through the slave
market, in the shadow of the viceregal palace and cathedral, where the colour of the merchandise ranged from
African ebony to ivory skins paler than those of the
wealthy Portuguese who were haggling over new purchases
for their harems, Francis went on to the two-storied houses
of painted stone. There men lay on the wide verandahs
fanned by slaves, and through the lattices of barred windows peered the lustrous eyes of veiled women whose talk
sounded shrill and meaningless as the chattering of the
green Mozambique parrots at dawn. Strange tales were
told, of poisons and aphrodisiacs, women strangled or
drowned by jealous masters, of corpses buried in gardens
or drifting down the river. To Francis, with his burning
love and equally ardent chastity, these things must have
been like the shrieks and stink of the damned. That hell
on board ship had seared his memory indelibly. Often, as
he went about, he was heard to murmur in horror: "Oh,
that Santiago!" After her shipwreck men said that so had
Father Francis foretold her fate. More likely the words

were the echo of the misery he had endured in her and with her cargo of desperate and miserable men.

Goa was infinitely worse. Those men lounging in vest and drawers on their verandahs as they gossiped or watched native snake-charmers, had within their houses not only women but children of every shade from black to white, most unbaptised, untaught except in evil and deceit. What could Francis do, his days already filled with work in hospital, prisons, leper-house, and begging? There was the bishop, old, overwhelmed with work, so gentle, as someone said, that he was incapable of killing a flea. There was Miguel Vaz, vicar-general since 1530, struggling with the organisation of a diocese which sprawled across half the world, and with the foundation of a college for native converts.

It seemed to Francis that the most crying need of this great city was instruction in the rudiments of the Catholic Faith. He put on a surplice over his loba, took a little bell and went through the streets crying: "Faithful Christians, friends of Jesus Christ, send your sons, your daughters, your slaves, men and women, for Christian teaching! Send them for the love of God!" As the ringing of the bell sounded above the din of Goblin Market, did its silver note sometimes catch him back to Javier, to that clear upland air full of the sound of bells—the bell of Santa Maria de Javier summoning to Mass, the brass bells of cows and sheep and goats among the brown rocks and yellow gorse, the tinkle of tiny bells on falcons' hoods and the twinkling feet of Basque dancers?

Men and women, boys and girls, rich and poor ran out to see what was afoot. A procession formed, crowded after Father Francis into the small chapel of our Lady near the hospital. "There everything that he did delighted those who listened and watched. If he raised his eyes to heaven he raised souls there to. Making the sign of the Cross he spoke aloud so devoutly that everyone, especially the children, imitated him. He taught them hymns which were a summary of doctrines and so fixed them in their minds. Then, with arms outspread or lifted skywards, he intoned a kind of litany whose every verse briefly enshrined some teaching of the Church. So the answers, sung afterwards, became an act of faith." (Gonçalvez, quoted by Cros.)

Whether Francis is really the author of the well-known hymn *O Deus ego amo te* or not, it was certainly struck in the Xaverian mint. Fr. Gerard Hopkins's translation runs:

> "O God, I love thee, I love thee—
> Not out of hope of heaven for me
> Nor fearing not to love and be
>   In the everlasting burning.
> Thou, thou, my Jesus, after me
>   Didst reach thine arms out dying,
> For my sake sufferedst nails and lance,
> Marked and marréd countenance,
>   Sorrows passing number,
>   Sweat and care and cumber,
> Yea and death, and this for me,
>   And thou couldst see me sinning:
> Then I, why should I not love thee,
> Jesu, so much in love with me?
> Not for heaven's sake; not to be
> Out of hell by loving thee;
> Not for any gains I see;
> But just the way that thou didst me
> I do love and I will love thee:
> What must I love thee, Lord, for then?
> For being my king and God. Amen."

The fire of love, the special devotion to the Passion, are typical of Francis; and he himself, how many griefs and torments, how many sweats of agony was he to endure, that, in those mysterious words of St. Paul, he might "fill up those things that are wanting in the sufferings of Christ!"

In the first letter to the "Fathers of Rome" that he wrote from India is a passage which deserves to be quoted at length, one of those rare moments when earth with its labours and troubles is left behind and, baring his heart, he soars eaglewise to the sun.

"The weariness of so long a voyage, the care of so many spiritual infirmities for which one is wholly inadequate, the stay in a country enslaved to idolatrous sins and difficult to endure because of its great heat, these troubles become great joys and reasons for great and innumerable consolations when one bears them for the Love which gives them. It seems to me that those who rejoice in the Cross of Christ our Lord find their true rest when they meet these sufferings and that, far from them, they find only death. What worse death is there than to live after having deserted Christ, once one has known Him, in order to follow one's own opinions and likings? There is no other torment so great as that. On the other hand, what peace to live a daily death, fighting our own desires, seeking not our own things but those that are Jesus Christ's. . . . I am confident that Christ our Lord will give ear to my prayers and will grant me the grace of using the useless instrument that I am to plant His faith among the Gentiles. For, if His Majesty so used me, it would greatly confound those who are capable of great things, and encourage those who are cowardly, seeing that I am but dust and ashes, even one of the most miserable wretches. Conscious as an eye-witness of the necessity of workers here, I will willingly make myself the permanent servant of all those who desire to come here to labour in the immense vineyard of the Lord." (Goa, September 20, 1542.)

CHAPTER X

CAPE COMORIN (SEPTEMBER 20, 1542–OCTOBER 28, 1542)

NEARLY five months had passed. Still there was no news from Mozambique, no signs of the arrival of Micer Paul and Mansilhas. Francis began to chafe. There was no lack of work in Goa; indeed there was enough and to spare for a score of souls as ardent and untiring as himself. But it was not to reclaim the Portuguese that he had left all and followed the call of his Master across half the world. Behind that narrow fringe of conquered territory, round the isolated forts with their little brass cannon and their thick stone walls, stretched that "immense vineyard of the Lord," the fields white unto harvest where innumerable souls waited for the coming of Christ.

Even in Goa as he went to and fro he found himself continually face to face with heathendom. Brahmins, who held some of the best Government posts, obstructed attempts at conversion. In spite of recent edicts forbidding the celebration of pagan feasts on the island, Brahminism was still practised even in the town itself.

Francis was not the only one horrified at the corruption of Christians and the abominations of the heathen. A little band of zealous souls had banded themselves together under the leadership of Diego de Borba, a secularised Franciscan who had come out with the bishop, and Miguel Vaz, vicar-general since 1530, and so better acquainted than anyone with the needs of the world's biggest diocese. He saw that a necessary preliminary to any successful attempts at conversion was the foundation of a seminary for native priests. Alms were collected for this purpose. The viceroy assigned a yearly sum from the revenues of confiscated pagodas. Needless to say Francis was wholeheartedly in sympathy with this project. In his letter to Ignatius of September 20 he describes the nearly completed church, "twice as large as the College of the Sorbonne in Paris" and begs for the despatch of Jesuits, specially "a preacher who can give the Spiritual Exercises to priests or give them lessons on Holy Writ or on Sacramental doctrine, for the priests who come to the Indies are not all very well educated" (a typically charitable understatement).

A request that he himself should take charge of the college, with its sixty native students, was however unhesitatingly refused. Goa was but a stepping-stone to his real work. Already his spirit was reaching south to the pearl-fisheries of Comorin, whose people, eight years before, had called in the Portuguese to protect them against Moslem marauders. Miguel Vaz with assistants had accompanied the troops. None could speak Tamil, so the thousands of Paravas who were baptised had no instruction and were then left to their fate. A rare visit from an unusually brave and energetic Franciscan, the presence of a captain and a handful of soldiers stationed at Tuticorin to collect the annual tribute of pearls, did nothing to keep alive the nominal Christianity of the fishers.

A ship was going to Cape Comorin. According to Texeira Francis seized the chance. The bishop could not withhold his consent, though it was given with tears. Don Martin agreed with more alacrity. As Admiral of the eastern fleet he had destroyed the Mohammedan pirates (1537) who were attempting to annex the pearl fisheries. One cannot help feeling too that he and others in high places did not feel averse to being free, even temporarily, from the presence of an apostle who did not conduce to official comfort and enrichment.

Like his Master, Francis had been the companion of publicans and sinners, and his manner of approach had given scandal to the rigorists. "I was certainly extremely surprised at the details given me about his method of drawing men to God," wrote Father Quadros thirteen years later, though with a noble attempt to be broadminded he added: "Truly, like St. Paul, he became all things to all men. He was a soldier with soldiers and the same with others, but with such prudence that his reputation never suffered."

Prudence, however, was not one of Francis's strong points. If it had been, probably the only commemoration of him would have been a dusty inscription in a corner of Pamplona cathedral, with a list of the dead canon's accomplishments. He had many friends in Goa, those who crowded to hear his instructions in the church of our Lady and crowded his confessional afterwards, his lepers and prisoners, the loungers on verandahs and hagglers in the slave-market who gave him alms for sick and poor. He could not leave them without a final attempt to regulate their lives, bring their mistresses and children into the fold. As he trudged up the Rua Drecha he would meet one, with his beguiling smile beg for an invitation to supper, "without ceremony, *en famille.*" Refusal was impossible, but that evening his host would greet him with embarrassment. What a picture! The host resplendent in silk and jewels, Francis in a loba green with age

and sun, the historic shoes, their soles and uppers "clown-
ishly sewn together" by himself, the women, swift and
silent as shadows while they placed dishes before the guest
and poured the wine into chased silver cups. Hindu
women in spangled veils, limbs brown through their muslin draperies, Burmese gay as butterflies in their bright
silks, Japanese, doll-like in their brilliant kimonos, with
little fans in their piled hair, Chinese, their mask-like faces
pale as the lotus in their hair or the white birds on their
gold-stiff coats—best of all, says old Torsellini, "both in
beauty of body and comeliness of person."

The evening ends; Francis takes a courteous leave. Not
a word of reprimand, yet somehow a subtle change has
come into the atmosphere of the house. His host, relieved,
meets him and invites him again. "And your sisters,"
asks Francis with an innocent air, "how are they all?"
One fancies an emphasis of sly humour on the "all." The
question is evaded, the visit repeated—irresistible charm,
unfailing courtesy from the guest. No more is said, yet a
few days later the man enters Francis's confessional, a
new life is begun.

He visits another of these houses. At his request the
children are brought in and, as usual, crowd eagerly
round him. He takes the smallest in his arms, on his
knees, blesses and caresses them, prays that they may lead
good Christian lives, questions the elder ones. Then,
greatly daring in this land of secluded women, he asks to
see their mother. One of those slender, pale women, gracious and beguiling, slips into the room. He hears about
her native country, her life, if she is a Christian, then compliments his host on her charm and beauty. "One would
have said a Portuguese. Her children will be worthy of
you." Then, unexpected as the thrust of a dagger, "What

prevents your marriage? Where would you find a better wife?" Often audacity was successful and he had the happiness of marrying the couple and baptising their children.

On other occasions he refused to eat without his hostess. She was perhaps a negress or an Oriental, black-skinned and coarse-featured. "Who is this monster? Are you harbouring the devil? What sort of children do you expect to have? Send her away and take a wife fit for you!" They are startling as an unexpected blow, these words of Francis, who is so gentle, so filled with love and sympathy. He knows that for some diseases there is no remedy but the knife. Those dark eyes see far. Marriage with such women as these can end only in disaster.

One day his friends could bear that tattered loba no longer. The hospital servant was bidden to replace it with a new one, which Francis put on without noticing it. At supper that evening with Peyva the other guests began to tease him. "Is it to honour us that you are so smart to-day in your new habit?"

"Then, casting his eyes upon his clothes he was much surprised to find himself in so strange an equipage. At length being made sensible of the prank they had played him he told them, smiling, 'that it was no great wonder that this rich cassock looking for a master in the dark could not see its way to somebody who deserved it better!' " (Dryden's translation of Bouhours.)

They might trick him into a new loba, but they could not persuade him any more than Castanheira had at Lisbon, to accept anything for his journey to Comorin. To his usual outfit of black habit, breviary, and rosary he added a surplice, some leather to resole his boots, and an *ombrello*, a necessary protection against the scorching sun of the Comorin desert. At the end of September or beginning of October, 1542, the fleet from Mozambique was expected daily, but the ship was ready for the south and Francis dared not miss the opportunity. He embarked with three students from the new college to serve as interpreters, and the voyage into the unknown began. At last he was to realise those vivid dreams on the Italian hills, which had awakened Lainez with the cry: "Jesus, I am crushed!" Lainez was now at Venice, where those dreams had begun. The beloved Peter Faber had just returned from Spain to Germany, where, at Maintz, a brilliant young Dutch student of Cologne was to hear him and find his vocation as Father Peter Canisius.

At every momentous step in life man looks back as well as forward. Perhaps now, as the palm-fringed coast slipped past, Francis realised that the thirty-six and a half years of his life had been but the training and preparation for the time to come, which he felt was to be only a short one. In the last letter from Goa (September 20) there had sounded the old note of self-distrust, the natural shrinking of the sensitive and finely-balanced mind from undivided responsibility: "Write to me at length, for God our Lord's sake, as to what line of conduct I should take with the heathen and Moors to whose country I am now going. . . . As for the mistakes I shall make while waiting for your answer, I hope in our Lord that your letters will make me realise them and enable me to correct them in the future." It is the last hesitation. From now on Francis stands alone, far from human help and advice. His true greatness is revealed. His decisions are swift and unfaltering, and, with scarcely an exception, irrevocable.

Thirteen times in the next ten years he was to travel the seven hundred miles from Goa to Cape Comorin, hugging the coast past hostile Mangalore and the tiny Portuguese station of Cananor with its Franciscan mission. There was Calicut, whose golden gates had opened to admit Vasco da Gama to its fairy splendour but were now closed against the white man. Not till 1597 were the Jesuits at last to enter it, at the invitation of the rajah himself. Beyond a chain of lagoons, where land and sea were inextricably entangled, rose the unending line of the Ghat mountains, their high terraces climbing like titan stairs into the dazzling sky. At Cochin, which Francis was to know so well, he must have landed to visit the Franciscans, settled in the port which was the starting-place of the yearly consignment of spices and pepper for Lisbon. Then on again to Cape Comorin, southernmost point of India, where the oldest local tradition declares him to have begun his missionary work.

The days at sea were not a time of idleness. As always he was everywhere, friends with all. "Nothing was more striking in him than the union of gravity and friendliness. . . . One can hardly imagine the charm of his face, his gestures, his talk, his words. His natural gifts, perfected by the grace of God, attracted and held hearts. A smile always gay, a freedom from reserve, sympathetic conversation—it was enough for a sick man to see him to feel better, a healthy one to be exhilarated and joyous. Many went to him to stimulate their souls with his heavenly force, to excite in themselves the desire of a good life, to set their souls on fire. Impossible to part from him feeling sad or depressed. . . . When he talked of divine things he was careful to prevent boredom by the spice of variety. A master of astronomy, he would enliven long voyages by telling the course of the stars" (Torsellini). A sailor with sailors, a soldier with soldiers, a merchant with merchants, the Spanish hidalgo, the Paris professor was equally at home with all, so that he said of himself with a smile: "I go in at their door so that I can make them come out at mine."

On one of these coastal voyages, perhaps this very one, a certain bluff soldier, Diogo de Noronha, who had heard a great deal about Francis but had not met him, asked a friend: "Where is this wonderful Xavier of yours?" He was shown Francis, busy playing dice with a soldier noted for his immorality. *"That* a saint?" he cried in disgust: "he is only a priest like the rest of them!" A little while later, when they had landed, curiosity made Diogo send one of his soldiers after Francis, who had gone away alone. The man ran back, amazed, calling his master. In a little grove of palm trees knelt Francis, rigid, immovable, eyes upturned, face aflame, caught up in ectasy.

Here was the secret of his success, those brief moments snatched alone with God, as on the deck of the Santiago. Here was his real life, the fountain from which he drew his apparently inexhaustible love and energy. The outward life of ceaseless activity, countless conversions, endless miracles, never for an instant interrupted that inner union with God which is the only true sainthood.

At Cape Comorin Francis and his companions landed. It was the first step into the unknown which never loses its terror nor its fascination for the mind of man. The sails of the caravel sank below the horizon. Francis was alone, with no trusted friend, no white man nearer than Tuticorin, seventy miles away; only those three half-educated young students, who were to prove of little use even as interpreters.

On this coast he was to stay a year, working among the Paravas. Now the four set out on their long tramp north to Tuticorin over the shifting sand which often buried whole villages. On the left the southern end of the Ghats rose over four thousand feet, their sharp peaks bare, their lower slopes fringed with coconut-palms. On the right lay the sea, dotted with the swallow-tailed sails of the pearl fishers' boats. Little villages of mud huts, thatched with palm-leaves, huddled in the shelter of palm-groves. Greybeards, with loincloths of rose, yellow or white cotton, squatted at doors or poured lustral water from brass vases over heads and hands. Naked children, brown and shiny, tumbled in the sand like puppies at play. Women, heavy and shapeless in their straight garments of cotton, moved slowly, the lobes of their ears pulled to their shoulders by great gold rings, wrists and ankles weighted by gold bands like fetters. Here a pedlar passed, his two baskets balanced on a bamboo, there a Brahmin stepped delicately to avoid contamination, chin in air, eyes above the heads of lower mortals as he fanned himself with a palm-leaf. After the chatter and clatter of Goa, the cheery sounds of life on board ship, there was something uncanny in the silence. Here men went noiselessly, as bare or sandalled feet sank into the soft sand.

One would like to know of Francis's first meeting with the natives, to be able to picture with some degree of accuracy the arrival in some little hamlet, as the sunset sky burned behind the Ghats and the boats were drawn up on the low shore. Was it only as the sudden darkness of the tropics fell that Francis realised for the first time the great gulf fixed between him and this dark, silent people, so gentle except for the cruelty of a religion of fear? Had he not thought before he left Goa, had the Franciscans at Cochin not told him, of the hopelessness, humanly speaking, of the attempt at conversion when he and the people had neither speech nor thought in common? Bitterly he was to realise this difficulty, now and later, in India, Malacca, the Moluccas, Japan. His young companions, during their time at Goa, had apparently forgotten Tamil, the pre-Aryan language of southern India, which Francis, Portuguese-fashion, calls Malabar. Before long he was to find it necessary to strike out a new line of communication.

"As soon as I arrived on the coast which they inhabit," he wrote to Rome fifteen months later, "I tried to find out from them what knowledge they had of Christ our Lord; and when I asked about the articles of faith which, now that they were Christians, they knew and believed more than they did as pagans, I received from them only this answer, that they were Christians, and, because they did not understand our language, they did not know our law nor what they ought to believe. And, as they understood me no better than I understood them—their mother language being Malabar, mine Basque—I collected the more educated among them and looked for some who understood their language and ours. After numerous meetings and with much difficulty we translated some prayers from Latin into Malabar, beginning by the way to make the sign of the Cross and the confession of three Persons in one only God. Next the Creed and the Commandments, Our Father, Hail Mary, Salve Regina and the general confession. When, having translated them into their tongue, I knew them by heart, I went through the whole village, a little bell in my hand, collecting all the boys and men I could." (Cochin, January 15, 1544.)

How emphatically he asserts that his native tongue is Basque! Spanish, Latin, French, Italian, Portuguese, he was familiar with them all, but still his heart echoed the tongue he had learnt from nurse and mother, in which he had stammered his first baby prayers and in which he was to murmur his dying words to Christ, His divine Majesty, at Sanchian.

There was an even worse barrier than that of language. Like all his European contemporaries Francis was entirely ignorant of the religion and character of the Oriental. He knew nothing of the Hindu. Islam, indeed, had been familiar to him as a symbol of the power of evil, subdued in Spain less than two decades before his birth. Here, however, it was Brahminism with which he had to deal, and of it he could form no conception save by the gross superstition and idolatry of the people, the cynical avarice and indolence of the priests. In languages which have no common formulæ, in minds which have no common thought, understanding is impossible. Once indeed, in conversation with a young Brahmin whom he hoped to convert, Francis caught a faint echo from the great pronouncement which is the summary of all Brahminist doctrine: *"Ekam eva advitīyam"* (there is but one Being without a second).

But the logical outcome of the belief that all things are but dreams and delusions, annihilation the greatest bliss that man can attain, is a fatalism that indulges in the basest sensuality. The pantheism of esoteric Brahminism became in vulgar practice the grossest polytheism. The worship of Siva, who embodied the chief attributes of Brahma, was more widespread than that of any other god, and one of his five principal sanctuaries was on the Fishery coast, in an island between Ramnad and Ceylon. At Cape Comorin itself was a place of pilgrimage dedicated to his wife, Durga or Kali, who, mounted on a tiger, demanded a yearly sacrifice of a young wife pregnant with her first child. Siva, lord of death, destruction and demons, with his necklace of human skulls, his images smeared with blood, also embodied the forces of fertility and reproduction, being represented as half male and half female.

Everywhere, as Francis journeyed from village to village, he saw great temples and monasteries with shining domes, their walls crowded with indecent sculpture, their long flights of granite steps worn by the bare feet of a million pilgrims. Under the stars, bright as diamond dust, sounded the throb of tomtoms, the wail of pipes, as nautch-girls postured before the images of three-eyed, four-headed, many-armed monsters, and jewelled snakes with unwinking eyes, darted forked tongues at golden dishes of food. By the wayside pot-bellied, elephant-headed images of Ganesha, reeking with oil, leered Silenus-like from the shadow of little mud shrines. At every turn the *linga* of Siva—obscene sign of phallic worship—thrust itself from the ground, smeared with blood-red, or was marked in white ash on the forehead of worshippers. It was a religion of fear, a darkness only lit by the lurid glare of secret rites when caste and division were swamped in sensuality. Night was peopled by demons, dread phantoms, all the host of Siva. Trees, rocks, streams hid, not the graceful dryads and naiads of Greek mythology, but Bhuts, sinister spirits only to be propitiated by sacrifices and offerings.

No wonder that Francis's heart burned within him, that he passed whole nights in prayer, as in the cave at Manapad where, looking out over the sea, he saw Ceylon as a dark shadow against the sunrise. "The people that sat in darkness have seen a great light, and to them in the region and shadow of death light is risen." But the beginning was not easy. He relates how he reached one village where none were Christians and all refused to be, "saying that they were vassals of a heathen lord who would not allow them to become Christians." In one of the huts lay a woman whose life was despaired of because, after three days' labour, she could not be delivered of her child. *Mantram*, spells and charms, failed to work. Francis heard of it and hurried to her.

"I began by reciting the Creed. The clerk, my companion, translated it. By the grace of God the woman believed the articles of faith. 'Do you wish to be a Christian?' I asked her. She answered that she desired it greatly. I then read the Gospels, in this case where, I think, no one had ever before heard of them; then I baptised her. What more? No sooner baptised than she was instantly delivered, as she had confidently hoped and believed in Christ Jesus. I then baptised the husband, sons, daughters and newly-born child. The news spread through the hamlet of what God had done in this hut. . . . I baptised the chief men with their households, then all the villagers, big and little."

In this same letter, one of the longest and most interesting of the series which poured like molten lava from his pen, he describes also the method he had evolved for instruction, the almost miraculous success of his work during the year he spent among the Paravas. Everything was based on the Creed, translated, emphasized, repeated, illustrated. Then came the Pater Noster, the Ave Maria and, always to finish devotions, the Salve Regina. Standing under the palms, amid the dusky crowd of men and women, the eager, pushing naked children, the chanted words of the familiar antiphon must have caught him back in memory to the abbadia at Javier, as the same words and music floated from the open door of Santa Maria across to the brown walls of the frontier castle.

He tells how his arms ached, his voice failed from the sheer physical fatigue of administering baptism; he tells of the tiny babies, still "unable to tell their right hand from their left," signed for heaven, of the children who crowded about him till not a free moment was left, till he was forced to send those who knew some prayers, armed with his crucifix and rosary, to visit the sick for him. "And then, thanks to the faith of the people and their neighbours, thanks to the sick man's faith, God our Lord granted great favours to those who were ill, gave them health of body and spirit."

Not a word of the miracles whose stories sprang up like spring flowers wherever he journeyed. Not a word either of trials and hardships almost past human endurance. The sand, shifting under the feet of the wayfarer or blinding him with fierce storms whipped up by wind from the mountains, the rocks so hot with the sun that human touch could not bear them, the drenching dews of early morning, the scanty food—a little rice and pepper cooked by himself, the rare luxury of a bit of fish—these were only some of the hardships. The fibre on which he lay, the mud floors of huts, were alive with vermin, with white ants which devoured everything, with scorpions, huge spiders, rats, poisonous snakes. He was credited with having restored to life a man dead from snake-bite; but he himself, like his namesake of Assisi, seems to have had that understanding with the animal creation which had been one of the joys of Eden.

In the nights, whose silence was broken by the call of mating tigers, the howl of jackals, the cries of huge bats, when fireflies, innumerable as the brilliant stars, flashed their tiny green lights among the trees, then at last Francis was alone, free from the eager crowding of men and children, at one with God. Caught into that sphere where is neither time nor space, where God is all in all, he was often heard to cry: "Less joy, O Lord. Admit me to Thy eternal splendour, for it is bitter to live here on earth, far from Thee, when once Thou hast granted an inward taste of Thy sweetness."

In the letter from Cochin (January 15, 1544), already quoted, Francis also tells of the Brahmin who, like Nicodemus, came secretly to him, and of an interview with the Brahmins of one of the greatest monasteries. Bellesort, who followed the steps of Xavier through India and Japan, gives a vivid picture of the scene. The great pillared court, with huge bats clinging head down to the sculptures, the Brahmins, grave, dignified, in their flowing draperies of white muslin, seated round. Against the columns lean the youths, slim, graceful, with the subtle smile and veiled lustrous eyes of women below the sign of Siva smeared across their smooth foreheads. In the midst Francis, with crucifix and rosary, his habit torn by thorns, gnawed by white ants, but always with shining eyes uplifted, radiant smile on the worn face, which still flushed like a girl's as he disclaimed praise and denied miracles.

How much of the thought of the other did each glean from the faltering sentences of a half-educated interpreter? In Francis's somewhat naive account of childish questions and pronouncements of belief, one fancies the subtle Oriental mind trifling with the western intruder, the caution of the Brahmin bound by deadly oath to reveal no esoteric doctrine. So too their satisfaction with his exposition of Christian doctrines was probably that formal Eastern politeness which allows no man to express his true opinion of a guest. In any case conversions remained limited to the Paravas and lower castes. Even the young Brahmin who "had studied in famous schools" refused baptism because it entailed an open confession of Christian faith.

There is a little personal note in Francis's account of the monastery interview. "They asked me . . . when a man dreams during sleep that he is in a place with his friends and acquaintances (and it is a thing which often happens to me, my dearest ones, thus to find myself again with you) if the soul, going to that place, ceases to animate the body. . . . My recreations in this country are constantly to remember you, my dearly loved brothers, and the time when, by the great mercy of God our Lord I knew and talked with you. I know and feel in the depths of my soul how much I wasted of the time we lived together, for I did not profit as I might have done from the many revelations which God our Lord made to you of Himself. Thanks to your prayers and the faithful memory you keep of me while commending me to God, God has granted me this great grace that, in spite of your bodily absence, He has allowed me, by your favour and help, better to understand the innumerable multitude of my sins and to give me strength to go among the heathen, for which I give heartfelt thanks both to Him and to you, my dearly loved brothers. . . . Among the numerous favours which God our Lord has granted me in this life and still gives me daily there is one which I desired to see above all others while still living—that is the confirmation of our rule and manner of life. Thanks be for ever to God our Lord that He judged it well to show forth publicly what He had secretly revealed only to Ignatius, his servant and our father." (To the Fathers of Rome, Cochin, January 15, 1544.)

CHAPTER XI

SOUTHERN INDIA
(OCTOBER, 28, 1542–DECEMBER, 1544)

AFTER a brief stay at Tuticorin, where he wrote a short letter to tell Ignatius of the progress of his work (October 28, 1542), Francis spent a year on the Fishery Coast, travelling to and fro to reach villages not yet visited and to revisit those already converted. The winter of 1542, the summer of 1543, with their scorching suns, torrential rains, burning winds and cruel sandstorms, came to an end at last. The trail was blazed, the way prepared, but still Francis was alone save for his three students. There was no sign of Micer Paul and Mansilhas, who were to have been sent on at once on their arrival in Goa. Money and helpers were necessary if the work was not to fail as the Franciscan mission had. Francis determined to return to Goa for men and money, but before he left he sketched a rough plan of organisation to keep the memory of his teaching alive by means of native catechists.

By October, 1543, his fame had spread from Cape Comorin to "Adam's Bridge." His energy, his charity, his miracles were already becoming a legend. The sick were healed, the dead raised, men bitten by cobras saved from swift death, others snatched by unseen power from raging torrents. In the village of Kombutureh a small boy fell into a well, and when rescued showed no signs of life. The distracted mother seized him in her arms, rushed to

Father Francis and flung herself at his feet with cries of despair. Francis kent beside the body, prayed, made the sign of the Cross and took the cold little hand in his. The closed eyes opened, the rigid limbs relaxed, the child sat up. The shout of wonder from the bystanders ran through the village, the countryside: "The Great Father has brought the dead child back to life!"

It was useless for Francis to bid men be silent. News travelled with that incredible Eastern swiftness which rivals wireless. Stories and wonders grew thick about him. Men saw him lifted from the ground during his Mass. Others watching in one of those short hours of rest saw his sleeping body float above the bare earth which was his bed, radiant with spiritual light. A century later the Dutch Calvinist missionaries were baffled by the children of St. Francis. "Work as many miracles as he did, or more," was the Paravas' only answer to the most eloquent Protestant persuasions.

By December Francis arrived in Goa with some young Paravas destined for the priesthood. Diogo de Borba welcomed him and took him with his companions to the college, now in working order. Micer Paul and Mansilhas were comfortably settled there—no explanation of their failure to obey orders and join Francis on the Fishery Coast. The college buildings were nearly completed. It was well endowed with a revenue large enough to support five hundred students. Micer Paul was installed as confessor and professor to these native students, some of whom were studying Latin with view to early ordination, while others were only beginning to learn to read and write. It was obvious that he could not be spared, for no one knew better than Francis the enormous importance of training a native priesthood.

The young Paravas who had come to Goa with Francis soon spread the fame of his work and miracles in their country. "Master Francis," inquired Diogo one day: "What about that boy you raised from the dead at Comorin?" "*I* raise the dead to life?" answered Francis, blushing crimson: "They brought the child to me, he showed signs of life, I said to him: 'In the name of God, arise,' he rose, and the people wondered." Words of humility, to which the swift blood that he could not control gave the lie.

During the few weeks' stay at Goa came the first letter from Ignatius. Written in January, 1542, it had taken two years all but a month to arrive, and "God our Lord knows what joy I received from it!" wrote Francis in answer. It contained the news that Ignatius had been elected general of the Society and that the five companions in Rome —Lainez, Salmeron, le Jay, Broet and Codure—had taken their solemn vows with him in San Paolo *fuori,* April 22, 1541. Accordingly Francis himself now made his solemn profession to the Bishop. The original of his vows was sent to Rome, a copy he wore round his neck till the day of his death, with a little relic of St. Thomas given him at Meliapor, and a signature of Ignatius, cut from one of his letters.

Since the despatch of Ignatius's letter much had happened. As well as the "old, dilapidated, hired house in front of the old church" in Rome a second house of the Society had been founded in Lisbon in the monastery given by King John (1541), a third in Paris the same year, and a fourth at Padua. In June, 1542, the college at Coimbra was put in the hands of Rodriguez, and two years later sixty Jesuits were being educated there. By 1545 there were houses and colleges of the Society at

Louvain, Alcalá, Cologne, Valencia, Valladolid and Gandia.

In mid-January, 1544, Francis was back at Cochin, with Mansilhas (whose incapacity for learning made it useless for him to be left at the college with Micer Paul), an Indian priest and Juan de Artiaga, an old soldier who, finding missionary work harder than any campaign, was soon to fall out of the ranks.

From Cochin Francis wrote a half-jesting letter to the Queen of Portugal, begging her to devote to the Parava mission the four hundred gold *pardaos* which was her share of the annual tribute from the Pearl Fisheries and was officially described as "for the Queen's slippers." Only one sentence of this letter has been preserved by Torsellini: "That she could have no better shoes or pantoufles to climb to heaven than the children of the Piscarian coast and their instructors . . . thereby to make herself a ladder to heaven; for she might be glad of such an occasion."

The annual fleet was ready to sail to Lisbon. It would be a year or more before Francis had another chance of sending home a description of results achieved in the past fifteen months. As he writes, with the rush and force of a flooded mountain torrent—so much to say and so little time to say it—he is suddenly overwhelmed at the smallness of the human material at his disposal, contrasted with the multitudes of those in Europe:

"How often I long to go through the universities of Europe, shouting at the top of my voice, like one who has taken leave of his senses! Especially in the Paris university, calling in the Sorbonne, to those who have more learning than desire to put it to good use! How many souls turn away from the road to glory and go to hell because of their carelessness! If they only studied the account that God will demand from them as carefully as they study letters . . . saying: 'Lord, here I am, what wouldst Thou have me to do? Send me where Thou wilt, even, if Thou judgest best, among the Indians!' . . . It has become the custom with students to say: 'I wish for learning in order to obtain some benefice or ecclesiastical dignity, then to serve God in that position.' . . . I have been on the point of writing to the University of Paris, or at least to our master De Cornibus and to the doctor Picardo, to tell them how many thousands and millions of pagans would become Christians if there were workers. Finally I did write to stir them up to seek out and encourage men who seek not their own ends but those which are Jesus Christ's. So great is the multitude of those who are converted to the faith of Christ in the country where I am that often my arms are aching from baptising and my voice is gone from having so often recited the Creed and the Commandments in their language. . . . Some days I baptise a whole village, on the coast where I am there are thirty Christian villages." (Cochin, January 15, 1544.)

Those students with their ambitions, their dreams of a famous future, how well he knew them, how he relived in memory those days at Ste. Barbe; himself, Ignatius, Peter Faber. He had painted his own dreams and ambitions so glowingly on winter nights in the room the three shared, or on long golden summer evenings by the Seine. And then those quiet, insistent words of Ignatius: "What doth it profit a man, Master Francis, if he gain the whole world and suffer the loss of his own soul?" How he longed now to cry aloud the dross and vanity of worldly position, when all about him he saw those "thousands and millions of pagans" dying without the Faith because he alone could not do the work of a hundred men. But still men followed the will-o'-the-wisp,

"Though conquest still the victor's hope betrays,
The prize a shadow or a rainbow blaze."

This great letter, red-hot from his burning heart, reached Lisbon six or seven months later. It was copied and read aloud at Courts, and from the chairs of universities. It was translated into French, and the *imprimatur* on publication was given by de Gouvea, Francis's old master at Ste. Barbe. Francis de Borgia, Duke of Gandia and Viceroy of Catalonia, wrote his admiration of his namesake's work, and Ignatius's cousin, Father Antonio de Araoz, declared that Francis Xavier was doing as much good in Spain and Portugal by his letter as in the Indies by his preaching. Peter Faber, who had seen the effects in Spain, told Ignatius that, thanks to this letter, the Society was known in Spain, palace and prison, Court and poorhouse. It was the means also of bringing into the Society Jerome Nadal, a Majorcan priest whom Ignatius had in vain tried to convert when both were students in Paris, and who afterwards, as Vicar of the Company of Jesus, promulgated the Exercises in the various Provinces.

The next eleven months Francis was travelling to and fro along the west coast from Cape Comorin, its southernmost point, to Punicale, northern extremity of the kingdom of Comorin. The return to daily life after the first fervour of conversion, the drudgery of organising work which has been begun on the high tide of enthusiasm, these are the things which try men's mettle and prove their perseverance. "Go and set all on fire," had been Father Ignatius's parting words to his son. They had been obeyed. Now the flame which had swept through the Fishery Coast like a forest fire needed care and thought that it might continue to burn with a steady glow.

Not for nothing had Francis spent those two years in Rome with the "great moulder of men," working at that correspondence which had already reached out through Europe and was soon to link up the ends of the world. Now, bearing alone the entire responsibility of the new mission, Francis showed something of his Father's Napoleonic width of vision, his grasp of the smallest details, and a practical care for finance unexpected in one of his temperament.

He had sketched a rough organisation, outlined in the letter of January 15: "When I go on to visit other villages I leave in each place someone to carry on the work I have begun. . . . Wherever I go I leave the prayers written out and beg those who know how to write to copy and learn them by heart, to recite them every day. I arrange for them to meet and recite them together each Sunday and that this may be done I leave someone in charge in every place."

Later the *canakapillai* or catechist, paid by the mission, had other officials under him—sacristans, beadles and the like; but Francis, who distrusted the village chiefs, too often pagan at heart, when possible named as catechist a younger man, trained by and obedient to himself.

The other human material at his disposal was only too poor, and hopelessly insufficient for the hundreds of square miles of the mission. Each of his three helpers was intrusted with a district in the northern part of Travancore, where at this time of the year the only population was old men, women and children. He himself remained in charge of Comorin. To each too he gave a paper written by his own hand and containing advice and suggestions for their work and a rule for their spiritual life.

Of the three one only, the native priest Francisco Coelho, was to prove successful. When Francis returned from Malacca in 1548 he was to entrust to Coelho the difficult task of making a Tamil version of the rhyming catechism he himself had composed for neophytes. Juan de Artiaga before a year was out had proved incompetent, and his post was filled by a Spanish priest. Mansilhas, who had been unable to learn enough to be ordained in Portugal and was equally incapable of helping Micer Paul in the Goa college, seems not even to have had the qualities of his defects. To stupidity he added impatience and bad temper, and his disobedience to Francis's orders to join him in the Moluccas in 1547 led to dismissal from the Society. Yet to Mansilhas we are most deeply indebted, for he treasured the twenty-seven letters written him by Francis between February 23 and December 18, 1544. These letters, which Père Cros calls the diary of the Parava apostolate, are the only basis for Francis's itinerary during the year. They are much more even than a treasury of advice, practical and spiritual. They are a personal revelation, all the more striking because written hurriedly, without afterthought, as it were leaves torn out and scribbled post haste for the eye only of their recipient.

Without them it seems that the man Francis vanishes in this whirl of ceaseless activity and movement, becomes a legendary figure, glamorous with strange tales of miracles and wonders, impersonal as "the voice of one crying in the wilderness." It is a psychological riddle why the great saint should have chosen such a confidant. Perhaps he alone, with his supernatural insight and charity, saw the gleam of gold in the dull dross, perhaps, with his usual ignoring of self, he did not realise how much of himself he reveals in these short, hasty notes to which he devotes so many of his few spare moments.

He who travels and toils ceaselessly himself asks little less of his helpers. The saint demands no less than sanctity from his fellow-workers. One cannot but sympathise with Mansilhas, the ordinary, dull fellow of the same common clay as ourselves, willing under Francis's magnetic influence to work for others but so often irritated with their deceit, laziness and obstinacy, asking for occasional rest and relaxation. "If you wish God to make you a great saint," said St. Ignatius, "ask him to send you great sufferings"; and to Francis it was unbelievable that any man should ask or desire less.

"I advise you to have no fixed home, but always to be moving in one direction or another, as I did myself when I was where you are now, and as I generally do now, except at the moment when I am without interpreter."

Francis knew the danger of familiarity with the natives, knew too their easy conversions and easier relapses, their incapacity for perseverance, knew the need of such patience with them as could only be shown by supernatural grace and charity.

"Pray God to give you great patience. You are in Purgatory, expiating your faults. It is the precious mercy of God that allows you to suffer for your sins in this life. . . . If you find yourself so overwhelmed with fatigue that you cannot attempt everything, do what you can and be content. Thank God that you are in a country where you could not be idle even if you wanted to be."

Again and again comes the call to patience and love, as it was to sound in turn to all his helpers. "With these people be like a good father with naughty children. . . .

If the people love you and are friendly with you you will do great work for God. Learn to forgive their weaknesses with much patience and remember that, though they may not be good at the moment, they will be some day. . . . Treat these people very lovingly always, and do all you can to make them love you."

There is plenty of practical advice, a stern message (in which one fancies an echo of laughter) that anyone drunk on palm-toddy would pay dearly for it, charming messages in almost every letter to little Matthew, a Parava orphan, with promises or rewards for good behaviour, unwearying encouragement for Mansilhas's flagging spirits. "Do not let yourself be discouraged by the evils you see round you. Do not despair, for you are doing more than you think. And if you cannot do all you would wish, be content with what you can do, since it is not your fault"—a counsel repeated later, with the addition: "as I do myself."

But human nature, with fine-strung nerves and frail body, cannot maintain unbroken such high serenity of courage. In these letters, as in no others, sounds some-times the cry of a sensitive nature strained to breaking point, of fierce anger against the Portuguese oppressors of the native converts, of physical fatigues and sufferings: "I cannot prevent myself from being cut to the inmost soul by the wrongs done by Portuguese to native Chris-tians. It is a wound that will not heal." "I have been ill for four or five days and bled twice." "I have been eight days on the sea, and you know what it is to be in a *dhony* [a small native rowing-boat] when the winds are as furi-ous as they were. . . . God our Lord knows what I had to suffer on this voyage. . . . God give us more rest in the next life than we have in this!" Then two notes of deeper discouragement and despair: "If I were to follow my own wishes and escape from all these troubles it would take little to make me embark on a *dhony* at once and sail for India and the country of Prester John, where there is so much work to be done for God without danger of persecution." "I am so sick of life I prefer to die in defence of our law and Faith rather than to have to see as many evils as I do without power to remedy them."

In June, 1545, a new peril was added to the continual Portuguese oppression of the pearl-fishers. The ruler of Comorin had died in March; the Rajah of Travancore captured his successor and annexed the kingdom and the Prince of Madura—a small state north of Comorin— seized the chance of invasion. The Badagas, a light cavalry, swept south like a cyclone, leaving behind them a desert of burning villages and massacred inhabitants.

Francis was at the village of Kombutureh, where the drowned boy had been raised to life, when news came that the Christians of Cape Comorin, who had fled from their homes before the Badagas, were dying of hunger, thirst, and exposure on the rocky islands off the coast. He rushed to Manapar, fitted out twenty *dhonys* with food and drink, and set out in the storm. Eight days and nights natives struggled, rowing and towing, against the monsoon ("God knows what I had to suffer on this voyage!") but they could make no headway, and in the end Francis was obliged to land and make a forced march with the convoy.

Throughout July he remained at Cape Comorin, where the Christians were daily augmented by refugees from Manapar and the surrounding country, "naked and poor, without food or clothing." Still the Badagas, on their swift Arab horses, kept up the reign of terror. At night the sky was red with burning villages where dawn found only mangled corpses.

One night, as usual, Francis had withdrawn to pray alone when a terrified Parava brought the news that the enemy were at hand. They were in sight, when Francis advanced alone against them. The men suddenly reined in their horses, turned and fled. When their leader inquired the reason of this sudden rout, tales varied. A man had appeared before them, tall, black-clad, awful, with a glance of searing fire. A form of superhuman size and majesty had materialised from the darkness, glowing with strange light. Their hearts had turned to water within them. The fact remained that the village had been saved by the Great Father's courage and prayers and who can say if the more than mortal shining in the night had not been the Captain of the hosts of the Lord whom the child Francis had so often invoked in the little Javier oratory, on whom the man Francis was again to call when the crash of earthquake threatened his altar and his little congregation?

On their retreat the Badagas sacked Tuticorin, whose inhabitants had to take refuge on the sandy islands near by—a specially unpleasant experience for Cosme da Paiva, the Portuguese captain, who had been feathering his nest very comfortably by the sale of horses to the enemy. There was soon to be open war between him and Francis, who wrote to Mansilhas: "He has sent me a letter in which he declares that, without grave scandal, he cannot write all the evil I have done him." And: "Help Cosme da Paiva to clear his conscience from the many thefts he has committed on this coast and from the evils and murders caused at Tuticorin by his great greed. More, as friend of his honour, advise him to return the money received from murderers of Portuguese, for it is a ghastly thing to sell Portuguese blood for gold. I do not write to him myself, for I have no hope of his amendment."

But the Badaga tide was receding. In August came an ambassador with peace proposals from the Prince of Madura and in November Francis set out to see the Rajah of Travancore. It was an adventurous journey. He was shot at and wounded by an arrow. One night he only escaped pursuit by hiding up a tree; another night enemy hands set fire to his bed of fibre—a story which later tradition embroidered by an addition that the Great Father was so wrapt in prayer that he was unconscious of the flames and smoke and was found kneeling at dawn in a heap of ashes.

Francis's only companion, a Portuguese interpreter, gives a maddeningly vague and laconic account of the interview with the ruler: "He was loved by all and found favour with the king." It is another scene which calls for a painter. The Great King, who made up for the inferiority of his Nair (warrior) caste by a symbolic birth from a golden cow, sat splendid in gold turban, tunic and slippers, his wide red trousers stiff with gold thread. With what curiosity, mingled perhaps with contempt, must he have watched the thin figure in tattered gown which had once been black, the scorched, scarred feet in broken sandals!

Willing to buy the Portuguese protection he needed by any concessions which cost him little or nothing, he listened to the stumbling Tamil of the interpreter with that Hindu mask of suave courtesy which hides such tortuous subtlety. Finally with gracious generosity he gave leave for the evangelisation of his Macua subjects and orders for a herald to be sent to these rough fishers commanding them to listen to the *Balea Padre*. No doubt the subtle smile lingered on his lips and those of the Brahmins after Francis had gone forth, the rags of his loba perforce covered by a surplice. Not one Brahmin or member of the higher castes would be converted. Outcastes and pariahs mattered to none except this strange white madman who believed all souls equal in the sight of his God.

Francis, knowing the quick changes of the Oriental mind, swept, swift as the raiding Badagas, along the flat, swampy country between sea and Ghats. Through shallow, sandy lagoons and fever-haunted rivers he went, across wide green undulating fields, over bare rocky hills and wooded terraces, through forests "whose scents and shadows lie heavy as a leaden cape on the shoulders." The dæmonic force drove him as relentlessly as the Furies chased Orestes. There was no time for careful teaching, for long instruction. On his arrival at a hamlet he would call together men and boys, in his halting, parrot-like Tamil he recited the Creed, the Commandments, some prayers, which he made his audience repeat after him when he had taught them to make the sign of the Cross. A question followed each article of the Creed: "Do you believe?" A murmur of many voices answered, as dusky arms were crossed on naked breasts: "We believe." Then came baptism and each new Christian received a palm-leaf on which the Father's own hand had written his Christian name.

Cold criticism may question the permanency of these lightning conversions (ten thousand were baptised in this month), but there was no alternative. Hundreds of children, doomed by the appalling rate of infant mortality, at any rate gained heaven in exchange for limbo. A generation later, too, old men who had been baptised as boys still cherished their palm-leaves, passports to heaven signed by the Great Father himself and believed more powerful than any of the old *Mantram*.

Perched in a tree, surrounded by listening crowds, leading tribes of children or villagers to destroy the rude images of Siva and Ganesha, moving from place to place with incredible speed—no wonder Francis seemed to the rough, ignorant Mascuas more than human; that over two hundred years later a Protestant missionary should find near Cape Comorin what he oddly calls "an idol" of the Basque apostle.

CHAPTER XII

It was fated that Francis should nowhere finish the work he had begun. Where, as pioneer, he had blazed the trail, others were to follow and cultivate the ground. In other places it was to revert to trackless wilderness.

He had reached one of the last Macua villages when he heard that the Rajah of Jafnapatam, in the north of Ceylon, had ordered a wholesale massacre of the six hundred converts on the island of Manar between Ceylon and the mainland. A brother of the persecutor found Francis at Cochin, whither he had travelled post-haste to catch Miguel Vaz, who was on the point of sailing to Lisbon. The Singalese prince appealed for Portuguese help in placing him on the throne which he claimed, and in return for such help promised the conversion to Christianity of his entire country. New fields, vaster vineyards, wider horizons opened before the vision of Francis, who was burning with desire to avenge his martyred children. The vicar-general agreed on the necessity for instant action. If he had not agreed the only difference it would probably have made would have been the postponement of his own departure.

On December 20, 1544, Francis left on a fast sailing boat. Christmas was passed at sea, and he reached Goa two days later, only to find that the Governor was at

Bassein, just north of the modern Bombay. Francis stayed in Goa long enough to hear that the three priests expected from Lisbon had not arrived, then pursued Don Martin to Bassein. He put before him the state of the Comorin mission, the ten thousand Christians in Travancore, the massacre of Manar, the offer of the refugee prince. Ignatius, with his greater detachment and wider experience, would have seen the danger of this game of political barter. Francis, his soul on fire with indignation at the deaths of his sons, with desire to win this new realm for Christ, did not hesitate.

"The Governor was so distressed when I told him of the murder of the Manar Christians that he gave orders to fit out a fleet to capture the king and put him to death. I had to soothe this holy anger" (January 27, 1545). More cynical than the saint, one is tempted to see in this "holy anger" a desire to be quit of one who was as comfortable a companion as a consuming fire would have been. Anyhow the fleet was promised. The island where Adam and Eve were said to have consoled themselves for lost Paradise might provide some pickings for a governor whose term of office was drawing to a close.

On January 20, 1545, Francis was back at Cochin after an absence of little more than a month. His time at sea had not been barren. Going north he had made friends with a rake of a soldier who turned a deaf ear to pious talk and roared with laughter at the word "confession." The boat put in for a few hours at Cananor, where the strange pair strolled toward a palm-grove. Under the trees Francis suddenly tore his loba from his shoulders and pulling out a discipline scourged himself so fiercely that the blood spurted. "That is for you. I would do all in my power to wipe out your sins, but you have cost dear Jesus infinitely more." The man snatched the discipline and flung himself on his knees in tears. "*I* am the one who should do penance. You have conquered me!"

On the way back Francis carefully embarked on the same boat as a sailor who was a notorious gambler and blasphemer. Disturbed while saying Office one day by a torrent of blasphemy and obscenity, Francis inquired what was the matter and was told the wretched man had gambled away everything he possessed. He took out a handful of *pardaos*—it was unusual for him to have any money—and sent them to the gambler, wishing him better luck. Sure enough, the luck turned; the man won back all he had lost, came to thank Francis, and ended by confession and reformation. A dangerous gamble in which only a Xavier could be sure of winning a soul.

From Cochin, where the last ships of the year were preparing to sail for Lisbon, Francis wrote four long letters, to the Fathers in Rome, Ignatius, Rodriguez, and the King. In the first, an account of the last year's work, occurs the first mention of Malacca, of which Francis had just heard from Antonio de Paiva, a merchant who the year before had reached Macassar and was taking to Goa four Malayans destined for the college of Santa Fé and the priesthood. In the letter to Ignatius, which is more intimate and personal, is an insistent demand for more news and more help: "Men without the gifts necessary for hearing confessions, preaching, or doing similar work in the Company would be of great use in this country . . . for in these healthen parts knowledge is unnecessary"— a fallacy, as Francis himself was afterwards to discover. In his emphasis on the bodily strength needed we get a glimpse of his own trials: "They must be able to stand immense physical fatigue, for a stay in this country is very trying on account of the great heat and the absence of drinkable water in many places. Bodily food is scanty and monotonous—nothing but rice, fish and chicken; neither bread nor wine nor anything which is plentiful in Europe. They must be healthy, not delicate, to be able to endure the endless work of baptising, teaching, travelling from one village to another." (Cochin, January 27, 1545.)

The long letter to the King, after a plea for him to name Miguel Vaz coadjutor to the bishop, now old and infirm, is an outspoken indictment of Portuguese rule in the Indies and of John's own weakness and incapacity to end corruption: "I seem to hear voices crying aloud to heaven from the soil of India, accusing your Majesty of avarice towards this empire from which you draw such treasures and to which you hardly allow in return a pittance for the supply of such immense spiritual needs. . . . Fear lest you hear these words spoken in wrath by God, the sovereign Judge: 'Why have you not punished your ministers and servants who have fought against My religion in India under cover of your name?' " (February 8, 1545.)

The postscript to Rodriguez's letter burns with passionate indignation: "Let none of your friends come to India with place and office from the king, for it is of such that one can justly say: 'Let them be wiped out from the book of the living and their names not written among the just.' . . . It has become such a custom here to do what should not be done that, so far as I can see, no one cares, for all run along the road of *I snatch, thou snatchest*. I am amazed to see how many fashions, moods and tenses of this same verb *to snatch* are invented by those who come out here. . . . The great need of India is a man who will defend its sheep from such ravening wolves" (January 27,

1545). Whatever particular instance had roused Francis to such anger there was worse to come.

From Negapatam, where he was waiting for the fleet to avenge the martyrs and invade Ceylon, he wrote Mansilhas an order for the dismissal of Juan de Artiaga and mentioned the possibility of a voyage to Malacca (April 7, 1545). In this letter is the jangle of taut nerves, worn with uncertainty and delay. His worst fears were realised: "Jafanapatam has not been taken. The king who promised to make his country Christian has not been put in possession of it. All has been left undone because a Portugal vessel from Pegu was wrecked on the coast and the King of Jafanapatam seized the cargo." (Meliapor, May 8, 1545.)

Pepper, spices, and jewels weighed heavier in the balance than immortal souls. Diplomacy forbade an offensive against a rajah who held such a rich cargo in pawn. The last illusion is stripped from Francis. He has plumbed to the depths the infamy of fellow-Christians and white men who set greed before religion, gold above their Faith. Alone, deserted, betrayed, he hears in the darkness only the tumult of a cruel rabble, the whisper of Judas who sold his Master for thirty pieces of silver. "For this is your hour and the powers of darkness."

On Passion Sunday he embarked to return to work at Cape Comorin, but God had other plans for him. Once more it was impossible to make headway against the southern monsoon. The little boat had to put back into Negapatam. A few days later Francis set off on foot, alone but for a Malabar servant, northward along the Coromandel coast. Then, after a week or more, there rose on the horizon a low, rocky hill, crowned by a rude little chapel which marked the traditional site of St. Thomas's martyrdom. Round it clustered the small Portuguese settlement of Meliapor, with its fringe of native huts, a miniature Goa in its greed, its vices, its crude luxury. Far out at sea fishermen declared they could see the ruins of the old Hindu city, lying fathoms deep under the clear waters of the Bay of Bengal. In the presbytery, separated only by a garden from the chapel, lived Gaspard de Coelho, the old Portuguese vicar, and one can imagine the delight with which he welcomed such a guest as Francis, whose fame had probably penetrated even to this sleepy backwater.

Only in solitude and silence can the bruised and bleeding soul recover poise and serenity, and these four months at Meliapor were all the respite granted to Francis in ten years of ceaseless journeys and toil.

There was the old vicar, with his good-humoured little jokes, his harmless gossip, his local lore, the white stone which sweated blood during the Mass of St. Thomas's day, the pilgrimages to the shrine of him with whom even the Saracens claimed kin. Had Francis heard at Venice the legend of the martyrdom brought home by Marco Polo two and a half centuries before? How, wounded in the right side like his Lord by a lance as he knelt in prayer in the palm-grove, Thomas had fallen asleep, surrounded by the peacocks after which Meliapor was named—a tale with the glowing, ethereal beauty of a Japanese painting. Patron of the sceptical who, at last convinced, believe without reserve, and of the unpunctual, St. Thomas it is to whose late arrival we owe the opening of our Lady's tomb, which revealed not mortal flesh but the sweetness of lilies.

Even here Francis could not be wholly idle. He was soon a familiar figure in the narrow streets with their smell of spice and fetid humanity. As in Goa, vicious unions were regulated or ended, sinners brought back to the sacraments, the sick healed, the dying comforted. One João d'Eiro who had followed Francis from the south promised to give up all and serve him. At the last moment his courage failed him. He was just going on board the boat he had brought for a secret flight when a small native boy came running to say that Father Francis wanted to see him. Afraid and reluctant he obeyed, and as he hesitated on the threshold he heard Francis's voice: "You have sinned! You have sinned! Go and confess your sin." Stricken with remorse, João rushed off, sold everything and flung himself repentant at Francis's feet. He afterwards became a Franciscan.

This is only one instance of Francis's power to read men's thoughts, sometimes to communicate his own to them without medium of a common language. It was no stranger for him to know events far off or still in the future, for to him who dwelt in such close union with God, the Eternal Now, space and time were sometimes obliterated "as a dream when one awaketh."

The days passed in prayer, reading, good works. In the cool of the evening, as they sat on the verandah under the stars, looking out across the sea, Francis's thoughts turned backward to childhood and youth, and the old man listened, open-mouthed and all ears, to those intimate revelations of student and professor days in Paris, of the all but miraculous preservation of the young man's chastity. Ignatius of Loyola, Peter Faber, Rodriguez, Lainez, Salmeron, they lived before de Coelho's eyes. To Francis himself there must have been one memory more vivid than any. On the Feast of the Assumption was the tenth anniversary of the taking of the first vows in the little chapel of St. Denis. Perhaps, as he knelt in the little chapel of St. Thomas, Meliapor faded from his thoughts and he stood again on the hill of Montmartre and saw the buildings of the Benedictine abbey, the long covered passage up to the parish church of St. Pierre with its tall spire, the busily turning sails of the windmill that crowned the hill, and, far below, the huddled roofs of Paris and the silver Seine winding through yellow corn-fields and wooded hills. Again he and his six companions broke the bread and drank clear, cold water from the martyr's spring as the long summer day passed swiftly in "loving talk."

Now, as after that day ten years ago, Francis had withdrawn from the tumult of man that in the silence he might hear the still, small voice revealing the Will of God. As always, when the soul asks nothing but to do the work and Will of God in God's own way, the answer came clear: "With His usual mercy God has been pleased to remember me. I have felt and understood, with deep interior consolation, that it is His Will I should go to the country of Malacca. I am so firmly decided to carry out what God revealed in my soul that if I did not do it I should feel I were fighting the Will of God and that He would not forgive me in this world or the next. And if there were no Portuguese ships sailing this year for Malacca I should go on some Moorish or heathen ship." (May 8, 1545.)

In this same letter to Diogo and Micer Paul at Goa are instructions about the Comorin mission, where a Spanish priest had replaced de Artiaga, and for the three fathers expected from Portugal. They did not arrive at Goa till Francis was on his way to Malacca. One of them was Antonio Criminale, whom Francis perhaps met at Parma on his way to Lisbon. Antonio had been received into the Society by Ignatius himself in 1541 and was then sent to

Coimbra. In March, 1544, Simon Rodriguez had sent for him to tell him to start for the Indies in twenty-four hours' time. Antonio had laughed gaily. "Italy, the Indies, Turkey, another country—I am ready to stay or go. All I wish is to work for the love and service of God." One cannot help regretting that this gay, brave, ardent soul, so like his own, was not to be Francis's companion in some of his far journeys and hard labours. The two were to meet only for a few days at Manapar on Francis's return from the Moluccas in the spring of 1548.

It came to the old vicar's ears that after he himself was in bed and asleep his guest used to steal out to spend most of the night in a corner by the chapel, reputed to be haunted. "Don't go there, Father Master Francis," he cried in horror. "There are devils there, and they will hurt you." Francis laughed and went just the same. One night his faithful Malabar, who slept like a dog on the ground by the door, woke to the sound of blows and cries from his master: "Our Lady, will you not come to my aid?" The next morning the vicar, missing Francis from Mattins, hurried anxiously to his room. "Are you ill? Did I not tell you not to go there?" Francis smiled and said nothing, but the Malabar told his tale and when Francis was up and about again two days later the vicar teased him as they sat at supper: "Our Lady, will you not come to my aid?" Again Francis tried to pass it off with a laugh, but again, as when he had been asked about raising the boy from the dead, the tell-tale blood betrayed his secret.

He still went out, though, to spend the dark hours in prayer and discipline. One Friday night as he was passing through the deserted garden on his way to his usual corner he was amazed to hear solemn Mattins chanted so loud that he could distinguish words and music. . . . He is a boy again standing outside the archway with its carved crescents, while through the night comes the chanting of Don Miguel with his companions in the church of Santa Maria de Javier. Far on the hills tinkle the little bells on the necks of sheep and goats, nearer the cry of a wakened bird. Overhead are the same moon and stars, the clear line of the Great Bear whose seven Rishis, say the Hindus, "adorn the north as a beautiful woman is adorned with a collar of pearls, a necklace of white lotus-flowers." The chapel of St. Thomas is dark, empty, every door safe locked, but still the Indian night is full of that solemn chant. Down twenty years of exile, across sea and ocean, the rivers and mountains of two continents, it reaches Francis, and "over all there is peace."

CHAPTER XIII

MALACCA (AUGUST, 1545–DECEMBER 31, 1545)

THE last few days of the four weeks' voyage from Meliapor to Malacca were slow and tedious. The ship anchored at night and only crawled by day for soundings had continually to be taken in the shallow straits between Sumatra and the Malay Peninsula. Malacca had been captured by Albuquerque thirty-four years before, but apparently no charts had yet been made. There is a good deal of probability in the theory that the rapid decline of Portuguese power in the East and the more rapid rise of the English and Dutch empires there was largely due to the superiority of the latter as sailors and pilots, for within a short time of English or Dutch occupation of a new colony maps and charts were made of shoals and rocks, coasts and rivers.

At last Malacca was sighted, the low hill which rose from the shore crowned by the white church of our Lady of the Mount and the citadel, built of stones from desecrated mosques and royal tombs. Below lay the fortress, the parish church (afterwards the cathedral of the Assumption), and the wooden houses of the Portuguese town, defended on the seashore by a wall and separated by the river from the native quarter. Originally a small fishing village, Malacca, under the Mussulmen who had taken it in the fourteenth century, had become a great trading centre and now was the chief clearing-station between India and the far East.

The harbour was crowded with shipping. Flat-bottomed Chinese junks and sharp-nosed *prahus* from Java lay beside Portuguese caravels and native fishing-boats. A soft blue haze veiled the town. The steel-blue sea was stained blood-red from the reflection of the scarlet clouds, which the sun pierced with long golden spears as it set below the Sumatra horizon.

Francis's fame had preceded him. The yellow sands were crowded with Portuguese, Javanese, coffee-coloured Malays with bright dresses and *krisses* poisoned and gilt, Arabs and Chinese. As he landed a shout went up in the soft, damp air: "The holy Father is here!" He was mobbed by children, surrounded by mothers and nurses with babies in their arms, who would not go without his touch and blessing. It was said later that he had called each child by its name, spoken to men and women of things he could have known by no natural means.

A proposal made recently to mark the spot of his first landing in Malacca could not be realised, because the lighthouse now occupies the site and to move it would necessitate changing all the charts of the world.

Francis's first care was to report to the captain, Garcia de Sa, who vied with a rich merchant, Diogo Pereira, and the old parish priest, Father Martinez, in eagerness to have the Great Father as his guest. He, however, insisted on taking up his quarters in a little house near the hospital, accompanied by the repentant João d'Eiro, and later, following his usual custom, moved into the hospital itself. A generation and more later the inhabitants of the little house declared that nothing would induce them to leave it, so impregnated was it with the spirit of the saint who had tarried there for so short a time.

One of the witnesses at the Goa process of 1556 gives a vignette of this time: "The Father had a tiny room to himself. He withdrew there to pray when my companion and I were going to bed. On a little table there were a crucifix in St. Thomas's wood, a cross and a breviary. Beside this table was a longish black stone, big as a head or bigger. When we were asleep the Father, dressed as in the daytime, mediated and prayed on his knees, his hands lifted heavenwards. I myself have watched him for some time. Two or three times I saw him rest his head on this stone or some others near the table. Before dawn he rose to say Mass and Office."

Those nights of prayer and ecstasy, with only such short sleep as an exhausted body forced on him, were followed by days as strenuous as those at Goa. "Every Sunday I preach at the *Séo* [cathedral], but I am not as pleased with my preaching as those who have patience to listen to me. Every day I teach prayers to the children for an hour or more. I live at the hospital, hear the confessions of the poor sick people, say Mass for them and give them communion. I am so overwhelmed by confessions that it is impossible to satisfy everyone. My chief occupation is translating prayers from Latin into a language understood by the people of Macassar. It is a most troublesome thing not to know the language." (To the Fathers in Portugal, November 10, 1545.)

Those crowded days—care of sick and sinners, processions through the streets with the little bell ringing to summon all to instruction—can have left little spare time. He became a familiar figure. The wealthy Diogo Pereira would only talk to him bare-headed. Even Mohammedans and Hindus called him the holy Father, kissed his hand and begged his prayers when they met him in the street. In the evenings, suppers in the houses of sinners, as at Goa, and with the same results—almost invariably penitence and amendment. There was another conversion, held to be miraculous. A Jewish rabbi, "hard-headed, learned and obstinate," whose influence prevented the conversion of other Jews, made a habit of attending Francis's instructions in order to scoff. Francis, who heard of this, managed to get to know him, had friendly talks, invited himself to dine, won and converted him. Strangely enough this is the only conversion since his arrival in the East where personal magnetism was supplemented by learning and the old armoury of university debate was once again brought into play as it was so often to be with the Japanese bonzes.

Had he ever a free moment to leave the town by the rough roads of red earth and wander through those fields of rice, sago and coconut-palms and bread-fruit, brought to such rich harvest by the daily showers of rain succeeded by burning sun? From the little house perched high on the rampart he could have looked farther, to the forest whose undergrowth was so tangled that even herds of wild elephants and bison or rhinoceros could penetrate only it by the winding paths made by their ancestors. In nests in the trees, surrounded by monkeys small or larger than themselves, lived the aborigines, the Sakai, safe from human intrusion once they had pulled up their rude ladders of hemp or creepers.

Nothing is told of Francis working among the natives. There was work enough and to spare among the Portuguese, but as Goa had been only a stepping stone to Comorin so Malacca was to be only a halt on the march

to further conquests. He had come with the Spice Islands
as his objective, the islands which had lured the west since
Pomponius Mela, ten years after the Crucifixion, had
marked "*Chryse*," the golden island, on his map as the
extreme eastern limit of the world.

Explored by the ships sent out by Albuquerque after
his capture of Malacca in 1511, the secret of the Moluccas
had been carefully guarded by Portugal for fear of rivals.
The golden age of Portuguese Malaya had been under the
governorship of Antonio Galvão, best of all his country's
administrators in the East, who, as we have seen, returned
to Lisbon in the fleet whose arrival Francis had witnessed
in 1540. It was he who had organised the first missions
in the Moluccas, but on Francis's arrival in Malacca
(September, 1545) the converts of many islands, including the important station of Amboina, were without priest
or instructor. His original intention had been to proceed
at once to Macassar (capital of the island of Celebes, over
twelve hundred miles east of Malacca), but he learned
from Garcia de Sa that a priest had gone there a few
months previously with the Portuguese fleet despatched to
drive away the Spanish interlopers from the New World.
It was unnecessary to follow and the three months of
winter monsoon, which blew steadily west, made it impossible to set sail yet to other islands.

The delay imposed on him was, as we have seen, filled
with abundance of work, and the arrival of a ship from
Goa in October brought a great joy in the shape of letters
from home and Goa. There was one from Ignatius
written in July, 1543, two years and three months ago, one
from Broët, and two from Peter Faber, early in 1544,
with news of his labours in Germany. "How great a
consolation! I read and re-read them and seem to be

still with you, my beloved brothers, if not in body at least in spirit." (November 10.)

There were too letters from Goa telling him of the arrival of the three Jesuit fathers, the first batch who had left Lisbon for the East since his own departure four years before. To Antonio Criminale, and a Portuguese, Juan de Beira, he wrote directions to go to Cape Comorin and put themselves under the orders of Mansilhas, "who knows the country and what you must do there." The third, Lancilotto, a consumptive but fiercely energetic Italian, was to remain at Goa to teach in the College. He outlines his own altered plans: "I am going to Amboina where there are many Christians and where apparently there is a good chance of making many more. From there I will let you know what the country is like and what fruit can be gained there. Thanks to the experience I gained at Cape Comorin and Goa, and which, please God, I shall gain at Amboina and the region of Molucca, I shall see and will let you know where you will best be able to serve God and spread the most holy Faith of Christ our Lord." (Malacca, December 16, 1545.)

He was not to leave Malacca till New Year's Day, 1546, but, during the weeks of waiting, yet a further horizon had opened before him. Since 1520 China had been closed to foreigners on pain of death, owing to the mad folly of the Portuguese marauder who had invaded Canton, robbed the native merchants and insulted a mandarin. Trade was still carried on, however, between Portuguese merchant-ships and Chinese, who met on Sanchian, a small island in the mouth of the Canton river. At Malacca Francis met a merchant just back from China. He had been questioned by a Chinese courtier about a people living in the mountains who would not eat pork—in reality a Jewish colony.

Francis asked many of the traders who were going to Canton to make exhaustive inquiries, and promised to send home any information he could gain about China.

In the same letter which first mentions China (Amboina, May 10, 1546), comes again the note about the language difficulty, the immense trouble he had had at Malacca in translating prayers, Creed and Commandments into Malay, the lingua franca of the Far East. This tongue, somewhat resembling French but with the more open vowels of Italian, was spoken by educated natives throughout the Malay peninsula and the islands. It had apparently not been written before the advent of the Mohammedan conquerors in the fourteenth century and was now written in Arab characters taught by the *cacizes*.

The gift of tongues, so freely attributed to Francis Xavier by many of his biographers, can only have been intermittent, for his complaints about the almost insuperable difficulty of learning the eastern languages occur continually in letters, each time he goes to a new country. It was his invariable habit to get interpreters to translate prayers and short instructions which he would learn off by heart—a probable explanation of some of the testimonies which describe him as speaking new tongues after a brief stay in the country. Naturally these translations were rough and ready, often inaccurate and misleading. There was the difficulty of an interpreter who only understood his own language thoroughly—not always even that!—and the worse difficulty of finding symbols for ideas entirely new and unknown. As soon as Francis discovered translations which were inaccurate or misleading he would take endless pains to rectify them, witness some of his letters to Mansilhas about the prayers and catechism in Tamil.

Such occasions as that on which the congregation on

the Coromandel coast, as on the day of Pentecost, heard
"every man in his own tongue," and the day when a
Japanese audience understood a sermon in Portuguese,
come into another category. To explain them by telepathy
would be to impose a greater strain on credulity than to
accept them as miraculous. The earliest biographers, such
as Torsellini and Valignano, do not mention the gift of
languages, but the Bull of Canonisation states most definitely: "The signs and prodigies by which God confirmed
the teaching of the apostles by the cradle of the new-born
Church He has been pleased to renew in the person of His
servant Francis. . . . He was suddenly inspired to speak
the unknown tongues of diverse peoples without having
learnt them."

The gift of tongues was only one among the "signs and
prodigies" that followed him in each new mission field.
Indeed the numerous miracles [1] of all kinds, such as healing the sick, raising the dead, driving out devils, calming
storms, saving those in danger of bodily or spiritual death,
have proved a sad trial even to the most sympathetic of his
Protestant biographers. It is difficult to see how anyone
calling himself a Christian can deny the possibility of
miracles, but human nature is a bundle of illogical con-
tradictions, and natural laws are considered stronger than
the omnipotent Creator.

With that absurd inaccuracy so often shown by the
would-be scientific investigator, Dickson White declares

---

[1] It is unnecessary to repeat and elaborate the list of miracles which
appeared in each new field. They can be found in the *Monumenta
Xaveriana,* in Père Brou's great *Saint François Xavier* (the standard
life of the saint till the completion of Father Schurhammer's monu-
mental work), or any authoritative modern life. It is a sad omission
on the part of English Catholic publishers and public that there are no
translations of Brou's life nor of Bellesort's vivid and picturesque
portrait of the saint.

(*History of the Struggle between Science and Theology*)
that every Catholic must, under pain of eternal damnation,
believe such stories as that of the crab and crucifix, a
charming incident in Seram which was related in the
Process of 1616, and will be found in a later chapter. The
fact that a miracle is accepted by the Congregation of Rites
and inscribed in a Bull of Canonisation actually imposes
on the Catholic historian or investigator only the obligation
of prudence and respect, for the infallibility of the Church
is not involved.

One may grant that a good many stories of miracles,
specially some of those related at the Process of 1616,
would hardly pass muster as evidence in a modern court of
law. Some are hearsay, at second or third hand, or popular
talk. Some are childish memories of men and women who
when they gave them must have been nearly or over a
hundred. Grant that such conditions as cataleptic trances,
which deceive even the most advanced medical science,
may well have been mistaken for death by a credulous
and ignorant people. Grant too the mythical element with
which such a people quickly surrounds anyone who has
deeply impressed them. Grant all this: there still remains
a large residue which cannot be explained by natural laws.
Of conversions indeed the word "miraculous" is too
loosely used, but it cannot be avoided when speaking of
sick healed, dying and dead restored instantaneously to
health and life by the prayers of the Great Father, and by
the touch of those life-giving hands or even of the rosary
which seems more often to have been on errands of mercy
than in its owner's possession. That the exorcisms worked
and the devils driven out by Francis were not only the
imagination of superstitious natives other Catholic missionaries, past and present, can testify.

Our Lord answered the disciples of John the Baptist: "Go and tell John what ye have heard and seen, the blind see, the lame walk, the lepers are cleansed, the deaf hear, the dead rise again, the poor have the gospel preached to them." And He added the warning: "Blessed is he that shall not be scandalised in Me."

CHAPTER XIV

AMBOINA AND TERNATE
(JANUARY 1, 1546–SEPTEMBER)

AT last the long weeks of waiting ended. The wind veered to the west, and on New Year's Day, 1546, Francis boarded a ship sailing to load a cargo of nutmeg in Banda. It was a perilous voyage, both from man and nature. The shallow straits between the Malay Peninsula and the flat, fertile shores of Sumatra were the haunt of the dreaded Achinese pirates, and the uncharted sea was full of reefs and sandbanks. "Once in particular . . . we were running before a tempestuous wind for more than a league with our keel continually grounding. If we had struck a reef during this time all would have been up with the ship. We should have stuck in the sand if the water had been deeper one side than the other. There were many tears on board!"

The narrative of "torments by sea and in the midst of enemies" is here broken by a psychological analysis of their results: "Proving clearly that the consolations vouch-safed at such a moment are greater than the fear of imminent death. Once sufferings are over and danger has ceased man can no longer relate nor describe his feelings in the moment of danger. All that remains in his memory is the resolve never to weary of serving such a good Master both in the present and future and the hope that the Lord, Whose mercy is infinite, will grant him strength for such

167

service" (Amboina, May 10, 1546). Sublime and selfless heroism such as the saints alone know!

Days and weeks passed. The rocky heights of Java and the long chain of volcanic islands south of Celebes lay astern. The horizon of the Banda sea was unbroken by sight of land. Francis's days were filled by work, his nights by prayer. The Portuguese captain and sailors were not the only captives of his charm. If the crew of Lascars did not always understand his halting Malay, at least they understood his works of mercy, his friendliness, his gay smile.

It was six weeks since they had left Malacca. Captain and pilot began to be afraid that the strength of the monsoon had blown them past their objective and that it would be impossible to beat west in the teeth of the gale. Francis came up to them. "Have no fear. To-morrow we shall sight Amboina." At dawn the northern horizon showed two rocky promontories, joined in the shape of a rough horse-shoe by a sandy neck. It was Amboina. The captain, who did not wish to delay, put off a small boat and crew to land Francis, d'Eiro and Araujo, a Portuguese merchant (February 14, 1546). As they were rowing ashore a fleet of canoes manned by apparently hostile natives appeared, and the Portuguese sailors, terrified, turned for the open sea. There they lay, the little boat tossed up and down with the sun beating down on it. Francis reassured the crew—a little impatience would have been pardonable— and presently they reached the calm of the bay.

The water of this splendid harbour was so amazingly clear that on the sandy bottom, seven or eight fathoms down, red coral, sponges and giant anemones could be clearly seen. Fish of strange shapes and brilliant colours swam through them, and huge jelly-fish made patches of rose and orange on the blue surface. On the south side of the harbour lay the town, the usual Portuguese trading-centre, with its wooden houses clustered round the stone fort, and on the east the native suburb, its thatched huts shaded by palms and banana-trees.

The Christians baptised nine years before had since then been left without care or instruction, and Francis's first job was to build a rough chapel of palm-leaves, his next to set out in search of the neglected converts. His own account is tantalisingly brief and unilluminating: "This populous island is twenty-five to thirty leagues round and has seven Christian villages. As soon as I arrived I visited them all and baptised the children, many of whom died soon afterwards."

To reach some of these villages it was necessary to clamber up the steep mountain-sides, slipping in red clay, scrambling over rocks, pushing a way through tall ferns and bamboos, between slender palms and under the low, thick clove-trees. Around Francis, as he went on foot, were quivering clouds of venemous insects, the flash of gorgeous emerald and sapphire butterflies with wings like a swallow's tail. The green gloom was filled by the shrill chatter of crimson parakeets, heavy with the scent of unopened clove flower-buds. Dozens of leeches clung to legs and ankles, face and body streamed in the steamy heat, the brain felt like bursting, the way seemed unending.

Suddenly, in the heart of the forest, was a little cluster of native huts. The place looked deserted. Not a soul was to be seen. Yet, under palm-thatched eaves and behind barred doors, was a rustling whisper. Men, women, and children, terrified as a wild animal at the steps of a hunter, had fled at first hint of a stranger's approach. Portuguese and Arabs were alike a terror bringing death, slavery, or conversion to some unknown faith. Exhausted, alone, almost despairing Francis stood and prayed for inspiration. Suddenly he remembered his own childhood, for what were these Alfurus but foolish frightened children? He remembered the clear hill air of Javier, full of music—songs of shepherds as the sheep huddled round the glowing fires, song of the farmer as the slow oxen ploughed the brown, rocky slopes, song of the men in the castle yard as they groomed the horses and polished their swords, songs of the women as they crooned over the cradle to the whir of spinning-wheels. The Basque was born, lived, and died with a song on his lips, and was he not a Basque and proud of it? In "the psalms and hymns" that we are told he began to sing was there not perhaps an echo of childhood's words and melody?

> "White pigeon on the wing, where will you go?
> The passes into Spain are full of snow.
> In our house for to-night lie low, lie low!"

Doors were pushed open. Brown, bearded faces peered out under a tangle of coarse, black hair. One naked child ran out, made bold to clutch the damp, stained skirt of the old loba. Other children followed, men and women. The conquest was complete, and before the swift darkness fell Francis was squatting in one of the huts sharing a supper of bread-fruit baked in wood ashes and tasting like potatoes mashed with milk. There was arrack, too, in the halves of dried gourds; and perhaps, hung in the shadows, the grinning of a human skull or the leer of a wooden idol.

> "In our house for to-night lie low, lie low!"

Soon there was no sound but the regular breathing of

sleepers, the whimper of a baby as it sought its mother's breast, and in the darkness Francis tasted that union with God that alone enabled him to persevere. The next day he went from door to door, preceded by a boy carrying a cross, and no doubt followed by a crowd of children. He asked at each house if there were children to be baptised, sick to visit, dead to be buried. "Often the body was healed as well as the soul." Before long the villages had all been found. From the heights as he looked over the clove-trees, between the red stems of the palms he could see the volcanoes of Seram on the north, while, to east and west, innumerable little islands were scattered like green and gold beads whose string has been broken.

Francis remembered the king's instructions to him, at their farewell interview in Lisbon, telling him to inspect and report on the state of religion in every Portuguese settlement. He remembered too the brief of Paul III appointing him Papal Nuncio in the East. Such memories were fuel to the ceaseless fire of love which consumed him, that passionate hunger for souls which was never to be satisfied till the worn-out body was buried at Sanchian.

He tells us nothing in his letters of his journeys to Seram and the surrounding islands. Perhaps here, as so often with him, it was a case of *"nil nisi bonum."* It was a happy chance which preserved some details of those wanderings (between mid-February and mid-May, 1546). An old Portuguese gunner, driven from Amboina by the Dutch in 1608, rewarded the hospitality of the Cebu Jesuits by telling them how he had been Xavier's companion sixty-two years before. In his testimony on oath is the story of the miraculous crucifix brought by Francis from Rome and still preserved among the former royal treasures in Madrid. On the crossing to Seram such a fierce storm rose that the native crew gave all up for lost. "Then Father Francis drew from his breast a crucifix of about a finger's length. He leant over the side to touch the waves with it. But somehow the crucifix slipped from his hand and fell. He was much distressed and did not hide it. . . . The next day . . . landing on the coast, Father Francis and I were walking together along the shore in the direction of Tamano. We had gone about five hundred yards when both of us saw a crab come out of the sea holding the crucifix, which it carried between its claws. I saw it go straight to Father Francis and stop by him. The Father fell on his knees. The crab waited to have the crucifix taken, then went back and disappeared into the sea. The Father kissed the cross, clasped it to his breast, and so remained for half an hour in prayer." This is the delightful story on which Voltaire has seen fit to sharpen his wit, and which Dickson White declares must be believed by Catholics on pain of eternal damnation!

In a *paragua,* a native canoe made from a hollowed tree-trunk, Francis went on to other islands. Here nature was at her loveliest and most languorous. In the green depths of the forests clothing volcanic slopes grew huge orchids of strange shapes and splendid colours. A myriad birds flashed to and fro or chattered in the trees—green barbets with blue and crimson heads, kingfishers bright as jewels, red-breasted doves, cuckoos with red heads and green beaks, gaudy woodpeckers, great golden pheasants, birds of paradise with copper-gold breasts and sweeping loveliness of honey tail-feathers; the Portuguese story of the bird of fire which never touched earth till its lifeless body fell there might well have stood for a symbol of Francis's soul. Other forms of life were less pleasant—clouds of flies and mosquitoes, armies of leeches, poisonous snakes and evil-looking bats. On the larger islands the passage of elephant or rhinoceros sounded crashing through the undergrowth, that of a tiger was known only by a half-seen streak of black and yellow.

Love and war were the two prevailing passions. Alfuru men, wooly-haired, bearded, crept silent as snakes through the trees as they blew poisoned arrows from their bamboo quivers and hacked the head from the warm body of an enemy to lay it bleeding at the feet of their anamoratas. Their rude domestic implements scarcely differed from the deadly *panda,* the double-edged, handleless war-sword worn, blade upward, on the hip. In their huts or in little thatched shrines stood idols roughly hacked out of wood, grotesquely indecent, with their round ringed eyes and suggestive hands. And at feasts in the place of honour was a human skull, with a sinister mask of clay half-hiding the bare bones.

When Francis returned to Amboina the little town was full of noise and bustle, the harbour of galleons. On Shrove Tuesday, March 9, 1546, the Portuguese admiral had come back from Ternate with the remains of the battered fleet which had left New Spain four years before. The Spanish attempt to colonise the Philippines had ended in disaster, for hunger and disease had forced the admiral to surrender to the Portuguese. The commander, who died on Good Friday, was only one of many casualties. The disease which they had brought with them spread so rapidly among the three hundred sailors that the shore of Amboina was soon an extemporary hospital. There were four Augustinian friars and four secular priests on the nine Spanish ships but, when Francis returned, it was he who took command of the situation.

"All these men remained at Amboina for three months.

During this time I had plenty of spiritual work, preaching Sundays and Feast Days, continually hearing confessions, making peace and visiting the sick. These occupations were such that I hardly expected to find such peaceful results, for I found myself in the midst of a people at war and estranged from religion. . . . God be praised for having so generously granted His peace to those who professed as little wish for peace with God as with their neighbours." (Cochin, January 20, 1548.)

Among the Castilians was one of those swift yet enduring conquests peculiar to Francis. A wandering spirit, Father Cosme de Torres, had drifted to the New World and on to the Philippines in search of adventure. When he saw Francis he found his vocation. Francis does not mention him, perhaps was scarcely conscious yet of his existence, but he had changed the man's whole life. Cosme sailed to Goa with the fleet, did the Exercises, entered the Company of Jesus, and sailed to Japan with Francis.

Francis's work as liaison-officer between Spanish and Portuguese was no sinecure; there were perpetual quarrels; knives were out, or *krisses,* with their waved blades and grooved channels dripping with blood. Men were persuaded to dismiss their coloured mistresses, to return to their duties and keep the peace, but, as always, the sick were the *Santo Padre's* special care. He went about begging for food, wine, medicine and money, and Araujo, the merchant who had landed in Amboina with him, was particularly generous. At last, however, even his patience gave out and he bluntly said that he would contribute no more, since he wished to keep a little for himself. "What?" exclaimed Francis when he received the message: "Does João de Araujo imagine that he will live to drink his own wine? Let him still allow me to give away his goods, for his span of life grows short."

At the end of May the fleet was to sail to Malacca and Francis snatched time for some letters, for it was to be his last chance for nineteen months of writing home. To the Fathers in Europe he gives a brief sketch of his stay at Malacca and Amboina and his plans for evangelising the northern Moluccas where: "There are innumerable islands, almost all inhabited. They do not become Christian because there is nobody to convert them. If there were a house of our Company at Molucca an immense number of people would become Christians. All my thoughts keep returning to this one thing—how to found a house in that part of the Moluccas, and the great service of God which would ensue. The heathen in those parts are more numerous than the Moors. Heathen and Moors are ill-disposed one to the other. Mohammedans wish either to convert or enslave the pagans who wish neither to become Mohammedans nor slaves." He adds somewhat trenchantly about the *cacizes* from Mecca: "The best thing about them is that they know absolutely nothing of their own false religion." The letter ends on a note of deeply human affection and loneliness:

"Know, my dearly-loved brethren, that I have cut off your signatures from the letters you have written me and have put them with my profession-vows, so that I may never forget you, but have a special remembrance of you. I always wear them on me, to my great comfort. I give thanks first to God our Lord and then to you, my very dear Fathers and Brothers, for the many consolations vouchsafed me while I wear your names. I will say no more now, for we shall soon meet again in the next life, where there is more leisure than here" (Amboina, May 10,

1546). One can almost hear the interruption that brought his outpouring to such an abrupt conclusion, the hurried summons to an unrepentant death-bed or to a furious quarrel.

In the letter to Goa he orders Mansilhas and de Beira, the Portuguese priest who had arrived with Criminale, to join him in the Moluccas; and there is an insistence on holy obedience so emphatic that the shadow of the future seems already visible to his inward vision: "Believe me, my brother, Micer Paul, that the surest means of succeeding is to wish always to be commanded without contradicting him who commands you. On the other hand it is most dangerous to do one's own will, while opposing what one is ordered to do. Even were you to succeed while acting in opposition to orders, believe me, my brother, Micer Paul, that the evil is greater than the success. In everything obey Father Master Diogo and do his will, for that will always be for you the Will of God. Believe me you can please me in no way more than by doing what I beg you so earnestly." (Amboina, May 2, 1546.)

At the end of May the nine great ships weighed anchor, and as he watched their sails fill with the north-east monsoon and the hulls sink below the horizon Francis's heart surely sank too. Another link with his own world had broken and after that liquid Castilian which is the loveliest language in the world the Portuguese which had been his tongue for the last six years sounded more harshly nasal and guttural than ever.

The rainy season had begun, when the lowering sky poured torrents on the sodden earth and roads were impassable. Francis had planned to sail north to Ternate after the departure of the fleet, but his body, which had borne such herculean labours and such devastating heat, failed him. He was in danger for several days, but gradually the fever subsided and about the beginning of July he was well enough to go on board one of the two boats bound for Ternate. D'Eiro was left behind to carry on the good work. Araujo determined to give the lie to the prophecy of his speedy death at Amboina by accompanying Francis, but there was no room for him, and in the end he too was left behind.

The little island of Ternate, off the west coast of Halmahera, was the furthest outpost of Portuguese empire. The fort, with its garrison of fifty men, looked across an open stretch to the harbour. Round it were the houses of sixty Portuguese traders with their native wives and concubines. On the north-east of the bay the native huts were clustered round the mosque and the palace where, at the moment, the widow of the sultan who had first welcomed the Portuguese thirty years ago reigned as regent. Here and there was a *débris* of stones, wood, and tiles, remains of houses ruined by the last earthquake. Behind the town rose the seven-cratered volcano, its lower slopes clothed with mango and durwan, spice and palm-trees. Above this was virgin forest and a slope of reedy grass which reached the foot of the craters, scarred and fissured, black with the dribble of lava. In the air hung always those ominous feathers of smoke, dark against the brilliant sky of noon, glowing sullenly under the star-pierced velvet of night. When man lives under the shadow of doom, as here and at Pompeii, fear and desire preach the Epicurean doctrine: "Let us eat, drink and be merry, for tomorrow we die."

Ternate was reported to be as much worse than Malacca as Malacca was than Goa, and in the little town the vices of every race and of the half-caste reigned unchecked. In this Cytherean island Portuguese and Malays lived only for sensual satisfaction. Malay was said to be a language invented for love-songs, and day and night such songs, to the accompaniment of wild doves' cooing, filled the spice-laden air. Turbans glittered with jewels, or were adorned with sweeping plumes of the bird of paradise. Embroidered waistcoats and damask slippers were stiff with gold. Men and women, traders and natives, were scented and jewelled. Lust of the flesh, lust of the eye, were apparently the be-all and end-all of existence, and voluptuous ease was deepened by the blackest ignorance.

One July day there anchored in the harbour a shallow-keeled native boat, with two low masts, square sails and high, curved prow sharp as the horn of a crescent moon. Through the drowsy evening air sounded the tinkle of a little bell. Men strolled out to see what was afoot. Children ran too. Women peered through the shutters. A man went through the darkening streets night after night, the little bell in one hand, a lighted lantern in the other, chanting prayers for the dead and those in mortal sin. Francis carried out his usual programme, with its usual results. Ignorance was such that men were surprised to learn that any sexual vice except adultery was a sin, women were amazed to hear that they, as well as their lords and masters, had an immortal soul.

The atmosphere began to change. Soon the transformation was almost miraculous. It was not the only sign of the holy Father's supernatural powers. While saying one of his first Masses on the island Francis suddenly turned at the Offertory. "Señor João de Araujo has died at Amboina. I am saying this Mass for the repose of his soul. Say a Pater and Ave for him in honour of the bitter Passion of Christ." There was much talk and wonder how the Father could have known what had happened so many hundred miles away. It was not till ten or twelve days later that a letter came from d'Eiro to say that Araujo had just died.

August and September were the spice-harvest, and a busy time in all the islands, but Francis had plenty of work among the women and children. Then another astonishing thing happened. The old Sultana was known through the island for her deep knowledge of Islam, her equally deep hatred of Christianity, to which she attributed the death and dethronement of her three sons, her own twenty years of exile. Suddenly, to the amazement of everyone, she became a Christian and was baptised Isabella. Francis, in his letters, only mentions the bald fact of her conversion, but it would have been strange if the credit had not been given to him.

His work at Ternate was finished for the time being. Native women were married or dismissed. Peace and order, prayers and hymns were the order of the day. "Day and night the boys in the streets, girls and women in their homes, labourers in the fields, and fishermen at sea sing holy hymns instead of frivolous songs. It has pleased God our Lord that in a short time I should find favour in the eyes of the Portuguese of the town and the natives of the country, Christian and pagan" (Cochin, January 20, 1548). He had finished his tour of the Portuguese possessions and might well, it seemed, now return to rest and quiet with the comfortable words ringing in his ears: "Well done, good and faithful servant."

As he stood on the eastern shore of Ternate he could see the volcanoes of the great island of Halmahera, and beyond their craters lay the shore and islands called by the Portuguese Isles of the Moors. There, twelve years ago, the natives had called in the Portuguese to protect them against the fanatical persecution of the Sultan of Gilolo. Baptised and then left to their fate, they had soon reverted to savagery, had burned their churches and murdered their priests. Twice since then a priest had landed, but had not dared to remain in their country. Already in Amboina Francis had mentioned his intention of regaining these lost sheep, but the suggestion met with a storm of protest. Sheep indeed! Wolves rather, or tigers, to whom no treachery was too base, no cruelty too devilish! Not only weapons were poisoned, but even the food set before guests, a sin against the most sacred laws of Oriental hospitality.

There is in his letter of May 20 a passage which, obscure as it is, seems to show that fear had almost made him hesitate in his decision—fear not of bodily hurt nor of the martyrdom which he always desired and hoped for, but of something deeper and darker, the shadow of that power of evil which lurked behind the show of natural beauty. If the man exists who does not know fear he is one without nerves, sympathy or imagination. A temperament such as that of Francis Xavier, highly strung, sensitive, sympathetic and imaginative, faces danger not with the blind rush of the angry bull but with a courage fully conscious of what it goes to meet, yet unswerving. Like his Master, Francis could not escape the agony which is the natural shrinking of human flesh from suffering and death; he felt, too, the horror of that dark night of the soul when it seems deserted even by God Himself.

"I have decided to go to these Isles of the Moors . . . exposing myself to every deadly danger but putting all my trust and hope in God our Lord. In my small way I wish to obey the words of Christ, our Redeemer and Lord, Who said: 'He that will save his life shall lose it, and he that shall lose his life for My sake shall find it.' Though neither the Latin nor the general meaning of this word of our Lord are difficult to understand yet when one examines one's own personal case and intends to be willing to lose life for God in order to find it again in Him, then in face of so many dangers, of the probable loss of life, all becomes dark. Even the Latin, apparently so clear, becomes obscure. In such a case he alone will understand it, however learned he may be, to whom God our Lord will, in His infinite mercy, make clear this particular case. It is in such circumstances that one realises the infirmity of our weak and feeble flesh. Many of my friends and people devoted to me have begged me not to go to such a dangerous country, but as they could not make me promise not to go they offered me all kinds of antidotes against poisons. I thanked them warmly for their love and goodwill but, not wishing to show fear which I did not feel, and still more because I had put all my trust in God and did not wish to withdraw it, I refused to accept the antidotes they offered with so much love and so many tears, and I begged them to remember me in their prayers, which is the surest means of counteracting poison which there is."

CHAPTER XV

THE ISLES OF THE MOORS, TERNATE, AMBOINA, MALACCA (SEPTEMBER, 1546–DECEMBER 4, 1547)

WHEN Francis announced his intention of sailing to the Isles of the Moors there was the same outcry at Ternate as there had been at Amboina. The savages of that coast were not only adepts at every kind of poison, but their hands were red with the blood of their wives, children, parents and priests. Seeing his resolution unshaken by tales of horror, Francis's friends took more practical measures to prevent his going. They persuaded the captain of the fort to forbid the sailing of any boat to Halmahera. Francis heard of this, and his anger broke forth publicly. In an impassioned sermon he denounced such methods and declared that neither torture, danger, nor fear of death should prevent him from carrying out his plans. His only enemies were those who would stop him from going. "Every man must die, so why should I fear? A good death is much to be desired. If I die it is because God wills it, and He will send other labourers." He ended by declaring that if he could get no boat he would swim the straits to Halmahera; and according to a local tradition he came straight down from the pulpit and went on board the nearest boat in the harbour.

In the end a *carcacora* was put at his disposal, and he set off on the cruise round the north of Halmahera and the adjacent islands. Here, as round Seram, the natives fled at sight of a white man till, reassured by seeing Francis alone and by hearing him sing in Malay, they came round him and listened to his talk and simple instruction. The first task was to reclaim lapsed converts. "I baptised many children. I visited all the places where there were Christians. I comforted them and gained great consolation from them." Luckily Valignano supplements this bald statement: "He sought to tame those he had with him, and though they were a stupid and brutal people nothing damped his courage nor his hope of doing them good. . . . The work was so well begun that others had only to follow in his footsteps." In his next long letter to Rome Francis makes no secret of dangers and hardships waiting those who were to carry on his work: "These islands are very dangerous because of the numerous wars raging there. They are a race of barbarians who have no books and know neither how to read nor write. They poison those they have a grudge against, and many are killed in this way. The earth is tortured. There are nothing but chains of mountains almost impossible to climb. The country is barren of bodily food. They do not even know what wheat and grape-wine are. There is no meat nor any kind of cattle except a few pigs, which are an object of curiosity. As for wild boars, there is a large number of them. Many villages have no drinking-water." He continues on a more personal note: "I give you all this information so that you may know how much these islands abound in spiritual consolations, for all these dangers and sufferings are treasures fruitful in spiritual consolations when borne gladly for the love and service of God our Lord only. In this way these islands are such that, in a few years, a man might lose the sight of his bodily eyes in consequence of such abundant tears of happiness. I never remember having experienced such spiritual consolations and so little realisation of physical sufferings as in these islands. Yet all the while I was wandering in islands surrounded by enemies or inhabited by treacherous friends, in country entirely lacking not only in any remedy for bodily illnesses but even in everything necessary to preserve life. Rather than the Isles of the Moors they should be called the Isles of Trust in God."

Far from any human help or any white man, alone with "stupid and brutal" savages, without even the necessities of life, surrounded by dangers from men, beasts, earthquakes, and shipwreck, Francis found the consciousness of bodily suffering left behind as he entered deeper and ever deeper into that union with God which alone enabled him to dare and endure. "Yet not I, but Christ in me." Again and again it is necessary to remind ourselves that this inner and spiritual life of the saint must not be obscured from us by the cinematic movement and change of his outer surroundings, his unceasing journeys, pioneer work, and organisation for those who were to follow him. It is this inner life which is the motive of the whole orchestration. Without it all would be but a discord of sounding brass and tinkling cymbals.

Sanctity does not consist in speed and hustle, in the number of miles covered in record time, in statistics of conversions, in a-hundred-per-cent efficiency of social organisation. Its Alpha and Omega is the love which subjects the human will to that of God, till man asks and desires nothing but what God wills for him. This absolute and unquestioning obedience, inspired by a fierce and consuming love, is the mainspring of St. Francis Xavier's life. Those forty days in Paris when, cut off from the

world, he had done the Exercises under the direction of
Ignatius of Loyola, had set an enduring seal on him.
Before each new enterprise we find him waiting for God's
Will to be made plain, as Ignatius had said. "Considering first to what purpose man is born . . . that he may be
aided in the service of God our Lord and in the salvation
of his soul. That love which moves me and makes me
choose the said thing should come down from above, from
the love of God."

Only a few months after Francis's stay in Halmahera
his "father" was to write to Francis Borgia, Duke of
Gandia, then at the parting of the ways: "God sees and
knows what is best for us, and knowing all He shows us
the way He would have us follow. But in order to find
it, by His grace, we have to seek diligently, even to try
several ways before journeying along the one intended
for us."

When Francis left Meliapor his goal was Macassar. God
had other work for him, further afield, in Amboina, Ternate and the Isles of the Moors. Now, when he reaches
Malacca again, a wider horizon still opens before him, the
islands of Japan, of whose existence he does not yet even
know.

He returned to Ternate about Christmas, 1546, after
three months of adventures about which he is silent—
shipwreck, narrow escapes from savage pursuit, Moslem
persecution, volcanic eruptions, showers of cinders and
ashes, violent storms. He mentions one earthquake while
he was saying the Michaelmas Mass, with remembrance of
the tiny chapel of San Miguel at Javier and his family
devotion to the great archangel: "The earth shook so
violently that I was afraid the altar would be flung over.
Perhaps it was the divine strength of St. Michael that

commanded and compelled the return to hell of the devils of the country who were disturbing the service of God."

The few days he had meant to stay at Ternate in the end extended themselves to three months. It was probably during this second visit that he composed the rhyming catechism in Malay for converts to learn by heart. The rudimentary exposition of the Faith in Tamil which had been done for the rude Parava fishermen needed elaboration for educated Malays and Mohammedans. This new catechism—like a Chartres cathedral in miniature—was a *résumé* of the history of the world from the day of creation to the Redemption, as well as a guide to the individual soul from its earliest acquaintance with the Faith till the particular judgment. The whole was built round and founded on the twelve articles of the Creed. When he left Ternate Francis left careful instructions that every day the catechist should explain a short piece of the text and make his audience repeat it after him till they knew it by heart, so that at the end of a year converts should be thoroughly grounded in the Faith and its application to the things of daily life.

Those superficial writers who have described the saint as rushing restlessly to and fro, always in the limelight, making a spectacular success in each new field, then, careless of the future, hurrying on to new conquests, ignore the careful organisation which he elaborated before he left any scene of his labours. At Cape Comorin he had drawn up the Tamil catechism for Mansilhas and his helpers to teach, and in his letter from Malacca had ordered Antonio Criminale to join them. Now in the Moluccas the same plan is followed: "Before leaving Molucca I gave directions that Christian doctrine should continue to be taught

in a church as well as the brief explanation of the articles
of the Creed which I had made. New converts were to
learn it instead of prayers. A priest who is a friend of
mine remained with them. When I had gone he was to
give a two-hours' instruction daily."

Another practice begun while the saint was there was
also continued. Every evening at twilight a man in the
habit of the Misericord went through the streets, carrying
a lighted lantern in one hand, ringing a little bell in the
other, as he recited prayers for the dead and those in mortal
sin. How well Francis understood the mentality of his
converts, the appeal to eye and ear, the daily stimulus
necessary to counteract the tendency to drift and the self-
indulgence inherent in the Malay character and enhanced
by the climate!

At Comorin he had been face to face with the crudest
manifestations of Brahminism. Here, in Malay and the
Moluccas he was at grips with Islam, in so many ways its
opposite. A Moslem delegate to the Round Table Con-
ference on India said that Moslem and Hindu "differ in
habits, in customs, in laws, and above all in their food
and in their clothes. They also differ in their cultural and
economic ideals." It seems strange to our modern outlook
that Francis was apparently little, if at all, interested in
such differences. Outside Christianity were a vast multitude of heathen, differing perhaps in "habits, customs,
food, clothes," but all alike in this, that they knew not
Christ. Francis's aim was not to compose a monograph
on comparative religion nor to describe ethnological peculi-
arities, but to bring the light of divine revelation to "the
people that sat in darkness."

From Pisgah he saw into the far-off Promised Land, the
black heart of Africa, beyond the closed ports of Cathay,

across unknown seas to the fabled islands of Cipangu. Love of God and souls was the dæmonic force which drove him to and fro, opened vision beyond the earthly horizon, gave superhuman strength to the worn body and pierced the torn veil of time and space to the eternal Now and Here. No wonder that such love consumed his mortal frame, that he would tear open the breast of his loba and try to cool his burning heart in the cold waters of the well in the Goan college garden. Yet, for all that—nights spent in union with God, times when his desire to be alone with God became so unbearable that he would break off in the middle of talk and slip silently away—no detail was omitted that might make the work of those who followed him easier and surer.

When he left Ternate he did not forget the wild islanders among whom he had found such wonderful spiritual consolation. Father Beira, to whom he had sent orders from Malacca, was to reap the harvest in the northern Moluccas, and when he left, in 1556, there were said to be over twenty thousand Christians in the Isles of the Moors, in spite of violent persecutions.

On his return to Ternate Francis had found the political position changed. The old queen was dispossessed and Hairoen, a new sultan, had come back from Goa, suave, treacherous and boasting of "my lord and master, the King of Portugal." The dry irony of Francis's description shows that by the "deep friendship shown so openly that the principal Moslems were irritated by it" he, at any rate, was not deceived: "The King refuses to accept Christianity not because of his devotion to Mahomet but because he will not give up the sins of the flesh. There is nothing Mohammedan about him except that he was circumcised in his infancy, and had been married a hundred times since he reached manhood, for he has a hundred chief wives and many lesser ones."

The smiling Sultan, after assuring the Padre that there was little if any difference between Moslems and Christians, since all adored the same God, then proposed a bargain. One of his sons should be baptised on condition that the Portuguese would guarantee him the kingship of northern Halmahera and the neighbouring islands.

In mid-February the Bufara was to sail to Amboina with the yearly cargo of spice, but Francis was persuaded to stay over Easter by the promise of a boat to take him to Amboina in time to catch the ship for Malacca. On Easter morning (April 10, 1547) the native wives of the Portuguese made their first Communions, and soon after Francis arranged to board the boat at midnight to avoid farewells. It was in vain. The news had leaked out. The shore of the harbour was crowded, the darkness was full of lamentations and sobs, "so that this night-time separation from my spiritual sons and daughters made me fear the harm my departure might do to their souls' salvation."

It was said that only two of the Portuguese inhabitants had remained deaf to his persuasions and still lived in mortal sin. In a letter from Amboina he sent them a message that he would return even now if by so doing he could save them, that in any case he would always remember them in his prayers. He was never to see Ternate again, but Valignano tells how men and women wept "whenever his name was mentioned, so tender was the memory he had left behind him."

His stay of three weeks in Amboina was filled by missionary work among the crews of the four ships in port and the townsfolk. He also revisited the seven Christian villages, where he had small chapels built and set up tall crosses which Valentijn found still standing a hundred years later. Yet in some he foresaw apostasies: "These three places will not persevere, they will produce only bad Christians." When leaving one village he shook his feet with the stern words: "I will not take with me even the dust of this place." His prophecies were fulfilled when the Sultan of Ternate revolted against the Portuguese and the junks of Javanese pirates ravaged the coasts of Amboina.

In mid-May the fleet was ready. Francis, accompanied by d'Eiro, refused the most pressing invitation to go on the Bufara. In the straits she struck a rock, and was saved from total destruction only by what seemed a miracle.

When Francis landed at Malacca at the end of June or beginning of July, after an absence of eighteen months, he found two Jesuit fathers and a brother who had just arrived in answer to his letter of May 10, 1546. All were strangers to him, for Mansilhas, who should have accompanied them, had disobeyed orders and remained in Cape Comorin. Father Beira, destined for the Moluccas, had arrived at Goa with Antonio Criminale in 1545, the other two a year later. They were the first recruits from home he had met since his own departure from Lisbon seven years ago, and they brought letters from Europe, Goa, and Cape Comorin, as well as news from Rome, Spain, and Portugal. "I had the greatest joy during the month we were together. I saw they were true servants of God and able to do much for the service of God our Lord in this country of Molucca."

After all these months cut off from his spiritual brethren, separated from Ignatius by the three years and nine months necessary to get an answer to a letter, the company of the Spanish and Portuguese Jesuits must indeed have been "the greatest joy" he could humanly desire. There was so much to hear about the great expansion of the Society in the last few years. The Pope had suspended the rule limiting the numbers of the Company to sixty, and had granted its fathers wide spiritual privileges. There were flourishing colleges now in Louvain, Alcalá, Valencia, Barcelona, Valladolid, Gandia, and Cologne, as well as the original foundations at Rome, Lisbon, Paris, Padua, and Coimbra. The college at Gandia was due to Francis Borgia, who had been admitted to the Society by Ignatius in October, that at Cologne had been founded by the joint efforts of Francis's fellow-student and greatest friend (after Ignatius), Peter Faber, and the brilliant young Dutch student, Peter Canisius, whom he had gained for the Society. In April, 1546, when Father Ribero's ship had left Lisbon, the Council was opening at Trent where Lainez and Salmeron, probably the youngest of all the delegates, were to become world-famous.

There was bad news from Goa, though; Miguel Vaz, the vicar-general, had arrived back from Portugal in the autumn of 1546 with full powers from the King to proceed against official corruption—powers no doubt largely due to Francis's outspoken letter to John from Cochin. Scarcely had he reached Goa than he was found dead, poisoned. The town hummed with the sensation. Even the old bishop was accused of having put out of the way the man most likely to succeed him—the poor old Franciscan, "incapable of killing a flea!" Diogo Borba, head and founder of the college of Santa Fé at Goa, on hearing the news of Miguel's death, collapsed in a fit, and a few days later followed his friend to the grave. The double loss was a heavy blow, an end to Francis's hopes that Miguel Vaz's firm hand would have been able to clear some of the corruption which blocked the spiritual advancement of the Portuguese and prevented conversions among the natives.

In the middle of August the three other Jesuits left Malacca, but anxious as Francis was to return to India, there was the inevitable wait for the monsoon to veer to the east. The days from August to November were crowded with "numerous occupations, all spiritual." The church of our Lady was too small; Francis was forced to adjourn to the parish church. His confessional was besieged. Those who did not manage to get in complained loudly. The new catechism was taught daily. A dead girl, already wrapped in her shroud for burial, was brought back to life. Devils were driven out, the sick healed, inveterate enemies reconciled, the future foretold. It was a common saying that Father Francis read the future as naturally as the sun gives light.

More than ever during these five months his "life was hid with Christ in God." At dawn the sacristan would find him on the altar steps where he had spent the night before the tabernacle—sometimes still lost in prayer, sometimes in the light sleep that exhausted nature forced him to snatch. "Often when one was talking to him he would get up and go away in silence. One would seek him, often for a long time, and end by finding him hidden in some corner or in the depths of a thicket, praying or taking the discipline. Then one would slip away without speaking, and leave him alone with God." (Torsellini.)

One night in late October Malacca was awakened by the clang of the tocsin in the fort, shaken by the firing of cannon from ships in the harbour. Armed Malays filled the streets and a cry of terror went up: "The Achinese!" The terrible pirates from Sumatra had surrounded the spice-ships from Banda to try to capture the cargoes and set fire to the fleet. The junks, however, driven off by the combined firing from fort and harbour, made off northward, their only booty some geese. The Malaccans would have been content to relapse into temporary security, but Francis saw further. He interviewed the captain, persuaded him to fit out a small fleet and send it in pursuit. The captain, after its despatch, declared that it was entirely the holy Father who had provisioned and equipped it.

The fleet was expected back within a week, but days and weeks—a month and more—passed without news. The Sultan of Biltang, hearing that Malacca was defenceless, prepared to attack it. Fear for their own safety was added to the anxiety for those with the absent ships. The streets rang with laments. Wives got ready their widows' weeds. Children and girls wept for lost fathers and lovers. The Sultan sent word that the Achinese were triumphant. Magicians and soothsayers, consulted by frantic women who forgot their Christianity, saw the total destruction of the Portuguese fleet, white corpses floating thick in the sea. The populace turned angrily against Francis, the cause of all their misfortunes; but he continued to preach patience and advise prayer while the tide of fear and anger rose.

At half past nine on the morning of December 4 he was in the pulpit, finishing his sermon, when he broke off suddenly while a strange light transfigured his face. "There are some here who commit sacrilege," he cried: "Bad Christians who do not trust in God! To-day, even to-day, your fleet is victorious. Before long you will hear the good news." Gazing into the unseen, he described details of the naval battle then in progress. At Vespers, in his sermon to the women, he again bade them be of good cheer and prepare for the home-coming of their men. A few days later the forces of the hostile Sultan withdrew, and when the victorious Portuguese fleet reached the harbour Francis was on the shore to welcome the men, crucifix in hand. The battle had taken place, the Achinese junks been sunk or destroyed at the very hour when he had interrupted his sermon.

CHAPTER XVI

MALACCA, COCHIN AND GOA
(DECEMBER, 1547–JUNE 6, 1548)

THE easterly monsoon had risen, and at the beginning of December the spice-ships were preparing for the voyage to India. Francis's thoughts turned to Comorin. There was much to do there, the new superior, Father Antonio Criminale, and his helpers to see. The state of things in Ceylon was bad, for, owing to Portuguese intrigues, converts were apostatising instead of increasing in number. A new superior was needed for the College of Santa Fé now that Diogo Borba was dead. And then? His dreams reached out beyond the outpost of empire in the Moluccas. During his last stay at Malacca he had been inquiring about China, that vast and mysterious country now closed to white men. In His own good time God would reveal His Will, point out the way. As so often in life the path that opened led far from the expected goal.

One day early in December Alvarez, the captain of one of the spice-vessels, who had met Francis before at Malacca, waited for him in the church where he was celebrating a marriage. With Alvarez was a little man of about thirty-five, with yellow face and slanting eyes like a Chinaman, but with an eager expression of curiosity. He was presented to Francis after the service as Angero (the Portuguese version of Yajiro), a native of the islands of Cipangu, east of China, only discovered by the Portuguese

195

four years before, when the ships of some merchants on their way to China were blown out of their course by a typhoon.

The Japanese has given his own account of this memorable meeting.

"Alvarez put me in his hands and told him my history at length. . . . With what great joy Father Master Francis looked at me and embraced me! The further I advance the better I understand this, and feel it in my soul. Already so satisfied, so comforted by the sight of Master Francis, I could also converse with him for I understood Portuguese a little and could speak a few words of it."

The story Alvarez told was a strange one. About a year ago Angero had killed a man, and to escape justice had fled by night to Alvarez's ship, which was in the harbour of Kagoshima, a port of the southern island of Japan. Leaving his wife and children behind, he sailed to Malacca. During the voyage Alvarez, who had picked up a little Japanese, told him of Christianity and its apostle, the Santo Padre, and, difficult as an explanation of the Faith must have been in such fragmentary talk, Alvarez managed at any rate to plant in his listener's mind a keen desire to see this foreign *bonze*. "From what I was told about his life and work I was seized with a great desire to meet him. . . . I already felt inclined to be baptised, a wish which increased from day to day."

When they landed at Malacca, however, it was only to find that Francis had gone to the Moluccas nearly a year before. The old vicar refused to baptise Angero because he had a heathen wife. It was for the best, since if Angero had been baptised and had gone home he would never have met Francis, nor would Francis, probably, have gone to Japan.

When they were in sight of Japan on his homeward voyage, a storm drove the ship back to the coast of China; there a Portuguese merchant whom Angero had met before was about to sail for Malacca. Angero accepted the omen, which was confirmed, for the first person he met as he stepped ashore at Malacca was Alvarez, who at once hurried him off to Francis.

Francis too saw in this meeting the finger of God, pointing not to China but to the virgin soil of Japan; but in his most vivid dreams he can scarcely have foreseen the splendour of the future. Dreamer and visionary he might be, but like all the great mystics he could be extremely practical when necessary. His last few days at Malacca were spent in collecting all possible information about Japan. As Angero spoke little Portuguese and understood less, Francis turned to Alvarez; he had been several times to Kagoshima in the past few years, and was accordingly set down to write a description of country and people for Francis to send to Rome after he had mastered it himself.

The first European account of Japan, it is surprisingly accurate in its analysis of the Japanese character—proud, sensitive, generous, hospitable, curious about foreign countries and peoples, sober, dignified, courteous. The strong sense of family life and the inferior position of women are noted, as well as the social and political influence of the bonzes, but, as is only natural, Alvarez is only vaguely aware of the difference between Buddhism and Sintoism, and, ignorant of the Shogunate, he calls the daimios "kings." His description of the daimio castles, their narrow entrances, moats, fortified enclosures and palisades, and the feudal system by which samurai swear fealty to their daimio lords, must have brought to Francis a vivid memory of life in the old border fortress at Javier, and *Las Siete Partidas* of Alfonso X.

Francis did not baptise Angero. Perhaps he thought that to do so would be too open a rebuke to the old vicar, perhaps also he saw that such a ceremony at Goa would be a useful means of furthering the new mission. The Japanese with his two servants accordingly sailed direct to Goa. Francis arranged for daily catechism to continue at Malacca, promising to send two Jesuits as soon as possible. His things were taken on a ship bound for Cochin. With him was to go d'Eiro, whom he considered to have no vocation to the Society, though he predicted his future as a friar; it was in his Franciscan habit that d'Eiro gave his testimony at the Process of Beatification in 1556.

All was ready for departure when Francis happened to hear the captain of his ship boast to some friends that he meant to go to India whether God meant him to or not. "Señor," expostulated Francis: "Say rather I will go to India *if* God wishes it." The man refused to retract. Francis had his few possessions taken off the ship. A few days after it sailed the corpses of the crew were washed ashore. A servant who relates this incident adds: "Christians and heathen revered him to such a degree that they knelt before they kissed his hand and called him, in their language, 'lord of the earth.'"

Francis had prophesied disaster to the lost ship. The one on which he himself sailed was nearly lost three-quarters of the way to Cochin, in the open sea between the Nicobar Islands and Ceylon. As Satan was given leave to try Job so the prince of the powers of the air was surely allowed to assail Francis, for there was hardly one of his many voyages without terrible storms and danger of shipwreck. For three days and nights the ship was driven helpless before the gale. Crew and passengers threw overboard everything possible to lighten her. All were prepared for death. Francis heard confessions, cheered, calmed, encouraged, then disappeared. One of the officers went to his cabin, saw him kneeling in such an ecstasy of prayer before the crucifix that, ashamed of intrusion, he stole away.

The saint himself was given a glimpse of his prayer in that hour of deadly peril "to all the angels, from choir to choir, patriarchs, prophets, apostles, evangelists, martyrs, confessors, virgins, all the saints of heaven . . . I took for patroness the glorious Virgin, our Lady, since in heaven she obtains all that she asks of God." There is one strange note: "I also took for mediators all the saints in the glory of Paradise beginning with those who belonged in this life to the holy Company of Jesus and, first of all, the blessed soul of Peter Faber." Seventeen months before, Peter Faber had reached Rome from Spain where he had given Francis Borgia the Exercises after the death of his wife. After eight days' illness Peter had died in Rome, August 1, 1546. The letter from Simon Rodriguez with the news had arrived in Goa in October, 1547, only two months before this voyage, and in order to send it on to Malacca a wait of several months for the spring monsoon was necessary, by which time Francis had already been back in India two months. Yet, in early January, 1548, he invoked as a saint in heaven the friend whose death he could have known by no earthly channel.

"Thanks to all the help and protection," he continues his story: "I felt as great joy in the middle of this storm as after our deliverance from it, even more, I think. When I remember this it fills me with amazement that such a great sinner should be granted tears of joy and consolation in such a trial. So, in the height of the storm, I begged of God our Lord that, if He saved me, it should be only that I might endure other perils as great or greater for His greater service." There is the echo from the Exercises, to desire sickness rather than health, poverty and failure rather than riches and success, a short life of danger, toil and suffering rather than peaceful old age after long years of ease and comfort. The prayer was answered as generously as it was made. He was returning to strife, corruption and treachery. Only four years of life remained to him.

The tempest abated. The shores of Ceylon were sighted, Cape Comorin rounded. As the ship hugged the coast on the way north to Cochin, Francis watched familiar scenes slip by—shallow, sandy lagoons and fever-haunted rivers, the wide undulating green fields and terraced forests which he had traversed with the sanction of the Rajah of Travancore. He remembered the murmur of Tamil voices: "I believe," the brown figures, old and young, crowding round to receive the palm-leaves inscribed with their new names. How long ago it seemed, though it was only three years—much longer ago and dimmer than those student days in Paris when he and Peter Faber had shared room, books, hopes, and ambitions.

Kneeling in his cabin before the crucifix till the worn body drifted into sleep, or lying on deck under the wonderful blaze of tropical stars, vivid dreams wove sound and colour into a living present. Again, during those first days together, he was captured by Peter's quiet simplicity, pure and limpid as a mountain stream, his eager charm, his quick sympathy. The four and a half years of study, their Masters' degrees, their first lectures, the walks by the river on summer evenings, the icy winter dawns, they passed and were gone. He woke with Ignatius's voice in his ears: "What doth it profit a man, Master Francis, if he gain the whole world and suffer the loss of his own soul?" If he might indeed gain the whole world, not for his own glory but for that of God! Japan, China, and beyond—his mind leapt out hungering for them all. The dawn rushed up flaming behind the mighty terraces of the Ghat mountains. There was a babel of talk, Portuguese, Malay, and the patois of Lascars—the rattle of the anchor-chain as it ran out. They were at Cochin (January 13, 1548).

It had been from Cochin that he had written the first of his great missionary letters four years ago. From Cochin he was to write the second epic of the eastern missions (the letter to the Fathers in Rome, January 20, 1548, from which all the quotations in the last two chapters are taken). Like a canvas of Michael Angelo it is crowded with figures of every nation, set against a background that stretches from Goa to Japan.

In the Franciscan friary, to which he hurried on landing, Francis found the old bishop, John d'Albuquerque, and the four Spanish Augustinians. The bishop, old and feeble, deprived at one blow of the support of two of his most capable helpers, must have welcomed his beloved Francis with even more than his usual affection. Into his sympathetic ear he poured out all his troubles. The powers of reform brought back from Lisbon by Miguel Vaz had been blocked since his death by the determined opposition of the Indian Council and venal officials. The new governor, John de Castro, was too busy with Mohammedan invasions to worry about domestic policy. Money sent by the king for the Bassein mission had disappeared. The Rajah of Travancore was persecuting Christians with impunity. The massacred converts of Manar had never been avenged. In Ceylon the convert ruler of Kandy had been betrayed by the Portuguese who were helping in every way the Rajah of Cotta. This was the prince whose assassination of his own heir and the Manar Christians had roused Francis to such anger three years ago.

Meanwhile the annual fleet was ready to sail to Lisbon and the long tale of woe had to be interrupted while Francis, beside the long official letter to Rome, scribbled a note to enclose in it for the Father General, one letter to the king and another to Simon Rodriguez (January 20, 1548). The letter to the king burns with fierce indignation, not perhaps wholly justified. Vaz had brought back wide powers from the king, largely suggested by Francis, and it was not the king's fault that Vaz had died before he had been able to put them into execution, nor that the Indian Council had offered stubborn opposition. The history of empires, from the Roman capitol to Whitehall, has always shown the inability of rulers at the centre of government to deal with problems that need experience on the spot combined with knowledge of local conditions and customs.

The new governor had been accorded a triumph like those of imperial Rome on his return to Goa after defeating the Moslem army, which had almost reached the gates of the city. He had found himself faced by instructions which, he and the Council agreed, were ill-advised, and which were accordingly shelved. John de Castro, a fierce, stern nobleman, burning with the old crusading spirit, cared little for city politics. His one desire was to raise men and money to crush Mohammedan power at Bassein for good and all. It was not likely that he and this "Father Master Francis," quoted so often in the offending orders, should see eye to eye. Nor could Francis be expected to take a just and impartial view of things which he knew only from the old bishop's tearful tale. He himself—fresh from adventures, triumphs and discoveries, on fire with plans for Japan—probably suffered some of that reaction that all experience when, a fair idyll finished, the return to daily life, with its dreary monotony and apparently barren futility, darkens mind and heart with a misery out of all proportion to its original cause.

After the strange beauties and vivid colours of the Spice Islands, the solitude transfigured by communion with the Divine Lover, after the dog-like devotion of Alfurus, Malays, half-castes, and the women he baptised and married, Francis found himself flung back with a jar into the world of corruption, avarice, lust, and intrigue from which he had fled in horror to Meliapor three years ago. It was still the old story, he felt now at Cochin—spices and gold valued more than human souls, European Christians setting greed before religion, jewels above the Faith: Judas and the thirty pieces of silver. This time Francis did not flee. Burning with indignation, he seized his pen and poured ink on paper in a molten torrent. Weak and ineffective as King John showed himself in dealing with bad officials, it must at least be written to his credit that he bore Francis no malice for such frank and angry condemnation as few rulers can have had to endure.

The same anger is in the letter to Rodriguez, though without the bitter irony about "holy jealousies": "It is time, dearest brother, Master Simon, to waken the King from his illusions, for the hour is nearer than he thinks when God our Lord shall call him to account saying: 'Give an account of thy stewardship.' . . . If only he would daily spend one quarter of an hour praying God our Lord to let him understand better and take to heart these words of Christ's: 'What shall it profit a man?' " Still the echo of Ignatius's voice and those oft-repeated words of warning! And to him Francis writes a cry of the heart, of doubt and discouragement: "God knows the ardent desire I have to see you again in this life, my beloved Father, so that I could consult with you about various things on which I need your help, as well as needing the spiritual healing which flows from you. For neither space nor great distances prevent obedience. Several of our brothers scattered in this country, and we ourselves, feel the urgent need of a doctor for our souls. I beg you in the Name of the Lord Jesus, O my good Father, to turn your eyes on your children in the Indies, and to send a man of energy and consummate holiness, whose zeal and fervour will cheer my fainting soul. . . . To convince you still more of my need I pray the omnipotent God to reveal to you by His light how deeply I need your help and prayers."

At the end of the long public letter he breaks off "because of the immediate departure of the ships." "How can I better end my letter than by declaring to all those of the Company: 'If ever I forget the Company of Jesus may my right hand be cast into oblivion,' so deeply do I realise my indebtedness to all those of the Company. . . . I end, then, by praying to God our Lord that, as He has united us in His Company during this unhappy life, so He will in His great mercy reunite us in His glorious Company in heaven, since our deep separation in this life is caused by love for Him."

The fleet sailed, taking so much of Francis's heart, so many of his hopes; and he too sailed, south to Cape Comorin. At Manapar, where he arrived at the end of

January, an unpleasant task awaited him, the dismissal of Mansilhas, who had left Lisbon with him and to whom he had revealed so much of himself in that series of letters. Mansilhas had flatly disobeyed the order to join his superior in the Moluccas. There was no place for him in an order which set such a high value on obedience. Transferred to work as a secular priest under the bishop, he retained to the end a devotion to the saint he had failed. His brief testimony in the Process of 1556 is true to character in the irritating stupidity of its vacant platitudes: "If I could make known all I know of his life and labours endured for God, I should never finish. What he did for God passes belief." On his death-bed (1565) Mansilhas would accept no ministrations save that of Jesuit fathers: "To see and hear one of you is my greatest consolation."

At Manapar the superior of the mission, Father Antonio Criminale, with the four Jesuits and three native priests under him, awaited the famous missionary. The young superior (he was only twenty-eight) remembered Father Francis's passage through Parma on the way to Lisbon when he himself had been a student at the university. How much, too, he had heard from his professor, Peter Faber, of the intimate friendship of student and regent days at Paris. At Rome he had heard more from the Father General, who had himself received Antonio into the Company (1541), and from yet another of the original companions, Simon Rodriguez, his superior during the novitiate at Coimbra.

At last the small boat was sighted and Francis landed. He had not changed much in these last eight years— looked as he did at Goa three years later when seen by Texeira, his earliest biographer, who has left the most detailed description of his appearance by an eye-witness:

"The Father Master Francis was tall rather than short, with good features, a red and white skin, his face gay and very charming. The eyes black, a wide forehead, hair and beard black. His under-garment was shabby but clean. He wore over it a thin sleeveless cassock, no cloak nor outer garment, like the usual dress for poor priests in India. And when he walked he lifted it a little at the breast with both hands."

There was much to hear and arrange. Criminale had taken the most difficult district of the mission, the Macuan villages where the rajah was persecuting fiercely. Father Anrique Anriquez, a Portuguese Jewish convert, was in charge of the Tuticorin country. He had nearly died on the voyage from Lisbon, had been little better at Goa and had cheerfully accepted the summons to Comorin as a death sentence. The harder the life, the more strenuous the work, however, the stronger he became and he spent fifty years on the Fishery Coast, the chief buttress of the church which Xavier had founded (died 1606).

For Francis these ten days were a gleam of sunshine between gathering clouds. Here were none of those miserable jealousies, only peace, enthusiasm, and affection. In Antonio Criminale Francis found a kindred spirit, a spiritual son, with his own dauntless courage and ardour, gaiety, generosity and personal magnetism. Antonio had too a capacity for organisation and a balanced judgment rare in youth which combined to make him the ideal superior. A year later Francis was to write of him to Ignatius: "He is a true saint, born for the apostolate in these countries. . . . Everyone loves him, Christians, natives, idolaters and Moslems. As for his companions, it is impossible to tell you how devoted they are to him."

Antonio had one advantage over his senior, a natural

gift for Oriental languages. Already he had begun to speak, read, and write Tamil, but in this he was outstripped by Father Anriquez, who could preach and hear confessions and so was given the task of composing a grammar and dictionary—the first grammar to be drawn up of the Tamil language. Coelho, one of the native priests whom Francis had known three years ago, was commissioned to translate into Tamil the Malay rhyming catechism.

Antonio's arrangements were approved. Indeed they were all on Francis's own lines, daily sermon and catechism, special weekly services for boys, girls, slaves, women.

In the manual of guidance Francis drew up for the missionaries the first and last rule, as it had been in his letters to Mansilhas, was love which does not shrink from necessary severity. Failure on the part of native priests, quarrels, difficulties, apostasies, were to be referred to the superior. Discretion of speech both with Portuguese and natives: only to speak of divine things was the best way to avoid entanglements and waste of time. And again: "Win love by good works and good deeds."

Francis was ready to embark. Did one of those swift glances out of time show him Antonio with the martyr's palm? Anyhow the last blessing to the young superior as he knelt on the sand, the last embrace to his spiritual son, must have held something of special tenderness. Again, as at Lisbon eight years before, "the yellow sands with tears are silvered o'er." The two Jesuits were to meet no more on earth.

For another year and a half Antonio went to and fro along the sixty leagues of Fishery Coast, bare-footed and sleeping on the ground. "His life was holy and without reproach, relations with him easy and pleasant," wrote of him Father Cypriano, a fiery and implacable old Spanish priest who worked under him: "Very obedient, of stainless purity, very poor, very zealous . . . he left everywhere peace and concord." One day in mid-June, 1549, he and his congregation at Vedelai were suddenly surrounded by Badagas. Pierced by lances, stripped of his garments, he managed to stagger into the chapel and fall on the steps in front of the altar before another savage raider hacked off his head. Francis, then at Malacca on his way to Japan, seems to have known of his death as he had known that of Peter Faber. "Very pleasant hast thou been to me: thy love for me was wonderful, passing the love of women." Criminale was the first martyr of the Society of Jesus and (though he is not yet raised to the altar) the first star of that constellation of young saints who shine so brightly in the new Order—Aloysius Gonzaga, John Berchmans and Stanislaus Kostka.

It is an open question whether Francis landed in Ceylon on his way to Goa. He makes no reference to such a visit in his letters, nor do his earlier biographers. The two young princes on whose baptism at Goa such hopes had been built were both dead. The King of Kandy had been coquetting with Portugal and Christianity for some time, but he seemed at last to have decided that it was possible to obtain Portuguese help while still an idolator. If Francis did stop in Ceylon his visit was fruitless, but he arrived in Goa early in March, 1548, accompanied by a Singalese ambassador from Kandy.

The governor, just leaving for Bassein, the headquarters of his campaign against the northern Moslems, had neither time nor inclination to receive the returned missionary nor the ambassador, and left without delaying his departure. Already the accusation of meddling in politics, which has stuck like a burr to the Jesuit habit, was being levelled at Francis, but, careless of talk, he left Goa a week after he had got there and followed de Castro north in a small but fast-sailing boat. De Castro's welcome to the missionary, who reached Bassein in Passion week, was to order him to the pulpit within an hour of his landing. Drily, with cynical detachment, he watched the thin figure drooping with fatigue, the dark eyes burning in the pale face.

The sermon began, passionate eloquence like the rush of lava from Ternate's seven-crated volcano. It was Passion-tide, when, forty-three years ago, his mother had followed the Way of the Cross with such fervour the last few days before his birth. The Passion of Christ had always been Francis's special devotion, as it has been that of his country. In that pulpit at Bassein there must have been before his inner vision the miraculous crucifix of Javier, the eyes closed in death, the head sunk, the narrow twist of thorns crowning the brow that was to be dewed with bloody sweat in three years' time when Francis's own life was drawing to a close. Exhausted, pale, drenched with sweat, Francis came down. His victory was complete, the governor won by a spirit akin to his own in its severity to self, its deathless courage, its burning devotion.

De Castro was no great age, only forty-eight, but the sands of his life were running low. His body was worn with fever and with bitterness for "the miserable state in which he saw India, without power to remedy it." He listened to Francis's proposals, promised help for Kandy if the king became a tributary of Portugal and the sovereignty of north Halmahera for the son of the Ternate Sultan. Francis's proposal of a voyage to Japan was also approved. The interview ended on a more personal note. De Castro exacted a promise from Francis that he would not start for Japan that year, so that himself, when on his death-bed, should have the benefit of that "special gift in preparing souls to appear before their judge."

On April 2 Francis was back at Goa, where he fulfilled his promise by sending two Jesuits to found a house and school at Malacca. He now made himself acquainted with matters at Goa, which he had not been able to do on the spot since he had left three years and three months before. He took up his quarters at the college. After the death of the founder, Diogo Borba, Cosme Anes had been appointed temporary head, while the superior of the fathers was Lancilotti, the Italian who had arrived with Criminale and Beira. Micer Paul, Francis's old companion, was jogging along quietly as professor and confessor to the native students.

With the Franciscan friary the college had now become the head of the Asiatic missions. Twelve or thirteen languages were spoken within its walls. Besides Hindus from all parts of India there were African negroes, Malays, Chinese and the Moluccans brought by Francis from Ternate. Diogo had hoped that all the students would be able to join the Society of Jesus. Lancilotti and Criminale had both seen the impossibility of such a scheme and wrote home an account of the disparities of age, race, caste, intellect, and morality of this ill-assorted collection.

It was inevitable that, with divided authority, there should be friction between the head of the college and the Jesuit superior. Lancilotti, ill and spitting blood, complained that he "could not write two words without causing a scandal." Accustomed as he was to the methods of Ignatius, he could not but be puzzled by those of Xavier, whom he had never seen in the two and a half years he had been at Goa. He wrote to Ignatius with plaintive sarcasm: "Master Francis can provide for our needs from where he is now [Ternate] as well as if he were in Rome. He does not know what is going on in the college. He has never been able to stay here."

One of the Franciscans grumbled: "Father Francis travels too much." When the remark was repeated to Francis, as such criticisms always are, he replied pertinently enough: "I cannot know the needs of countries unless I visit them. Without such experience I cannot give the necessary instructions to the fathers, for one of the chief ingredients of knowledge is personal experience." Others too felt the need of a guiding hand: "Because Master Francis is not here all kinds of disorders are rife."

There was some justification for all this; but, as Francis had not added bilocation to the list of his miracles, it is difficult to see how he could avoid absence. It was one of his greatest misfortunes that, during his ten years in the East, besides Criminale and Barzée, he never had another competent and faithful helper able to hold a position of authority.

Meantime discipline was tightened among the students, and on Whit Sunday, 1548, Francis had the satisfaction of witnessing the baptism in the cathedral of Angero and his servants—an occasion for much pomp. The three Japanese lived in college. Paul of the Holy Faith, as he was now called, wore a lay-brother's habit, went frequently to confession and Communion and worked hard at Portuguese. Meantime Micer Paul had a dozen novices in his care, and among those now admitted to the Society by Father Francis were Cosme de Torres, the Spanish chaplain who had found his vocation when he saw Francis at Amboina, and Affonso de Castro. The latter had been one of those young nobles at the court of Lisbon whom the king had put under the direction of the two Jesuits. Francis had given him the Exercises, had set before him the Two Standards. The boy had chosen not the bare minimum for salvation but the highest of which he was capable. He hid as a stowaway on the ship in which Criminale sailed from Lisbon, serving his novitiate during the voyage, and Xavier rewarded his zeal by giving him the post of greatest danger. Ordained priest just before Francis started for Japan, he went with him to Malacca, on then to the Moluccas, where, after nine years of missionary work, he was martyred by Mohammedan pirates.

De Castro, now Viceroy, mortally ill as he was, had not given up command. He ordered two fleets, from Bassein and Goa, to drive the Moors from Aden, a key-point of the Portuguese route to the East. As the fleet was hoisting sail at Goa Francis appeared on the shore, breviary tucked under his arm, and strolled up to one of the officers equally famed for his dare-devil courage and his extreme dissipation. "On which ship are you sailing? Good, then we shall be fellow-passengers." Captain and crew were amazed at the sight of the Santo Padre stepping on board with the reprobate. He had already made friends with him on shore and, hardly out of sight of Goa, suddenly asked him when he had last been to confession. Eighteen years ago, was the answer, when the vicar of Goa had refused absolution; so, since a man was already damned, what was left but to get what fun he could out of this life? The ship put in to water before striking due west to the Red Sea. The padre landed with the reprobate, who made his confession kneeling in a little wood; then, as once before on a like occasion, Francis was seen, crucifix in hand, his bare shoulders bleeding till the penitent snatched the discipline from him to use on himself. The ship sailed, and Francis trudged the sixty miles back to Goa.

Then came the summons to Bassein. Before the old bishop, three friars, and Francis, gathered round his bed, the Viceroy took a solemn oath that he had made no illegal profit from his office, had exhausted his private fortune in government expenses. Francis was with him till he died (June 6, 1548) and saw him laid out for burial in the Franciscan tertiary habit and the white cloak of Knight of the Order of Christ. His coffer held three small pieces of silver, a blood-stained discipline and a lock from his beard which he had given the Goan bankers as security for money to pay his troops. Greatest of all the Portuguese viceroys, with the austerity and courage of a crusader, he is the final figure of future Portuguese greatness in the East in Vasco da Gama's vision in the *Lusiads*.

CHAPTER XVII

GOA, COCHIN AND MALACCA
(SEPTEMBER, 1548–JUNE, 1549)

On September 4, 1548, about six weeks after Francis's return from Bassein, the fleet from Lisbon was sighted off Goa. One ship, the Gallega, with five Jesuits on board, was missing, but five missionaries landed from the San Pedro and were warmly welcomed by Francis, who had never forgotten the horror of his own voyage out. One of the new arrivals was João Fernandez, a worldly young elegant converted by a sermon from that Padre Estrada who, in his own young days, had enjoyed teasing Francis for his inability to answer letters or keep up a fire. Fernandez had had his vocation tested by one of Simon Rodriguez's typically eccentric orders: he had obediently ridden through the city, dressed in his smartest silks, facing the tail of his ass. Nine months later he was judged ripe for the Indian mission, and by his amazing natural gift for languages was to prove Francis's right hand in Japan.

Father Gaspar Barzée (Berse), who landed with him, was Flemish. A wandering spirit, like Cosme de Torres, he had taken his M.A. degree at Louvain, and had been a soldier of Charles V, a hermit at Montserrat, a minor treasury official at Lisbon, till he too found his vocation in the novitiate at Coimbra. With Antonio Criminale he

214

was practically the only Jesuit in the eastern mission on whom Francis could wholly rely, and who was capable of successfully filling the delicate and arduous post of superior.

He tells an amusing story against himself. On our Lady's birthday, four days after he had landed, he was told by Francis to preach in the church of San Pablo and warned that it would be crowded by those anxious to hear one of the famous new European orators. Gaspar however—from nervousness—spoke so low that those at the back of the church could not hear a word and went out grumbling during the sermon. One of the older fathers, probably Lancilotti, was heard to exclaim in pardonable disgust: "This is a nice business, for them to send us an idiot like that!" Francis, who was leaving the next day for Comorin, gave practical advice as well as consolation. Gaspar accordingly trained his voice by speaking every night in the empty church, and by the time Francis got back, two months later, had the town enthusiastic about his sermons.

A budget of letters from home had come with the fleet, letters from Ignatius's secretary for Lancilotti, Criminale, and Cypriano. For Francis, who had not heard from his beloved father for two years, there was nothing; and that he was deeply wounded by this strange silence is evident from a sentence in Lancilotti's answer to Ignatius, in which he says that Father Francis was "astonished there was nothing for him" and begs the General to write Francis a letter which shall be forwarded wherever he is.

Francis bade Lancilotti to hand over command to the new superior of the college when he arrived on the delayed Gallega, and then left for Comorin. He wished to bid the Paravas good-bye before sailing for Japan and to find out on the spot the truth about renewed persecution in Travancore and Badaga raids in the north of Tuticorin.

Francis's welcome by the Paravas was reminiscent of Palm Sunday. Converts tore off garments to lay under his feet, strewed the way with palm-branches and flowers, and finally lifted him and carried him on their naked shoulders into church—a form of devotion no doubt pleasanter in theory than in fact. There was good news and bad. Father Anriquez, with all the keen intellect of his race, had made amazing progress with his Tamil, the grammar and dictionary. Criminale had the reputation of a saint, only lesser than the Santo Padre himself. Beside the unwearying heroism of the missionaries there were heartening tales of native bravery under persecution, even under torture. But there were apostasies too and, as always, the sickening difficulties with officials. The new captain of Tuticorin was carrying on the tradition of Francis's old *bête noire,* Cosme da Paiva, by his greed and cruelty. Francis was not again to visit the Paravas, the first fruits of his missionary harvest which Father Anriquez was to garner so successfully, sometimes the only European there. The Christianity of Cape Comorin was to survive many difficulties and persecutions, the substitution for Jesuits of native priests from Goan prisons, the conquest by the Dutch who exiled the Jesuits and turned churches into factories. The endeavours of Calvinist ministers to protestantise the Paravas met with the dogged answer: "Work as many miracles as our Father Francis, then we will believe you." The Dutchman, Baldeus, discouraged by the failure of his propaganda, declared irritably about the natives of the Fishery Coast: "They know nothing but the Creed, the our Father, the Ten Commandments and the Hail Mary."

Comorin Catholicism was strengthened by Xavier's rule of daily catechism and visits to church, frequent confession and Communion. Amid the ruin and apparent annihilation of so much of his work it is consoling to the human heart that this, his first mission, still survives. Still that good-night prayer of the *Salve Regina* is sung by the dusky congregation under the tropical stars as it is in the basilica of Javier where the apostle of the East was born.

At Cochin (October 22) Francis found Lancilotti and one of the fathers, landed a fortnight ago from the Gallega and already on his way to Comorin. The latter wrote home an account of the meeting: "He is a true servant of God. I have seen none like him. Brothers, this is certain that even the sight of him, before he has spoken a word, inspires such a fragrant desire to serve that one can give no idea of it. . . . To hear him sets hearts on fire. . . . He was never tired of asking about the brothers and all that is being done in Europe. He wishes one to speak of Father Master Simon and above all of Father Ignatius." There was the same enthusiasm in other letters. All fell victims to Francis's charm, to his extreme holiness, his burning love, combined with sympathy, enthusiasm, and gaiety. Only one seems to have remained unresponsive to this magnetic personality—Father Antonio Gomez, the new rector of the college.

Back again in Goa (mid-November, 1548) Francis found the place full of admiration for the sermons of the Flemish priest but still more for those of Gomez. Goa hummed with his eloquence, his noble birth, his intellect, his good breeding. The old bishop, drifting with the tide, proposed to appoint him preacher-in-ordinary of the cathedral. He was the social success of the hour and fully conscious of it.

During Francis's absence a rumour had spread that he had been killed by the Badagas. Gaspar wrote home:

"It is impossible to describe the grief of his friends. They said that if his relics were to cost them thirty thousand *cruzadoes* they must have them, and get him canonised." Such generosity was indeed surprising among the votaries of the verb "to snatch." Perhaps the more far-sighted realised that those thirty thousand *cruzadoes* might prove a really gilt-edged security. The body of a dead saint is an unfailing source of trade and income, the presence of a live one generally exceedingly uncomfortable to the average worldling.

Francis had brought with him a long list of accusations against the Tuticorin captain, which he now laid before the new governor, Garcia de Sa, who had been captain of Malacca on Francis's first visit there. The old man (he was over seventy) had none of de Castro's fire. He asked for nothing but peace and comfort, and at the moment was enjoying the eight days of fête with which the city was celebrating the baptism of a rich and well-known Brahmin. The most he would do was to give Francis a letter to protect the Paravas against undue cupidity on the captain's part, and he was the means of causing a new missionary project to fall to the ground. This was the despatch of two Jesuits to Socotra, whose poor ignorant, neglected Christians Francis had never forgotten. Garcia, however, had just concluded peace with the Mohammedans and did not wish to upset them by Christian propaganda.

Francis returned to the college. Cosme Anes, its co-founder with Borba, had handed over its entire administration and authority to the new rector. Gomez had been such a success in Portugal that people had deserted even the bull-ring to listen to his sermons, an amazing token of popularity. A favourite of Rodriguez at Coimbra, he had come to India bristling with ideas for academic innovations. "No sooner was he in charge," wrote Lancilotti drily to Ignatius, "than he began to reform everything. He wished, he said, that as regards studies the house should be run in the Parisian manner. For pious exercises he will introduce our Coimbran customs."

The newcomer held forth to Francis. He explained at length the Coimbran methods and their advantages as well as the ideals of the Company of Jesus, and was so pleased with himself that he wrote home a detailed account of the interview: "He was so content, so delighted that all this seemed to him too good to be true. . . . He was perfectly satisfied with all this as well as the full information I gave him."

They were an incongruous pair—the rector, pompous, suave, smart in his black silk habit, swelling with self-satisfaction, and Francis, thin, worn, silent, shabby as usual, but perhaps for once with dark eyes downcast and unsmiling mouth. Behind that silence there was probably a tangle of motives. Humility, patience (though that was not one of his strong points), a realisation of the need for better discipline among the welter of mixed students, and deep down in his heart a hurt wonder why he alone had not received a letter from Father Ignatius, whose name fell so frequently and fluently from the rector's tongue. His silence still unbroken, Francis returned to Cochin with the governor's letter. There was nothing special demanding his attention at Cochin, but the eastern winter monsoon made a start for Japan impossible for several months, and it was better just now to be away from Goa, where he always found trouble and frequently made it.

The days of his two months stay at Cochin were filled

with the usual work, specially the care of the sick; he would himself carry them to hospital and then go round begging for them. When he met a poor man shivering in the street he would snatch off his own cloak to cover his nakedness and then accept a new cloak from his friends with a shrug and a smile—"Well, for the love of God"—knowing that before long that would have gone too.

In January, 1549, he wrote six letters for despatch by the fleet going to Lisbon. As a year ago, the letter to the king is burning with anger against officials: "It is a martyrdom to witness the destruction of all one has gained with so much labour without even being able to protest. . . . Experience has taught me that your Highness is powerless to spread the Faith of Christ in the Indies but powerful to amass and possess all the temporal riches of India."

There is a strong note of discouragement in the last letter to Rodriguez: "I fear none but God, fearing lest He should punish me for my negligence in His service, for my uselessness and incapacity to spread the Name of Jesus Christ among the peoples who do not know It."

In the long Spanish letter to Ignatius (January 12, 1549) sounds an echo of the same note, perhaps too of the wound inflicted by his Father's strange silence: "The natives of India are a barbarous race, so far as I can see . . . very ignorant, at least all those I have met till now. Those who come out to convert them need numerous virtues, obedience, humility, perseverance, patience, love of neighbour and a great chastity."

"Great chastity and humility," "great obedience," "friendliness and gentleness," "using every means possible to make oneself loved"—again and again the need for these qualities is emphasised, the very qualities in which the new rector was so conspicuously lacking. "It is my opinion that the Company of Jesus should mean the company of love and sympathy, not that of severity and servile fear." "I tell you this, O my soul's father, because those of the Company here have been disedified by the order given by [Gomez] to seize and send in irons to Portugal those whom he does not consider edifying here."

As well as the necessary virtues, he describes the dangers and hardships waiting for missionaries sent out, gives a list of Jesuits already in the East—four in the Moluccas, two at Malacca, six at Comorin, two at Coulam, two at Bassein, four at Socotra (a hope which did not materialise). He shows the impossibility of Gomez's and Anes's idea that the native students of the college should all become Jesuits: "From my experience in these parts I see clearly, O my only father, that it is unthinkable that the Company should be recruited from the Hindus, for Christianity here will survive as long as we do, we who are here and those who shall come after us." He gives a long account of Angero, from whom he encloses a letter, and of Japan before concluding: "I end, then, kneeling on the ground as I write, as if I had you before me in person, and beg you constantly to recommend me to God our Lord in your prayers and Masses, so that He may give me the grace both to understand His holy Will and perfectly to fulfil It."

In February Father Gaspar arrived at Cochin, commissioned by Gomez to found a new house of the order at Chaul—a scheme on which Francis had not even been consulted. The Goan news was discouraging. The famous "Coimbran method" was proving most efficacious but scarcely in the direction intended, for the students, unaccustomed to such iron discipline, had responded by climbing the garden wall and running away. This crystallised Francis's half-formed decision to dismiss Gomez from the rectorship and send him to found the mission at Ormuz, on the Persian Gulf, while Gaspar Barzée replaced him.

Francis followed the governor to Bassein to obtain his approval to the despatch of the two new missionaries to the Moluccas and Francis's own voyage to Japan. Early in March he was back at Goa.

Gomez received his orders for Ormuz and, deeply hurt in his pride, went straight to Cosme Anes, a fervent admirer for whom he had promised to use his own influence in Lisbon. The news spread. The city was in an uproar over the idea of the popular preacher's being exiled to waste his rounded periods on ignorant heathen. Garcia de Sa, the bishop, and all the best society joined in a fervent petition for Gomez to stay. Gaspar, in this case more prudent than the saint, saw the impossibility of his own position as rector and quietly but firmly begged to be allowed to go to Ormuz himself as had been originally arranged. Francis was forced to reverse his decision. Gaspar sailed early in April. Gomez remained as rector, but no longer as superior of the Jesuits. This post was entrusted to the faithful and self-effacing Micer Paul de Camerino, "one of those beautiful souls whose perfume the world only realises when it treads them underfoot" (Bellesort). Such an arrangement could be nothing but temporary and uncertain. It was, however, a working compromise, and Francis, his nerves worn by petty quarrels and intrigues, had only one desire, to escape from Goa.

As he looked back over the last year, it seemed that his

only pleasant hours there had been those he had spent with Angero. The Japanese had learnt Portuguese, spoke and understood it and could write well enough to send a letter from his own pen to the Father General, enclosing a specimen of Japanese writing. When asked by Francis why Japanese did not write from left to right like Europeans, he had made the shrewd reply that, as the head was man's most important member, it was only sensible to begin at the top and end at the feet. He had made the Exercises under Cosme de Torres and declared that what he considered the most important things in Christian practice were confession and Communion—an echo of Francis's insistent teaching. His descriptions of his own country and China were as accurate as could be expected from a small provincial who knew only his own corner of one island. The mysterious "Chengico," beyond China and Tartary, the original home of Japanese religion, was probably Thibet, the "great universities" of Japan the monastic schools of the bonzes.

Francis had written that, questioned about the possibility of the conversion of the Japanese, Angero had been hopeful: "He answered that the people of his country would not at once become Christian, and said that they would first ask me a great many questions and judge by my answers how well I understood things and above all if I practised what I preached. . . . After so testing me for half a year the king, nobility and other people of quality would become Christians, since, said he, they are a people governed only by reason." That roseate vision of wholesale conversion in six months was doubtless more tinged by the saint's enthusiastic optimism than by Angero's practical experience, but it was a radiant hope that enabled him to endure the criticisms and discouragements of Goa better than would have been otherwise possible. But the hour of deliverance drew near, and Francis drew a breath of relief: "I am leaving for Japan. There, at least, there are neither Jews nor Moslems, only heathen, a people eager-minded, greedy of new things, curious about God and nature. The thought of my determination to go consoles me."

As usual his friends tried to dissuade him. As usual he turned a deaf ear and continued his preparations. The ship was to leave for Malacca before Easter. Written instructions were left with Gomez and Micer Paul. It is perhaps not surprising that those of Gomez have not survived. Francis was of course taking with him the three Japanese as well as his fellow-Jesuits, the Valencian Cosme de Torres and brother João Fernandez. In the courageous and intelligent young man who spent three or four hours daily in prayer Francis had recognised a rare soul, and he accordingly told him to prepare for ordination. João, terrified at the idea, flung himself on his knees before his superior and begged him with so many tears to allow him to remain a brother coadjutor that, for the second time in a month Francis, who so seldom reversed a decision, consented and withdrew his order.

One of the fathers in Goa wrote home soon after Easter: "We have scarcely been able to enjoy Master Francis. He allows himself no respite. The more work he has to do for Christ Jesus the more he rejoices. He left us during Holy Week, 1549, and hopes to arrive in Japan in the month of August. He begged us to live with noble thoughts. After having lived so scattered on earth there remains the Heavenly Jerusalem where nothing can separate us from the most tender embraces of our brothers." What a true Xaverian ring about the words, "to live with noble thoughts" and that vision of happy reunion in heaven!

Easter Day (April 21, 1549) was spent at Cochin; then the voyage to Malacca was resumed and, wonderful to relate, completed without adventure. "We took a little over forty days to reach Malacca and arrived in good health, Father de Torres, the rest and I. No sea-sickness! The weather was beautiful. There were no storms and the Achinese pirates did not appear, God be praised."

The landing at Malacca was a delirious triumph. Surrounded by his companions, escorted by the entire population, to the sound of hymns sung by the children, the Santo Padre made his entrance into the town, blessing as he went. Then, summoned to the death-bed of the vicar, he hurried to his house. The old man, conscience-stricken as he looked back over his thirty years in Malacca, so sadly barren of good work, believed himself already damned. As he heard the welcome to the Jesuits he tottered across his room, crying aloud in his woe, and sank on the threshold as Francis crossed it. It was in vain that Francis spoke to him of the infinite mercy of God. The agony of despair continued. Kneeling by the bed Francis promised many Masses if this poor soul might find rest. At last the storm abated and the old man, having made his peace with God, died quietly in Francis's arms.

Father Perez, the Jesuit sent by Francis, had been working in the town single-handed. "I am lost in admiration of the good he has done," Francis wrote: "he certainly is a worker in the Lord's vineyard, not an idler. He has not even time to eat or sleep. . . . As for me I am ashamed to see how much good is done, with our Lord's help, by a man of such delicate health and always suffering."

On Trinity Sunday Affonso de Castro, whom the bishop had ordained at Goa before their departure, said his first Mass with great solemnity in the cathedral, such a thing as had never been seen before at Malacca. He left soon after for the Moluccas, appointed superior if Father Beira were dead, as an unfounded rumour reported.

Once more Francis wrote farewell letters, twelve in all, to make final arrangements for his long, possibly last, absence. Between Corpus Christi, June 20, 1549, and June 23, there were ten letters, to Ternate, Goa, Rome, the king, Rodriguez and Ignatius, with an account of the voyage, directions, and information about Japan. Gomez is specially bidden to exercise "charity, friendship and love." The devil is doing his best to prevent the voyage to Japan, but "neither savages nor tempests nor demons can harm nor hurt us more than God allows and permits."

All preparations were now complete. Francis had found the captain of Malacca, son of the great Vasco da Gama, ready and eager to help. A Chinaman, Avan by name, commonly called the Pirate, consented to take the three Jesuits and the Japanese to Japan in his junk. The captain saw that he gave a written undertaking to sail direct to Kagoshima and forced him to leave his wife and money at Malacca as hostages. Don Pedro da Gama also gave Francis enough to pay for the journey and his stay in Japan, as well as to build a church there. "If we were his brothers," wrote Francis to the king: "he could not have done more for us."

The departure was fixed for the evening of Midsummer Day, the feast of St. John the Baptist, and Francis closes what may possibly be his last letter to Rome: "I have continually before my eyes and mind what I have so often heard our blessed father Ignatius say—that those who wish

to join our Company must strive hard to conquer themselves and to drive out all those fears which prevent men
from having faith, hope and trust in God, by taking all
means to do so. And though all faith, hope and trust are
a gift of God Who gives them to whom He will, yet He
most often gives them to those who strive most earnestly
to conquer themselves. There is a great difference between
those who trust in God after they themselves have provided all that is necessary and him who trusts in God having stripped himself of all that he could retain in order
that he may more perfectly imitate Christ. . . . In seems
to me that those who live in continual danger of death
only to serve God, without any other end in view, would
soon come to regard life with horror and would desire
death that they might live and reign for ever with God in
heaven, for this life is not life but a prolonged death and
an exile from the glory for which we are created." (June
22, 1549.)

CHAPTER XVIII

VOYAGE TO JAPAN, KAGOSHIMA
(JUNE 24, 1549–SEPTEMBER, 1550)

THE junk was loaded, the eve of the departure came at last. Francis spent the night in the little church of Our Lady of the Mount, instructing a young man who had just applied for admittance to the Society. Left alone, he kept vigil before setting out on his new and perilous adventure, as Ignatius had at Montserrat.

Between the lines of his letter to his "father" is the shadow of some great sadness that darkened his soul, something that lay deeper than the memory of treachery and opposition, or anxiety about Gomez and affairs at Goa. There is some obscure instinct in man, perhaps no more than an atavistic fear of jealous gods, which makes him shrink as the prize he has so long striven for is within his grasp. But in this case it was stronger and more deepseated, a foreshadowing, perhaps, of the struggle with the powers of evil which lay before him. Only a few days earlier Antonio Criminale had been martyred by the Badagas, his pierced and headless body flung down before the blood-stained altar. There seems little doubt that Francis knew of his death without human agency, as he had of Peter Faber's, for in his detailed letters of arrangements and instructions there is no mention of the young superior of the Comorin mission.

228

Midsummer day dawned. Francis said his last Mass for many days: would the next be in Japan? Then, in the evening he boarded the junk of the Pirate, accompanied by Father Cosme de Torres, Brother João Fernandez, Angero and his two servants, a Portuguese, a Malabar and a Chinese servant. Don Pedro da Gama watched them go with misgiving, but the Father had refused to sail on a Portuguese ship because that would have meant wintering in China and a delay of a year in arriving in Japan.

The junk, manned by a Chinese crew, was a fair size, three to four hundred tons, flat-keeled, square-built, with low bow and a high stern; there were three masts, and sails of straw matting on bamboo yards—an unwieldy vessel, yet frail to face five hundred leagues of open sea and possibly typhoons and cyclones.

All promised well at the start—good weather, and the wind steady from the south-west. The dreaded straits between the Malay Peninsula and Sumatra were negotiated without a sight of the terrible Achinese. Before turning north a load of timber was taken in for ballast and packed in the hold with Don Pedro's presents for the king of Japan, a quantity of pepper, and a cask of Mass wine. In spite of orders to hurry, the Pirate began to dawdle leisurely up the coast, calling at each island on the way to Pekan, about a hundred and fifty miles north of Singapore. With each delay the chance of reaching Japan this year grew less, for by August the favourable wind would die down.

Francis was never one to suffer delays in God's service gladly, but on the junk was something worse even than this waste of opportunity. In a shrine on the high poop sat the patron god of the boat, a grotesque, leering figure carved in wood. Before this idol the Chinese sailors, who wore pigtails, little round caps, wide trousers, and short coats of blue cotton, were continually burning coloured candles and joss-sticks. Almost hourly the god was propitiated by offerings of food and drink before being consulted by casting lots; and with each prostration of the blue figures it seemed to Francis that the evil on board grew stronger and stronger.

The gulf of Siam, the wide plain of Cambodia and the mouth of the Mekon river were passed; then, on July 21, the wind rose with such force that it was necessary to anchor. The junk lay rolling helplessly on the angry sea. It was impossible to keep one's feet. The Chinese servant, Manuel, fell head first into the ship's pump and was hauled out apparently dead, streaming with blood from a wound on his head. He had hardly recovered consciousness under Francis's administrations when a cry was raised that the Pirate's daughter had fallen overboard. She was drowned under her father's eyes, battered against the side of the junk by the waves.

Night fell to the howling of the wind and the wails of captain and crew, a night whose blackness was unpierced by star or moon and was thick with the presence of evil. The candle-flames in the shrine winked like lewd eyes. The smell of burning spice mingled with that of the steaming blood smeared on the god's feet from a sacrificed cock. Again lots were cast, and a grim answer was given to the Pirate's agonised question why he had lost his girl: "Had the Chinaman not been brought back to life, the girl would not have died." The blood of cocks was not enough. The angry god demanded human sacrifice. Was one life lost enough to save the rest?

Silently, with fear and prayer, the little band of Christians huddled together. One by one they slept, till only

Xavier remained awake to face the struggle with the powers of evil without human help. His allusion to what followed lifts the veil but little. The experiences of the spirit, whether good or evil, can be expressed only by symbol. "That day and the following night our Lord granted me the special grace to feel and know by experience and to the depths that terrible and agonising fear which the enemy knows so well how to inspire, when God allows him." Francis knew, as every master of the inner life knows, that fear is one of the devil's strongest weapons; not ordinary fear of exterior dangers and misfortunes, but that mysterious terror which, in the dark night of the soul, rises from the inmost depths of the being and, if it join forces with that other fear, which is evil itself, will submerge the very citadel of the soul and sweep all to ruin.

This was not his first struggle with the power of evil, but it was deeper, longer and more terrible than any before or any we know of later. Still the wind raged between black sky and blacker sea, a blackness pierced only by those little flames in whose flickering gleam that lewd face in the shrine smiled horribly, as if certain of triumph.

"I do not write of the only remedy to oppose to such terrors, not because the lesson is useless but because time is lacking. I will only say, in one word, that one must show courage in the face of the enemy, absolutely emptied of all trust in self, trusting absolutely to God. Then, having put all one's strength and all one's hope in Him, supported by so mighty a defender and protector, one must prevent oneself from showing the slightest fear, and be certain of victory." In this same letter, from Kagoshima, November 5, 1549, he returns again to the last assault of the powers of evil at the moment of bodily death: "In that hour temptations will increase. There will be troubles and dangers of body and soul such as we have not yet felt."

With dawn came calm. Sail was hoisted, and the voyage was resumed "with great sadness," a sadness which seems to have cast a lengthening shadow till nearly the end of the saint's stay in Japan. A few days later the rocky island of Sanchian was sighted, at the entrance to the Canton river, a neutral spot where Portuguese and Chinese merchants could meet to trade now that entrance into China was forbidden to the foreign devils on pain of torture and death. The Pirate announced his intention of wintering here, but Francis's threats to appeal to the Portuguese in the harbour as well as to Don Pedro induced him to resume the voyage.

He had, however, no intention of proceeding to Japan. Lots had been cast again to know if they would reach Japan safely. Yes. And return safely to Malacca? No. The Pirate determined to cheat fate, as Araujo had tried to, and, like Araujo at Amboina, he failed.

The junk made for the harbour of Chang Chow, opposite Formosa, where the Chinaman was going to winter, but as she rounded the promontory a passing junk warned them that the harbour was full of pirates. More likely it was the Chinese fleet which the outlaw had no desire to face, so he put about and prepared to make again for Canton. Suddenly the south-west monsoon, which had died down, rose again with such force that there was nothing to be done but to run before it. A fortnight later land was sighted once more, and on August 15, 1549, the junk entered the bay of Kagoshima, the home of Angero, in the south of Kiusiu, the southernmost island of Japan.

It was the anniversary of the first vows at Montmartre, fifteen years before.

Francis has told nothing of his first impressions of Japan, but Father Valignano, thirty years later, wrote home an account of this strange country where everything was the opposite of Europe: white was the colour of mourning, black teeth a sign of beauty; their food and drink and music were all equally distasteful to the Western palate and ear, their clothes, houses, and ceremonies unlike anything known to the Portuguese and Italians.

Kagoshima then, as now, was a little town at the foot of a hill lying at the edge of the great land-enclosed bay from whose still, clear waters rose the steep island of Sakura with its active volcano.

The "foreign bonzes" were taken to his house by Angero—Paul of the Holy Faith. Three years before he had fled from justice, but now came home in triumph, full of stories of the wonders of Goa, his studies there, his new religion, and proud to be the only interpreter of these ambassadors of a mighty foreign power.

The meeting between him and his wife took place with that total absence of emotional expression which was not one of the least marvellous things in the eyes of the southern Europeans; then a meal was served. Francis, who had been told that the bonzes ate neither fish nor meat and drank no wine, had resolved to observe the same abstinence. He was accustomed to the most frugal diet among the Paravas, but even so the first Japanese meal must have been a sore trial. There was the double difficulty of squatting on the floor before the little low tables with their tray-like edges and of trying to eat rice with chopsticks. The soup was an easier problem, though unattractive both to taste and smell, for the bowl containing it was emptied at a gulp.

With many prostrations and in-sucking of breath the three Jesuits were shown the room they were to share, its wooden framework, the sliding paper panels for doors and windows, mats of yellow straw on the floor. On the floor too were the three quilted mats which served for mattresses, and the wooden pillows. Every sound was audible through the sliding paper panels of the walls— the murmur of Angero's voice as he regaled his wife with travellers' tales, her bird-like exclamations of wonder and admiration, the cry of a child who woke suddenly afraid of the ghost foxes and badgers who prowl at night. There was an occasional mutter as Cosme de Torres or Fernandez turned in his sleep on the hard *futons*. From the town floated up the throb of drums, the shrill call of pipes, the discordance of a five-stringed *kiwa*. The room looked into the garden, set out to plan with its miniature lake and islands, the little mountains and dwarf trees, the three symbolic stones of Worship, the Guardian and the Two Gods. The full moon was rising over the promontory of Shibushi, and a long path of silver stretched across the mirroring water to the yellow lights of Kagoshima.

Was Francis already beginning to realise what a world lay between him and the country he had felt he knew so well from Angero's talk? The feudal castles, their lords and vassals, the monasteries, with monks, friars and abbots vowed to chastity and poverty, with beads, vestments and chanted liturgy, these were only surface points of contact which masked a gulf of difference almost unpassable, a difference of belief, ethics, social manners and customs. He had met and battled with the gross Brahmin poly-theism, with the trenchant creed of Islam. This was to be his first encounter with Buddhism, which, brought from China a thousand years before, had absorbed where it had not superseded the old Shintoism—a glorified ancestor-worship without images or moral teaching.

The three Jesuits were the centre of interest when they went through the narrow streets crowded with women in queer straw hats and long kimonos, with paper parasols over their heads and sandals on their tiny feet. Among them pushed the coolies, clad only in a short tunic of blue cotton, thin yellow arms and legs bare, begging friars in grey habits, pedlars whose wares were slung over their shoulders by bamboo rods. Every now and then a samurai mounted on a small horse and followed by servants rode by, his two swords crossed in his belt, his face immovable as his slanting eyes gazed with scorn at the *ijin*. *Ijin*, foreigner, was no doubt the first word the missionaries learnt in Japanese, for the children, swarming round and almost under their feet, collected friends by the cry.

Angero's house was filled all day and part of the night with a stream of visitors who, after the complicated ceremonies of prostrations, compliments and self-depreciation, began interminable questions. These were interrupted only by the still more elaborate ceremonial of tea-drinking, invented, said legend, by a Shogun to wean a young emperor from his career of dissipation. Francis and his companions must have found tea as disgusting a drink as did Father Valignano a quarter of a century later. Like him, they were probably thankful that the china cups were no larger than "sparrows' drinking troughs." Angero, swelling with importance, was kept busy translating questions into Portuguese and answers into Japanese, and by bedtime the three guests were certainly glad to be alone. A modern writer says that the Japanese are tiring company, because their curiosity in insatiable, their questions a queer mixture of the profound, the shrewd, and the childish, and they take without giving information.

Days and weeks of blazing heat passed. Francis had intended to go straight to the capital on his arrival, for he knew by now the immense importance of the favour of the Oriental ruler. As it was he was only meeting Angero's friends, none of them belonging to the *Shi* or noble class.

About fifteen miles south of Kagoshima lay the castle of the local daimio who belonged to the Shimatsu, one of the three great clans of the island of Kiusiu. Since 1188 the emperor had been a mere cypher, imprisoned in his palace at Kyoto and invisible, while all the power had been in the hands of the Shogun or general, a post held for centuries by the same family, the Ashikaga. Now they too had grown degenerate, so that, without a powerful central government, the country had been ravaged with civil wars, and only the daimios (big feudal nobles), had any authority. Lawlessness was rife on land and sea. The country swarmed with wandering bands of uncontrolled soldiers, the seas with pirates. Farmers hardly dared to sow their crops, so problematic was their chance of reaping them. The capital of Kyoto (or Mioko), once a city with half a million inhabitants, magnificent palaces, temples and monasteries, was now half-ruined, with a population of only twenty-two thousand. The island of Kiusiu, where Kagoshima was situated, was in better state than that of Nippon, for in it the three great daimio families reigned supreme, exercising their rights of levying taxes, giving judgment and punishment, enlisting and training soldiers for their own troops.

Day after day a veil of rain was drawn across the grey-green tiles of the roofs, the grey sea, the wind-bent pines and the swaying feathers of bamboo. It was September, the wettest and most flowerless month of the year. Then, one day, Angero was summoned by the daimio. Francis gave him a picture to take with him, a painting of our Lady, one of those early Portuguese masters whose hieratic symbolism holds so much more religious feeling than the splendour of a Raphael or a Titian. Angero returned from his audience radiant. The daimio had questioned him closely about the *Nambanjin,* the southern barbarians, and he himself had drawn such a glowing picture of the wonders of Goa that an interview had been fixed for Father Francis and his companions. "The duke knelt before the picture of Christ our Lord and our Lady and adored it with great respect and reverence. He ordered all those present to do the same."

So the ceremonial reverence towards the possession of a distinguished stranger was transformed by Angero's enthusiasm and Francis's hope into an act of worship. Shimatsu's mother had admired the painting and asked to have a copy, which was impossible, as no oil paints and no competent copyist were to be had. She had also asked about the beliefs of the strangers; so for days Angero was busy writing out an account with brush and Chinese ink, in those Chinese ideographs which had puzzled Goa and would soon be amazing Rome.

It was a happy augury that the audience was fixed for the feast of St. Michael, the patron saint of Javier, chosen by Francis as the patron of Japan. If Javier was in Francis's mind when the party started, still more was he reminded of home when they reached the huge castle, one of those almost impregnable strongholds which were all destroyed in the final struggle between the emperor and the nobles in the middle of the nineteenth century. Beyond the outer enclosure was the narrow bridge across the moat, which was defended on its inner circumference by stone walls so thick that they looked like a truncated cone. Inside the entrance passage, so narrow that it could be traversed only in single file, lay a veritable little village of houses and gardens.

The three Jesuits were conducted along endless tiled verandahs, through one room after another, till at last the hall of audience was reached. The great Shimatsu sat on the dais, his robes of state spread stiffly round him. His plum-coloured silk kimono was embroidered with giant golden chrysanthemums. In his silken girdle were the *daisho,* the two swords of the samurai, with lacquered sheaths and gilded hilts, the long blade for fighting, the short for cutting off the heads of conquered enemies or committing hara-kari. His face had the fine bones and aquiline nose of the aristocrat. In the expressionless ivory mask the slanting black eyes were the only live thing. One slender hand held a painted fan. Round him were grouped his samurai, and below the dais, on the floor, their inferiors lay prostrate. On the wall behind hung perhaps one picture by Sesshu, greatest of all Japanese painters, who had died the year Francis was born—two wild birds in flight against a wide lonely expanse of silver sky and steely sea.

The ceremonious greetings were finished. A richly-bound Bible or missal was shown to the daimio, who admired it and handed it back with the non-committal advice "to keep with care the books containing the Christian law," since, if true, it would prevail. Little enough on which to found much hope of speedy and numerous conversions! Yet Francis writes that he had kept "this splendid news to the end of my letter to gladden you and make you give thanks." The results of the interview, however, were good. The missionaries were granted a house and given permission to preach their doctrines. Shimatsu saw that such encouragement would bring more Portuguese ships to his port of Kagoshima, and such ships meant not only trade and money but something which he valued even more, the fire-arms that his armourers could learn to copy. Francis's request for a junk to take him to the capital met with a temporising answer: the wind would not be favourable till next spring; the roads were too much infested by robbers for a land journey to be safe. Shimatsu saw no necessity to enlighten the foreign bonze on the true state of affairs in the half-ruined city of Kyoto, where the aged emperor was a prisoner in his decaying palace, while the Shogun's palace was a heap of ashes and the Shogun himself, a mere child, had fled into exile.

One would like to know where the first Mass was said in Japan—perhaps not till the two priests had their own little house and some quiet was occasionally obtainable.

October came and went, with the chrysanthemums glowing like beaten gold and copper against the grey stone lanterns in temple gardens or the granite torii which marked the entrance to Shinto temples. It was the time of the rice-harvest, when the little fields, like a pattern of "crazy" paving when seen from the hills, were filled with men whose sickles flashed like crescent moons. Francis was anxious to send news of their safe arrival to Malacca and Goa; he was anxious too about Gomez and what was happening at the college of Santa Fé. The channel of communication on which he had relied was closed, for the Pirate had fulfilled the devil's prophecy by dying. Then, early in November news came that a Portuguese ship was in the harbour of Hirado, at the extreme west of the island

of Kiusiu. She was about to sail for Malacca while the
north wind still held, and at once (November 5, 1549)
Francis prepared his letters. He dictated one of his longest
reports (over twelve thousand words), probably to Cosme
de Torres, as it is in Spanish. Only the last words, "your
brother in Christ, Francisco," are written in his own
hand.

One can see him striding about the small bare room
while the ideas poured out, jostling each other in the
struggle for expression; no literary finish, no sequence of
ideas, no construction, a live and detailed account of the
voyage suddenly interrupted by an analysis of fear. A
long description of the Japanese people follows the arrival
at Kagoshima, and the regard paid to noble birth rather
than to riches is emphasised as a welcome trait after the
avarice of Goa. The story of the visit to Shimatsu and
plans for visiting Kyoto are continually interspersed by
long exhortations to love, humility and obedience and to
living in brotherly love. When Gomez read these passages did he take any of them as meant for him, or did his
lip curl a little sarcastically when he received the recommendation to remain quietly working where God had
placed him instead of rushing off to gain greater kudos
elsewhere?

In spite of the eager flow of words, ideas, and hopes
from the interview with Shimatsu and for the journey to
Kyoto, in spite too of orders for Goanese Jesuits to be
ready for a summons to Japan, there is a strain of doubt
and discouragement underlying the surface. Perhaps
Francis was beginning to realise that, as a brother Jesuit
quaintly said of him, he had fished in India with nets, here
only with a line; at present converts numbered only Angero's wife, his family, and some of his friends. "We

live in great fear that God our Lord, Who knows all our continual imperfections and great faults, will withdraw His favour from us and no longer give us grace both to begin to serve Him and to persevere to the end, unless He grants us greatly to improve."

There are several letters to Goa, one to Gaspar Barzée at Ormuz ordering him with two other fathers to Japan. The personal letter to Gomez, filled chiefly with administrative details, has a distinct reserve, warnings against ambition and the "great things" which Gomez is hoping and planning for himself. The fathers are to bring with them presents for the "king" whose conversion should bring "great temporal benefits" to Portugal by opening a rich market. "For, after my experience of the Indians, I have little hope that they will send a ship only for the love of God, to bring the fathers and for no other reason." There is a postcript in Portuguese, written in Francis's own hand: "For the love of God, I entreat you to make all the brothers of the Company love you, those in the house, and the others by your letters. . . . I desire you specially to write to me about your interior life, for you know how happy I should be to be relieved of a deep anxiety which weighs on me without ceasing . . . for I shall not be satisfied to know that you love them [his fellow-Jesuits] but still more that they love you."

In the letter to Don Pedro da Gama, the captain at Malacca, there is much more of the old Francis—hope, enthusiasm, and gay humour: "I live in confident belief that before two years I shall write to your Excellency that we have built a church of our Lady at Meaco [Kyoto]. . . . If your Excellency will favour me by appointing me your agent in this country I will promise you one thing, a gain of a hundred for one, thanks to means used so far by no captain of Malacca. It is to give all for the poor souls who become Christians. The profit will be absolutely assured and without risk, for it is certain that he who gives one for Christ lays up a hundred for himself in the next life." He adds a postscript about the bonzes sailing on the Portuguese ship which is taking these letters, emphasising the need "to receive the bonzes well and supply them with everything necessary, so that they may leave with the desire to learn Christ's law, in order to gather fruit among the Japanese in the future."

The winter, with its rains and north-west winds, had now set in, and Francis had been down with an attack of fever; yet he was determined himself to accompany the two bonzes from Kagoshima to Hirado. The distance is a hundred and fifty miles as the crow flies, across a sea sprinkled with innumerable little islands and past the port of Nagasaki. It was a mad venture, and no doubt his companions tried to persuade him that Diaz—the Portuguese who had come to Japan with them—was escort enough for the bonzes, or that one of themselves could go. Francis proved deaf to persuasion. The fever which was wasting his body was only an outward symptom of that which burned inwardly.

From the time he left Malacca on the way to Japan there is a change in him. The gaiety and radiance of youth, the hope that springs phœnix-like from the ashes of each failure, seem dimmed. Only now and then they flame up with the flicker of a sinking fire. One sees a new hardness, an authority and reserve, in the letter to Gomez, an oft-repeated assertion that all who die without the Faith are in hell—a position from which he did not recede even when pitifully pressed by the Japanese, whose strong filial piety and family devotion made it almost impossible for them to believe their dear dead to be eternally damned. The explanation for these assertions probably was his shuddering horror of the almost universal vice prevalent in that warlike society, and of which the bonzes' monasteries and schools were hotbeds. Then too "the care of all the churches" weighed on him as it had done with St. Paul; and always the anxiety about Gomez was like the hurt of a thorn in a festering wound. Perhaps too that night struggle with the powers of darkness had left wounds not yet wholly healed, if they ever would be in this life. Yet the words from *El Conde Lucanor* rang in his ears, as they had done in Paris days: "Let us not leave the battle for the wounds we have; those we shall receive will make us forget the old ones."

At the end of November he arrived at Hirado with Diaz and the two bonzes, and was warmly welcomed by the captain and crew of the ship. Hirado was a busy little port, the nearest Japanese harbour to China, a missionfield which Francis had not forgotten, so he judged it politic to visit the local daimio. This was no great ruler like Shimatsu but a petty potentate, more pirate than prince, whose vanity had been flattered when the Portuguese had treated him as a king. It was to his interest to encourage trade with the barbarians, so he received Francis graciously and gave him leave to preach and proselytise. Ten years later the first Christian blood to flow in Japan was shed by order of this young man. The ship sailed, to reach Malacca in April, 1550. So great was the joy of captain and people to receive news of the Santo Padre, whom they had feared dead, that the place was *en fête;* the bonzes were treated with the greatest distinction and both baptised with high solemnity. Before the end of December Francis was back at Kagoshima. One would like to fancy him in time to say the first Christmas Masses in Japan.

The winter months crawled by. Fernandez was hard at work learning Japanese, a language which Francis at first had hopefully declared was easy, but a few months later was to confess he had found hopelessly baffling. Fernandez, however, proved as apt a pupil as Antonio Criminale had at Tamil, and before long was able to speak for Francis without calling in the aid of an interpreter, generally a bar rather than a help to understanding. A book of Christian doctrine and practice was compiled too; a queer production the lettered Japanese must have found it, in Fernandez's stiff Japanese, written in Latin characters!

Some time this winter Francis visited the home of a kinsman of Shimatsu, whose small castle of Ichicu lay a little north of Kagoshima. In this atmosphere of family and feudal life he must have felt something akin to his own upbringing at Javier. Perhaps here he learnt of the *ronin*, those masterless samurai who vowed fealty to no lord but wandered through the country seeking adventure, righting wrongs and defending the weak in the true tradition of the knight-errant.

At Ichicu all the household were baptised except the samurai himself, who could not reconcile this new religion with the traditions of his ancestors. The steward was baptised as Michael, the new patron of his country, and was left in charge of the little mission. When it was visited early in the seventeenth century by a Japanese priest there was still the memory of Francis's teaching, and relics of Christianity such as rosaries and Agnus Deis were treasured.

Francis was well known in the streets as he went through the throngs of country folk looking like thatched cottages in their queer mantles of rice-straw from which the rain dripped. The women, their high-piled greasy hair wrapped in white mufflers against the damp, made a clatter as they shuffled along on their *geta* with high wooden soles. The town had the miserable look of all Japanese towns in rain, as the wet poured from upturned eaves, like roofs of birdcages, on to the straw hats of coolies carrying their mistresses in funny little litters like hammocks.

Francis had begun to visit the local monasteries, "going in and out as if he were at home," says Fernandez—a lack of ceremony scarcely likely to popularise him in this land of elaborate ceremonial. Among the bonzes, with their shaven heads, their voluminous black-and-white habits, their frugal meals, their beads, their meditation, he felt at first an odd familiarity, but soon he was to see the opposition of their beliefs and practices to all he lived and taught, to consider that the devil imitates the things of God in order to increase his catch of souls.

He watched students and scholars in the monasteries, boys and youths of the better classes and perhaps learnt something of the *Bushido,* the way of the warrior, which was the samurai religion and rule of life, and of its lessons of frugality, loyalty and filial piety, the iron discipline that had been inaugurated as a protest against the effeminate luxury of the Shogunate—a noble rule, but a pitiless one; a life of the sword which, in case of failure, ended by the wearer's own hand and sword. Francis, watching the expressionless yellow faces, the still hands, the immobility of bodies trained to the hardness and suppleness of steel, listening to the low talk, with the broad vowels and soft consonants a little like Italian, no doubt contrasted all this with the rowdy good humour of Paris students, the eager chatter and quick gestures of Bologna and Lisbon.

"A samurai must live and die sword in hand"; how much more then the knight-errant of Christ! Francis, naturally so charming and gentle, had been hardened and sharpened like a steel blade in the hands of the swordmaker. He did not fear now to draw his blade, and condemned the vice of the bonzes in no measured terms. No doubt something of his incisiveness disappeared in translation, but enough remained to make his audience realise his horror. Some of the bonzes received his attacks with noncommittal silence, some with shrugs of the shoulder or mocking laughter. A few, interested in the strangeness of his appearance and teaching, embarked on some of those Japanese conversations which seem to flow endlessly on.

With one, the abbot of a Jenzu monastery, he made friends. This was a Buddhist sect whose belief was summarised in the statement: "Nothing exists, all is delusion." This Ninjit was of noble birth, and, like many of the great abbots of the Middle Ages, after having passed his youth and manhood in fighting, had retired from the world in old age. Like many of his fellows he was cynical, but more frank than most. One day when Francis visited his monastery he saw all the bonzes squatting in one of the meditations which took place a hundred times a year. He inquired the subject of the meditation; it was nominally the nothingness of man and all things, and man's ultimate goal, annihilation, Nirvana. "Some are calculating how much they got out of the people last month," replied Ninjit with cynical and amused detachment; "the rest planning how they will dress and amuse themselves."

Francis and the old man had endless discussions about the soul and immortality—endless, because neither understood the other's point of view or used words in the same sense. To the Buddhist the soul or individuality is only a quantity of drifting delusions drawn together by the force of desire as iron filings are attracted by a magnet, to disintegrate and vanish when that centralising force ceases, as the body decays in the grave.

Part of one conversation has been preserved. The two men in their black habits paced perhaps to and fro on the verandah, with its red-lacquered pillars of wood, or walked in the garden, while the pale winter sun shone gently on grey stone and twisted pines, and in the shade the camelia-flowers were red as splashes of blood in the sprinkling of snow. "In which part of your life have you been happiest?" asked Xavier: "your long-dead youth, or your present old age?" "Youth." "Why?" "Because then the body is strong, and one can achieve all one's ambitions." "When seamen sail from port to port, which time seems best to them, the hour in mid-ocean buffeted by every storm, or the moment when they are in sight of home?" There was a silence before the old abbot answered slowly: "I see your meaning, but that is not my case. I know not where my journey will end. For him who knows, to whom the harbour lies open, happiness is there. As for me I know nothing of where or what is my ultimate goal." Few words, but in them sounds all the sadness of paganism, the despair that underlay the splendour and courage of old Greece and Rome, as it underlies the neo-paganism of to-day.

The New Year was past, with its children's festival of toys. February too was gone, with its biting showers from the northern hills, and in March began the spring, with its first exquisite loveliness of the plum-blossom, symbol of selfless humility. April brought the feast of

cherry-blossom, *Sakura,* the soul of Japan and of *Bushido.*
All the world went holiday-making under the rosy mass
of fragile petals flushed like the clouds of dawn. Little
paper butterflies, little pink cakes, lanterns, all were the
shape or colour of the blossom. Pedlars sold twisted papers
which, when burned, revealed their message before crumbling into grey ash: "The cherry-blossom falls when it
must," the samurai saying that when his hour has come
a man should die without fear or regret; or mottoes that
young lovers watched as they flamed and were gone:
"Bitterness endures but for a little while; if you wait, the
dew will taste sweet to you."

The cherry-blossom had gone too, softly as the ending
of those little Japanese poems that hold a world of love
or loneliness in a score of words. The fire of wild azaleas,
rose, gold and flame, that blazed across the hills was dead;
so were the huge black butterflies that had fluttered lover-
like above them; dead too the trails of mauve wistaria, the
battalions of irises, proud as samurai among the grey
sword blades of their leaves. The lotus-buds opened at
dawn on the ponds where the frogs had croaked all night.
The sound wind rose and blew over the hills and beyond
the Inland Sea to Kyoto.

A year had passed since the missionaries had landed in
Japan. Christmas numbered perhaps a hundred—far from
Angero's glowing prophecy of the conversion of the whole
people. There was talk of miracles, a leper healed, a child
raised from the dead, a blind man made to see. "Sorcery!"
cried the bonzes, and they began to come when Francis
preached in the streets, to shout him down: "He is a
devil in human form!"

A sinister rumour crept abroad, probably started by the
indiscreet talk of some half-instructed catechumen, a

rumour old as the earliest Masses in the catacombs: the foreigners were cannibals; blood-stained cloths were found at the door of their house. They were stoned and cursed when they went out; at night stones and lumps of wood or metal crashed through the flimsy walls of their house.

The bonzes requested Shimatsu to expel the *Nambanjin* who were causing such disturbances. The daimio had heard of Francis's visit to Hirado and its daimio. Another Portuguese ship was now in the Hirado harbour. If trade were deflected from his territory there was no longer any point in favouring the foreigners. He issued an edict punishing by death any conversions to the new religion, then courteously offered a junk to further the missionaries on their way to Kyoto. No doubt there was a little smile on his fine-cut lips as he sat among his samurai and thought of the disappointment waiting the priests at the end of the journey. The conventional greeting to a traveller was at any rate to be amply fulfilled: "Honourably tired."

"We left for another part of the country and took leave of the Christians," wrote Francis briefly (Cochin, January 29, 1552): "They bade us good-bye with many tears because of the great affection they had for us, and with much gratitude for the trouble we had taken to teach them how to save their souls."

For ten years war and persecution made it almost impossible for missionaries to revisit Kagoshima; then, in 1560, a Japanese Brother came to the town and Ichicu, and found old Ninjit still abbot and eager for news of Francis, then eight years dead. Even in 1607 Padre Frois, S.J., met a few old people who still remembered Father Francis and fragments of his teaching, but a permanent mission was rendered impossible by the bigotry of daimios and bonzes.

As for Pablo de Santa Fé, once Angero, left by Francis in charge of his little flock, his end was for long wrapt in mystery and edifying stories. According to the most reliable authority, however, that of Luis Frois, he was forced to flee from his home once more, whether from justice or persecution, became a pirate on the Chinese coast, and was finally killed on a raiding expedition. It was a strangely ironic end for one who had been the first Japanese Christian and had been the means of introducing the first Christian missionaries to Japan.

CHAPTER XIX

HIRADO, KYOTO, YAMAGUCHI
(SEPTEMBER, 1550–FEBRUARY, 1551)

SOME time in September, 1550, Francis left Kagoshima, accompanied by his two fellow-Jesuits, a Malabar and a Chinese servant, and Bernard, a relation of Angero's who had been baptised and was to act as interpreter when necessary. After a short stay at Ichicu, Hirado was reached by the end of the month, and again a warm welcome was given by the crew of the Portuguese ship in the harbour and by the daimio. Within a few days about a hundred Japanese were baptised—as many as in a year at Kagoshima—and a small chapel was built by the Portuguese. This success was largely due to João Fernandez, who now spoke Japanese fluently.

Francis, though, regarded Hirado only as a stepping-stone on the way to Kyoto. He had seen enough of the Japanese to know that, humanly speaking, Christianity had little chance of succeeding unless embraced by the nobles. He remarks in a letter that noble blood is the thing held in esteem, not riches. As for the emperor, the Son of Heaven descended from the sun-goddess, whose ancestors had reigned for over two thousand years, Francis did not realise that he was now but a symbol of vanished greatness, an aged and effeminate being who was a prisoner in the ruins of his palace.

At the end of October he left Hirado with Fernandez, Bernard, and another Japanese convert on the journey of five hundred miles or more. Father Cosme de Torres remained in charge of the mission at Hirado, but his superior gave him no letters for despatch to Goa or Europe. Francis had not written to his beloved Father for two years, had not heard from him for four years, and there is no letter written by Francis while in Japan after those from Kagoshima of November 5, 1549, except an Italian copy of the long one of that date. The long silence, though he did not know it, had already been broken. A letter from the General, recalling him to Rome to report fully on the eastern missions, had been at Malacca since the spring, waiting for a vessel to sail to Japan.

Skirting along the north-west coast of Kiusiu, the little band reached a famous monastery of Ninjit's sect. They were well received, for the rumour of strangers from the land of the gods had preceded them. They were brought into the presence of the abbot, where an appetising meal was ready; and Fernandez no doubt looked forward to a good night's board and lodging. Francis, however, hardly waited till the ceremonies of welcome were finished, cast not a glance at the food, but standing before the bonzes uttered a scathing denunciation of their vice, which he had heard was rampant in this particular monastery, and then went on to blame them for their extortion of alms from the poor. There was a general stupefaction. Some broke into laughter. Probably Francis's broken Japanese was baffling enough to their ears, but there was no mistaking the message of his blazing eyes and burning cheeks. He finished his say, turned on his heel and swept out. "We continued our journey," says Fernandez briefly.

As they went the western slopes of the hills were scarlet

with the maples whose leaves fall with the first touch of frost, and drift across the still water like a rush of blood along the steel of a sword-blade. To reach the island of Nippon it was necessary to cross the Inland Sea on a junk. "Pirates swarmed. In order not to be seen we often had to hide in the bottom of the hold. Those five or six days were very hard." (Fernandez.)

At last Yamaguchi was reached, a town of about fifty thousand inhabitants, at that time practically the capital of Japan. Its daimio, Yoshitaka, was one of the most powerful in the empire, with vast territories in Nippon and Kiusiu. At his court were the *kuge,* descendants and relations of the emperor, effete, luxurious, pleasure-loving, despised by the samurai because they preferred poetry and art to the hardships of war. It was against their degeneracy that the Spartan code of *Bushido* was taught. Life at court was a series of fêtes and amusements, drama and recitation, an appreciation of art in all forms, the collecting of paintings, embroideries and exquisitely carved figures in jade and ivory. Bonzes were everywhere. On all sides rose huge temples and monasteries. The air was filled with the silver tinkle of the bells at the corners of the wide, curled eaves, which projected over the red lacquered pillars of the entrances. Beyond the bronze green of giant cryptomerias and the blackness of pines long flights of stone steps led to the temples where Buddhas sat cross-legged with folded hands on the lotus of Enlightenment. Behind rows of torii, granite or painted wood, were Shinto temples, with the stone foxes of *Inari,* the rice-god.

Into this town of luxurious splendour tramped the weary Jesuits and the two Japanese, and, like the travellers at Bethlehem, found "there was no room for them in the inn." Again and again they were turned away, because of their shabbiness and strange looks. Soon they were mobbed in the streets; and when at last they found shelter in a humble inn the curious crowd pushed in to stare.

It is difficult for the European to realise how grotesque he appears in Oriental eyes. A contemporary Japanese painting of Portuguese landing from a ship and a description of their looks shows what a strong physical repugnance the early missionaries had to overcome before they began to preach a belief so strange to their hearers. Their large heads, tall stature, prominent round eyes, red skins, loud voices and vivacious gestures were astounding in Japanese eyes and ears. They were more unpleasant to Japanese noses, for the smell of a European has always revolted the nostrils of a race whose sense of smell is so fine that it can distinguish the most delicate scents. Francis, though, was undaunted. He would go out into the streets, and, in the poorest, most populous quarters, would climb on to the coping of a well or stand at the corner of a square, make the sign of the Cross, and begin to preach. Or he would let Fernandez preach, when he himself had read aloud from the book of doctrine; and he would stand by, lost in prayer.

Idolatry, unnatural vice and infanticide, the great crimes of the country, were singled out for denunciation. Opinion in the audience was divided. Some free spirits, disgusted by the bonzes, agreed with their condemnation. Others laughed, jostled the preachers, and threw things at them, while the children pursued the black bat-like figures, calling them opprobrious names. The better class saw them passing and, ready for a new sensation, called them in. Once in the house Francis wasted no time. He signed himself and began to read. Sometimes one of his listeners was struck by the noble austerity which pierced the awkward language or by the courage of the man himself. Once, when they were laughed at, Francis's hidalgo blood boiled; he bade Fernandez to reply with the same insolent familiarity as had been addressed to them. Another day, as Fernandez was reading the story of the fall of the angels, their host broke into laughter and sneers. "However powerful you may be," said Francis, "if you do not humble yourself and weep for your sins God will cast you too into the torments of hell." The only reply was more laughter and jeers, and the old hot temper flared so that Francis's eyes blazed and his face flushed: "Wish it or not, if you do not humble yourself you will go there!" And he strode out of the house.

These audiences were a sore trial to poor Fernandez. As he read fierce condemnations out of the book the corner of his eye caught the sinister flash of gilded hilts from the two swords tucked conveniently into silken belts. When he was told to answer with the insolence which had angered Francis, he thought the end had come: "Evidently the Father wished at all costs to die for the Faith of Christ! When I answered as he told me I felt that a sword-stroke would sever my head from my body. But all the consolation he got from Francis was: "Before anything else fortify this fear of death. Only by contempt of death can we show ourselves the superiors of this proud people. . . . The disregard of death which our teaching inspires will show them that it is of God."

A noble to whom Francis had an introduction at last arranged an audience with the daimio; Yoshitaka was anxious to see the barbarian who had made his courtiers laugh and was not afraid to rebuke the bonzes to their face, nor to preach to a hostile crowd. Francis did honour to the occasion by putting an old habit over his loba, and, accompanied by Fernandez, was conducted by his introducer through the outskirts of the palace. Verandahs and galleries were crowded by curious *kuge,* rustling with silks and the murmur of soft, mocking voices. Yoshitaka was alone in the hall of audience except for the abbot of one of the principal monasteries. His wide trousers of blue silk and his sandalled feet were hidden by the billowing folds of his green coat, stiff with embroidery and gold. The magnolia-wood sheaths of his swords were finely varnished and lacquered, their hilts were carved jade. Under his high curled black headdress his face, pale with a dust of orris-root, was like a delicate mask of ivory, and the painted fan in his slim fingers looked better suited to them than the swords.

The ceremonial prostrations over, Francis answered a murmured question as to whose ambassadors they were: "The God of heaven and earth." The daimio expressed no surprise but put a few more questions about India and Europe before the crucial one: "What is this new law you have brought to Japan?" At a sign from Francis Fernandez began to read, cheerfully and fluently enough at first; but as he approached the censure of vice he faltered. Another sign told him to proceed, and he read that the man who was the slave of such vice was "filthier than a pig, worse than dogs and other brutes." He cast a hurried glance at the ivory mask and fancied that it had whitened. Already he felt his head roll upon the floor. But the daimio had the imperturbable self-control of his caste. For an hour he listened without word or movement to thought and language which must have been penance to him, then in silence made the gesture of dismissal. The two Jesuits left, Fernandez still uncertain if his head was in place. What the introducer thought we are not told.

Every word had been heard by the thronging courtiers, and as the black-robed figures came out they were surrounded, hustled and abused. In the streets the people shouted after them: *"Deos! Deos!"* Francis had at first used the word *Dainichi* for God, but, discovering it had a material and sometimes evil meaning, substituted for it the Portuguese word. Unfortunately *Dai uso* in Japanese means "great lie," so that the common nickname for the preachers became "Great Lies."

Monasteries, temples, palaces, shops hummed with talk about the audience. Doggedly Francis went on with his morning and afternoon preaching. He and Fernandez endured twice daily the taunts and missiles of the rabble, and the bitter cold—for already the winter had set in with unusual severity. No progress was made, not one converted or baptised. Time was being wasted, so after two months of barren labour Frances, Fernandez, and Bernard set out a week before Christmas on the three-hundred-mile tramp to Kyoto. The Jesuits carried the wallets containing their personal belongings, a surplice, three or four shirts and an old rug. The Mass vestments and vessels had been left at Hirado. Bernard had, hung from his belt, a bag of roasted rice, in case, as often happened, the country inns could supply no food. They went on foot rather than by sea, though the roads were infested by robbers. "A truly brave and confident heart was needed to embark on such an enterprise. Those who knew in what state Japan was then will agree that it was a mark of really heroic and supernatural confidence to penetrate into the interior of the country, to travel in so strange and new a costume, to pass through the samurai of Japan without guide, without hope save in God." (Valignano.)

Everywhere the snow lay deep. Nearly every day more fell. After the scorching heat of the Fishery Coast, the enervating hothouse atmosphere of the Moluccas, Francis needed a body of iron or steel. Another traveller, meeting the three as they struggled knee-deep through the snow, called to them: "Hey! You from the country of the gods, tell them up there to send down a little less snow!"

The rivers, in summer a mere trickle along their wide, pebbly beds, were now raging torrents, which the companions had continually to ford, waist-deep in icy water. Francis's old shoes disappeared, fallen to pieces or washed away in a ford. He went barefooted, feet and ankles raw and swollen with chilblains, bleeding from stones and thorns. The few inns were filthy, as they still are in remote parts of the country, "like stables," says Fernandez. The bitter wind came in through holes in the flimsy walls and paper screens. The household huddled round the charcoal fire in a hollow of the floor, lying like a starfish so that at any rate their feet were warm against the bamboo grating that covered the ashes. The travellers were lucky if they managed to push in near enough to feel a little warmth, and got stinking soup and boiled rice for supper. Often their only meal was a handful of rice from Bernard's bag. In vain Fernandez and Bernard tried to thaw themselves by lying on the rice matting and putting the filthy *futons* over themselves. Fernandez would wake shivering to find that Francis had covered him and Bernard with the rug and his own mattress. They did not know the country, so continually lost their way, and had to scramble to the top of a hill to regain their direction. If a pedlar was going their way they would thankfully follow him. The main roads were crowded with troops, so it was wiser to avoid them.

It was just fifteen years since Francis and his nine companions had made such another winter journey from Paris to Venice, "clothed in coarse and old habits, everyone with a staff in his hand," avoiding bands of soldiers, losing their way, scrambling over rocks and through snow.

"All the passes are full of snow . . .
  I am not afraid of the snow and darkness,
  My beloved, for you I would pass through night and day."

Did the memory of the Basque song echo in Francis's ears? Did Peter Faber walk beside him through the snow as the angel went beside Tobias—under the pines bent with their load of snow and the maples whose flame had vanished like the rosy clouds of cherry-blossom?

Fernandez's vivid pen gives a sketch of Francis during these days: "To have any idea of what he endured it is necessary to have seen him as I did. Everything breathed penance, even his prayer as he went. Meditation and contemplation were habitual with him. There was nothing to be seen but snow on mountains and valleys, nothing round us to distract him. And all the time as he prayed Father Francis never lifted his eyes or looked from side to side. His hands and arms were still; only his feet moved, and very quietly. Certainly he showed by the modesty and reverence of his gait that he walked in the presence of God." Fernandez notes that Bernard, young and inured to hardship, bore all with true Japanese stoicism. Of his own physical misery he says nothing. The elegance of the delicately clothed and nurtured young worldling had been replaced by a noble and selfless courage which, however, left room for humour and observation.

Francis's own account is as brief as usual when he speaks of what he himself endured: "We experienced great wearinesses and many dangers because of the wars which disturbed the country we went through, to say nothing of the great cold and the many robbers who infested the roads."

At one point they boarded a junk bound for Osaka. It was crowded with passengers, so that there was no room except to squat on the high stern, exposed to the bitter wind, or to crouch in the filth of the hold. One day by mistake Francis occupied a corner reserved by a man who poured a torrent of abuse on him. His only answer was a long look of sad reproach. A young merchant fixed on him as a butt for coarse and brutal jokes. After long endurance Francis broke silence to say: "Why do you treat me like this? Know that I love you and desire nothing more than to show you the way of salvation"—words received with more laughter and jests.

At one landing-place a samurai who saw and spoke to them gave them an introduction to a friend in Osaka, which they reached at last. The snow had turned to unceasing rain. The beauty of the sheltered bay, the island of Awaji, one of the loveliest in Japan, the three-storeyed pagoda which dominated the huddle of curved roofs, all were blurred by the grey veil of rain. To and fro went the three through the muddy streets, drenched habits clinging to frozen limbs. No one would take them in. Nowhere could they find the man to whom their letter was addressed. Stoned by children, at last they left the town in despair and rigged up a rough shelter of pine-branches in a little wood. It was inadequate enough, and Francis was beginning to burn and shiver with fever. Fernandez was distracted. Francis said little: "Only one thing grieves me, that we cannot preach." Ultimately they found the house and were hospitably received. None too soon, for Francis went down with a violent attack of fever. It was sharp but short, and he was no sooner on his feet again than he went out and began his catechism.

Their host did all he could to further their journey to Kyoto. He was probably anxious to see the last of guests who might easily bring trouble as well as ridicule upon him. At length a samurai was found who gave permission for the three to join his train of servants on the way to the capital. So Francis and Fernandez, with Bernard, had to trot with porters, archers, and valets after the samurai and his mounted friends. How the little Japanese, hard and wiry, running light-footed and untiring through the mud, must have mocked the tall, awkward barbarians, stumbling along on swollen feet and ankles, sometimes even falling by the way. At night they were made to groom the mounts, fiery little beasts, with small heads and thick necks and as great endurance as their masters.

Suddenly, as they approached Kyoto, with the unexpectedness of a burst of sunshine through the clouds, Francis regained the youth and gaiety which had seemed to have left him for ever. "Never have I seen him so gay," wrote Fernandez gladly. Bernard elaborates the picture: "Sometimes he jumped and gaily threw into the air an apple, then caught it again, his face wet with tears of joy." The Basque in him had revived. Those poor, bruised feet were light as the feet of the *danza tchikiaki* in the intricate entrechats of the sword-dances of Corpus Christi. He played with the apple as he had once flung and caught the ball at pelota.

Kyoto lay before them, pagoda and monastery towers rising like great rocks from a sea of black roofs. On three sides the snow mountains gleamed under the winter sky as they entered through the city gate of grey stone. The streets, like those of a Roman camp, ran in straight lines, intersecting each other at right angles, but their symmetry was marred by the charred ruins of burnt houses and temples. It was a city where desolation and debauch jostled each other. The famous temple of Hongwanji was a heap of ashes. So deep was the veneration of the people for this national shrine that when it was rebuilt the women gave their hair to weave the ropes to hoist the new roof-beams into position. Pillaged and ruined palaces, monasteries fortified to almost impregnable strength, shops sacked of their merchandise, alternated with little houses whose insignificance had saved them, and the warren of the *kuruwa*, where women sat at the windows, motionless as painted idols in their scarlet kimonos. Samurai in full armour clattered through the deserted streets, their faces half hidden by the visors of their horned helmets, the stiff plates of steel damascened with gold changing them from human semblance to the grotesque fierceness of demons of war. Round them rode their following of lesser samurai; after them trotted the soldiers, armed with lances, and bows and arrows.

The friend to whom the host of Osaka had recommended the Jesuits was equally anxious to be quit of them. He sent them to his son-in-law fifty miles away, who sent them back as promptly. The children in the streets mobbed them with jeers of: *"Dai uso!"* and: *"Ijin!"* Their shrill mockery mingled with the ceaseless clang of temple bells, the clash of steel, the groans of wounded men, the screams of dying horses as armed bonzes descended to join in fights between rival clans.

Francis wandered from one place to another in the

attempt to arrange an interview with the "king." He and
Fernandez reached the *Gosho*—palace, park, temple and
fortress—which occupied the whole north-east quarter of
the city. The broken walls of the palace were open to robbers, and through their breaches the half-starved wives of
the emperor haggled with pedlars for a meal of sweet
potatoes. The *kuge,* with their silken robes and painted
faces, had long fled, like a flock of gaudy birds before the
wind of winter; but still the Son of Heaven remained,
surrounded like an idol by intricate ritual. Every morning his wives washed his old body, decked it in new robes,
scented and incensed it. Every vessel he had used was
burnt or destroyed so that it might not be contaminated
by a common touch. He was borne from room to room
in a palanquin so that his sacred feet should not be defiled
by contact with the earth. The water in which those feet
had been washed was holy. One day a little was brought
to the house where Francis was staying and offered to
him after those present had sprinkled their heads with it.
With a little smile he put the basin aside in silence.

With Fernandez he wandered round the palace, tried to
force an entrance, but the guards maintained contemptuous
silence or asked: "Where are your presents?" His thoughts
turned then to the Shogun, whose family had held sway
for three hundred years, while the emperor had been only
a shadow. But the Shogun, a boy of fifteen and a helpless
tool in the hands of the daimios, had fled from the smoking ruins of his palace and from Kyoto. Another authority might prove more hopeful, the abbot of the famous
monastery and university. Francis found that, in revenge
for the warlike bonzes having sacked and burnt half the
town, the Myoshi clan had burnt the monastery and
massacred the monks.

Preaching in the streets met with no response but abuse, stones and beating with sticks. Eleven days went by. Useless to waste more precious time among ruins and war. But the experience was not wasted. Francis had learnt two lessons—that Emperor and Shogun were empty titles while the real power was in the daimios' hands, and that poverty and humility were not the right methods of approach to "this proud people." With his two companions he boarded a junk bound for Osaka. As long as Kyoto was in sight he stood on the stern looking back and murmuring: "When Israel went out of Egypt. . . . They have eyes and see not, mouths and speak not, ears have they and hear not."

The return journey to Hirado was as hard as that coming to Kyoto. The February wind blew icy from the northern snows. The travellers crouched in the hold, sick and stiff with cold. The last part of the journey was by land. Francis spent the little money left on dried fruits, which he stowed in his pocket or the sleeve of his habit. When they reached a village he would gaily call the children, bribe their shyness with the fruit, and, when they clustered about him, would give them his blessing.

CHAPTER XX

YAMAGUCHI, BUNGO, DEPARTURE FROM JAPAN
FEBRUARY, 1551–NOVEMBER, 1551

FRANCIS's safe return in February, 1551, after an absence of over three months, was a great relief to Father de Torres at Hirado: "You can imagine what suffering my separation from Father Master Francis caused me as well as the thought of the dangers and hardships endured by him and his companions. . . . Neither cold nor snow nor fear of penetrating into the midst of unknown peoples could stop Father Francis, so keen is the fire of the love of God and the zeal for souls which burns in his breast." So wrote de Torres a few months later.

To Francis the greatest joy of his return must have been that he was able again to say Mass, after so long a deprivation. He found the Portuguese gone, but the little Japanese congregation had increased. Father Cosme had converted the owner of the house in which he lodged, as well as all his family. A few of the better class had also been baptised.

The missionaries had now been in Japan for eighteen months. A hundred or more Christians had been left in Kagoshima, a little over a hundred won in Hirado. Francis's arduous journeys and efforts of the past four months had brought no tangible results, but he had learnt his mistakes and was determined not to repeat them. However admirable poverty and humility were as virtues of the religious life, shabbiness and meekness were the last qualities to impress the proud, practical, independent Japanese. He resolved to return to Yamaguchi, no longer as a wandering preacher whose strange appearance brought ridicule on the Faith he taught as well as on himself, but as the accredited ambassador of the mighty King of Portugal. The worn-out loba was replaced by a "court-like habit." A junk was chartered and laden with Mass vessels, vestments, wine, and the presents provided in Goa, as well as the parchments on which were inscribed the letters of recommendation signed by the Viceroy and the bishop.

Torsellini tells us that, before starting on this fresh adventure, Francis renewed his vows: "He used this custom oftentimes by himself with great fervour, finding by experience that by often renewing his vows he found his vigour and strength of mind again renewed like the strength of an eagle." Indeed the gaiety which Fernandez and Bernard had noticed at the approach to Kyoto seem to have marked the lifting of that dark shadow which had fallen during the night of struggle on the pirate's junk. In his bitter denunciations of the bonzes and of Yoshitaka there had been something dark and hard, such as had not been caused before by all the disappointments he had had to endure. The children, who had run to him and clung about him in India and Malacca, had jeered at him and stoned him. He who had always been radiant-faced, with eyes lifted to heaven, the breast of his loba torn open to cool the burning of love in his heart, had gone along the *via dolorosa* to Kyoto with eyes downcast, head bent, his hands motionless in the sleeves of his habit.

All this year and a half in Japan there had been "that

deep anxiety which weighs on me without ceasing" about Gomez and affairs at Goa. There had been that strange, long silence on the part of his dear Father for which he knew no reason, unless it were displeasure with his own methods, criticised by so-called friends in letters home. That anxiety was not relieved. That silence was not broken. But the shadow had gone, that shadow which had been like a veil between him and the divine brightness.

Only a few days were spent at Hirado in preparations, then Francis started again, with Fernandez, Bernard, and Matthew, another Japanese Christian. This time Yamaguchi was reached without adventure.

Yoshitaka bore Francis no resentment. It was a new sensation to welcome as a royal ambassador the tattered wanderer who had not been afraid to denounce him to his face. Graciously the daimio accepted the incomprehensible parchments and the presents which included a clock, a kind of musical-box, some cannon, a piece of brocade, crystal flagons, mirrors, spectacles, and a Portuguese costume. Japanese chroniclers have related the marvels of the clock, "which rang exactly twelve times in the day and twelve in the night, a musical instrument which played of itself, and glasses for the eyes which enabled an old man to see as clearly as a young one."

With his acknowledgements Yoshitaka sent handsome gifts and a large sum in gold. "We sent them back to him and said that we only desired one thing, leave to preach the law of God and liberty of conscience for his subjects." The daimio was so much struck by the contrast between Francis's disinterestedness and the greed of the bonzes that he granted the Jesuits an audience that very day and himself gave them leave to preach. Nor did the matter end there, for notices were posted in the town announcing permission for the foreign bonzes to preach and for Japanese to accept the new faith. A deserted monastery was assigned to Francis, and the Sacrifice of the Mass was now offered in the temple that had housed Buddha and the innumerable little gods who sheltered in his shadow. The former worshippers, country folk and poor townspeople, no doubt still frequented the shrine, prostrated themselves at the foot of the stone steps and left their humble offerings on the verandah, as Bellesort says they did a few years ago in the little temple in Yamaguchi which had been handed over to the Catholic missionary.

Francis began to preach again, sitting on the parapet of the well in the Street of the Nobles. From dawn till late at night his lodging, in the house of a samurai, was besieged. Bonzes, samurai, Buddhist nuns, rich and poor, all came. There was a ceaseless flow of questions and objections. The old Paris days seemed to have returned when, as Ribadeneira says, "one discusses before dinner, during dinner, after dinner, in public, in private, everywhere." Now indeed Francis's university training was to stand him in good stead, for his questioners were no longer ignorant Parava fishermen nor Moslems who knew little of their own religion, but minds formed, as his own had been, in universities, or in the famous monastery schools.

Fernandez has kept a list of questions (without him our knowledge of the two years in Japan would have been sadly small), some profound, some curiously naïve: "From what matter, it was asked, does God make the soul? What is its shape, form and colour? What is the nature of God? Does the soul see God when it leaves the body? Then why not now? How is it that the soul, if it is not the body, is not God Himself? What are the devils? How do you reconcile their existence and the evil they do to men with the goodness of God? The same difficulty about man's natural inclination to evil. Why is the road to heaven so hard? . . . What becomes of men not intelligent enough to know God?"

"Curious and questioning to the point of importunity, anxious for knowledge, they never finish asking questions and elaborating our answers. They know nothing of the shape of the earth and the course of the sun. They question us about comets, lightning, rain, snow, and other phenomena. Our answers delight them. They take us for deeply learned men, which adds value to our teaching."

Francis by implication describes his own life at Yamaguchi when he warns Ignatius what the Jesuits who come to Japan must expect: "They will be worried by visits and questions at all hours of the day and part of the night, called to the homes of the principal men of the country, for we cannot escape it. They will have no time for prayer, meditation or contemplation, nor any spiritual recollection. They will not be able to say Mass, at least not at first. They will be endlessly busy answering questions. There will be no time to say Office, nor even to eat and sleep" (Cochin, January 29, 1552).

He had learnt the chief doctrine of Buddhism (that all is delusion and nothingness), and its results. When all is a dream, man himself only a dream within a dream, then the end is despair. But apart from this esoteric doctrine was the exoteric one taught to the people—heaven and hell, one to be won, the other escaped, by help of the bonzes, who, alone able to observe the commandments, must be paid by the people for their help. Francis had never been afraid to tear the veil from the lives of the majority of the bonzes, to expose their vice, their avarice, their self-indulgence and their quarrelsomeness. The pupils of the monastery schools began to desert them for this new teacher. "There is none among the heathen peoples I have seen," Francis wrote, "who will listen to reason more easily than the Japanese." His exposition of the Faith, the creation of the world and of each individual soul, redemption and judgment, by its unanswerable logic convinced many hearers. Conversions began, but slowly. There was at first none of that success which has swept the Fishery coast like a forest fire, but the saint saw that the national qualities of courage and loyalty to an ideal would conduce to perseverance, even under persecution: "Those converted showed us great respect and affection. I think they will prove true Christians."

One of the new converts was a learned man who had studied at the university of Bandu with the intention of becoming a bonze, but, losing his belief in Buddhism, had remained a layman and married. Another was a strange contrast to him, a one-eyed street singer and story-teller gifted with a quick wit and good memory. He heard the saint preach, visited and questioned him, and was so struck by his charity, zeal and selflessness, that he accepted the Faith. Baptised Lawrence, he was afterwards received into the Society by Cosme de Torres and became the first Japanese Jesuit.

The months passed. September was here again. Francis had been over two years in Japan. The short-lived beauty of the blossom, the Morning Glory which blooms at dawn and fades at noon, all was a symbol of the swift passing of life, the transience of all earthly things. One wonders if Francis, with his vision out of time, knew that in a little more than a year his body would be lying in the

quicklime at Sanchian. So much was still to do; time
was so short in which to plan and perform.

The Christians in Yamaguchi now numbered about five
hundred. His work there was finished. He had opened
up the field for those he had summoned in his letters of
two years ago. He began to cast round for some new
country to conquer for Christ. He knew that the religion,
letters, art, poetry, and social system of Japan were all
derived from China. He was accustomed to the objection
that his law could not be true because the Chinese sages
had not heard of it. His thoughts returned to his first
visit to Malacca, his long talks with the merchants who
had traded with China and knew something of its people.
The folly of a marauding Portuguese admiral had closed
China against the foreign devils, and isolated the town of
Macao, which was now cut off from the mainland by a
huge wall. Yet somehow or other, if God willed, he
would manage to enter the forbidden land and by con-
verting its emperor and people would make the conversion
of Japan more swift and certain. "China is an immense
and peaceful land. War is unknown there. . . . The
Chinese I have met in Japan and elsewhere are refined,
much more industrious than the Japanese who work.
Their country is rich in every product. There are great
cities with well-built stone houses. From what one hears
its greatest riches are silk."

At the end of August a rumour had reached Yamaguchi
that a Portuguese ship was in the port of Figi, on the
south coast of the Inland Sea which divides Nippon from
Kiusiu. Matthew was sent to find out the truth of this tale
and before long returned to say that not only was the
ship there but that its captain, Duarte da Gama, an old
friend of Francis's, had spoken to the daimio of Bungo in

his favour. Matthew brought a letter from the daimio, inviting the missionary and promising him an honourable welcome.

There were other letters, sent on from Goa and Malacca, including two from Ignatius. The first was the one already mentioned—two and a half years old now—recalling Francis, but it was superseded by another (October 10, 1549), appointing him Provincial of the newly-constituted province of the Society in the East Indies.

It was laid down that, in case of the absence of the Provincial, the rector of the college at Goa should act as vice-Provincial. That rector was still Antonio Gomez, and the report from Goa proved how well justified had been Francis's anxiety about the state of affairs there. Deaf to advice, Gomez had been dismissing the native students in large numbers and replacing them by Portuguese hardly able to read or write. A number of these had already been ordained, and it was the rector's aim to get rid of the remaining native students and so destroy the object with which the college had originally been founded. There was obviously urgent need for the Provincial's presence in Goa, so he summoned Cosme de Torres from Hirado and left him with Fernandez in charge of the Yamaguchi mission.

One of the Japanese converts has given an account of the last meeting and Francis's words of farewell to his children: "In this present life you will always have to endure troubles, persecutions and dangers. It is the surest way to heaven. I leave you Father Cosme de Torres and Brother Fernandez as your good guardians. They will help and instruct you, but learn to put your whole trust in God alone." The tears pouring down his face, he lovingly and lingeringly embraced his fellow Jesuits, with words prophetic of trouble: "I recommend you all to God our Lord, now more than ever. He will give you all the strength you will need. He will know how to defend you." There was another of those heart-breaking good-byes, his bereaved children lamenting till he could hardly tear himself from them. He took with him only two samurai who had been baptised a couple of months before. No one but himself was allowed to carry the heavy bundle containing the Mass vessels and the vestments of brocade, which had so struck Yoshitaka with admiration that he had told Francis he looked like a god in them. He had no longer the strength to walk as in old days, and it took two days to reach the port where the junk from Bungo was waiting. His feet, which had never recovered from the walk to Kyoto, could hardly support him. It was a short crossing to the harbour where the Portuguese ship was lying, but when he landed he was suffering from fever and a blinding headache, so the salvo of artillery with which the crew greeted him can hardly have been an appropriate welcome.

In a short while he was recovered enough to hear the news from Goa and Malacca, for he had been entirely cut off since he had left Goa in Holy Week, 1549. He heard the details of Antonio Criminale's martyrdom, of which he had apparently known by no natural means. He heard too of the baptism of the Japanese who had left Kago-shima with him. In Ormuz Gaspar Barzee's work among Christians, Moslems, Jews and heathen had been crowned with wonderful success. The old viceroy, Garcia de Sa, was dead and had been succeeded by Jorge Cabral.

Francis began his apostolic work among the merchants and crew of the ship even before the day appointed for his audience with the daimio. The Portuguese were only too willing to help to make his appearance before the ruler as splendid as possible. Such splendour would heighten their own value, but there was something better in their willingness than calculating greed, for Francis once more had won all hearts.

Among those on board was Mendez Pinto, author of a book of travels bristling with inaccuracies but racy and full of colour. His account of the reception, that of an eye-witness, may need to be taken with a large pinch of salt, but it is the only one we have, except for a few words of Valignano's and a bald sentence in a letter of Francis: "The duke received me very well and the Portuguese cared for me greatly."

The ship was dressed. The boats in which the company rowed ashore were gay with flags and silks, the Portu-guese decked in their best—small feathered hats, starched ruffs, and, under their short coats of silk, red trousers that ballooned above their high boots. They were a strange sight for the crowds that lined the landing and the streets. They marched to the music of drums and fifes. Francis refused to use the magnificent gilt and lacquered litter that was waiting for him, and walked through the town. "He had put on a very fair gown," says Torsellini, who had seen Pinto's manuscript, "over which he wore a fine linen surplice; and about his neck there hung a priest's stole of green silk grogan down to his knees, with a fringe of gold." He was followed by the smartest of the young Portuguese with his breviary in a silk bag, others carrying ceremonial slippers of velvet and a parasol, last of all a picture of our Lady, borne under a canopy of crimson damask, guarded by the rest of the Portuguese, marching in square formation.

No doubt Pinto's imagination is responsible for the

well-turned speeches of welcome on arrival at the palace:
"Your arrival is as dear and pleasing to the King as
summer rain to a thirsty field of corn," and other compliments. The daimio, a young man of twenty, received
the missionary most graciously and invited him to dine,
an offer which was refused, though scarcely for Torsellini's reason—that he was "not acquainted with Japanese
dainties." Francis had had many chances of acquainting
himself with Japanese food and drink, both equally distasteful to the European palate, except *saké,* the rice-wine
which at its best faintly resembles a slightly acid sherry.
The refusal may have been due to the need of keeping a
certain distance or to knowledge of local rumours that the
daimio had reached his present position only by the
assassination of his father, mother and small brother.
Anyhow the result of the interview was all that Francis
had hoped—leave to preach and convert. He began work
in the town with such energy that the Portuguese grumbled
that he left himself no time to eat, sleep or attend to them.

It was probably here that one Sunday, after Francis had
finished preaching, a well-known merchant, who had been
blind for years, pushed his way through the crowd and
asked to be healed. The saint prayed and made the sign
of the Cross over him. The blind man saw, returned next
day to give thanks, and was baptised with his wife, family, and friends. "I know that, because I was there and
saw it with my own eyes," was the testimony given at the
process of 1616.

All was quiet at Bungo, but at the end of October the
servant whom Francis had sent with letters to Yamaguchi
returned with the news of a revolution which had broken
out there a month before. Yoshitaka, forced to flee, had
avoided capture only by hara-kiri, and the two Jesuits

had escaped almost miraculously thanks to a hiding-place provided by a friendly, though unconverted, samurai. "If things quieten down," wrote de Torres to Francis: "we will try to get the new rulers to confirm the concessions of the late King. If they refuse I will return to Thomas [his host at Hirado] till there is a new king. After that if we are forbidden to preach in public we shall preach secretly and, I believe, shall still make converts."

The mantle of Francis had certainly fallen on the Valencian priests, and when he died, in 1570, the church in Japan numbered thirty thousand souls. But it was even more to Fernandez that Japanese Christianity was due after Francis's departure. The Vice-Provincial, Nunez, wrote a glowing eulogy of him to the General, adding, after a list of his virtues: "It is he above all who helps on the progress of the Gospel. First there is the good example of his humble and mortified life. . . . He has all their manners and gestures, those of the most ceremonious people I have ever seen. . . . Father Cosme de Torres assures me that without him nothing would be done in Japan." He composed the first Japanese grammar and dictionary, and the language became so much his own that it was in Japanese that he invoked Jesus and Mary in his last agony, 1567.

Meantime the situation at Yamaguchi improved. The new ruler was a brother of the Bungo daimio and granted liberty of propaganda to the missionaries. At Bungo the number of converts seems to have been small. The daimio showed no signs of becoming a Christian, and the bonzes began to stir up strife. One in particular had been present at the reception and, according to Pinto, had been dismissed for his insults and interruptions. War was now openly declared and, in Torsellini's words, the bonzes paraded the streets calling Francis "a foul, stinking dog, the most beggarly fellow alive, and a devourer of dead men's carcasses"—the old, horrible calumny. Pinto too gives an exciting but incredible story of a great argument between Francis and the bonzes which lasted five days, with the daimio as referee! On one occasion Duarte went ashore in a small boat to bring Francis back to safety on the ship and found him instructing a catechumen in a poor house. He told him his life would be forfeit if he did not escape at once. The answer was typical: "I for my part know well I am not worthy of so great an honour."

The ship was to sail in November, and Francis determined to go on board. His presence was urgently needed in India, and the missions at Hirado and Yamaguchi were in good hands. The results of two years and three months' apostolate had not been what Angero's optimism had led him to expect. All told, the Christians in Japan numbered between fifteen hundred and two thousand—about a thousand at Yamaguchi, a few hundreds at Bungo and Hirado, the little group at Ichicu, and less than two hundred at Kagoshima. Through the varying fortunes to come the loyalty and courage of his Japanese children were splendidly to justify Francis's belief in them. Priests and laymen remained faithful through the most ghastly tortures and horrible deaths. In 1643 the last European Jesuit to land was burnt alive, yet for over two centuries the Christians of Japan, cut off from all communication with the world, deprived of all human teaching, kept the Faith alive, and supplied the Church with one of the most wonderful pages of her history.

What were Francis's thoughts as, in mid-November, 1551, the ship of Duarte da Gama steered slowly through the myriad rocky, wooded islands of the Inland Sea?

Nothing that he had planned had been accomplished in Japan. He had been buried in a remote corner for over a year, had failed to see the emperor or make a single convert in the capital, had never penetrated to any of the universities, left behind him less than two thousand converts. He has told us himself how little this apparent failure discouraged him; how he saw, beyond the present, the rich harvest waiting the reapers.

"The fatigues of working among intelligent people, anxious to learn in what religion they would best save their souls, bring with them immense satisfaction. . . . The number of people who came to question and discuss was such that I can truly say that never in my life had I so much spiritual joy and consolation. . . . I end without being able to end, for I am writing to my fathers and brothers whom I love so much. More, because I write about the Christians of Japan who are so very dear to me." (To the Fathers in Europe, Cochin, January 29, 1552.)

CHAPTER XXI

MALACCA, COCHIN, GOA
(NOVEMBER, 1551–APRIL, 1552)

THE days slipped by as Duarte da Gama's ship sped westward. There was time for "prayer, meditation, contemplation, spiritual recollection," even to say Office. It was strangely peaceful without those crowds of eager Japanese with their endless questions and arguments. As Francis looked astern over a sea that was iridescent with blue, green, and gold like the peacocks of Meliapor, he remembered some of those inexplicable incidents that Bernard has recorded: "Father Master Francis asked the heathen who visited him to question him as they would. There were ten or twelve there, each one presenting his objection. With one answer the Father answered all. . . . That did not happen once only but continually. Without doubt it was a special gift of God." The gift of languages had not been granted to him in Japan. To the end of his time there it was a painful struggle for him to express himself in Japanese, yet God had spoken through him, not by the cramping medium of words but direct to the hearts and minds of his listeners.

About two-thirds of the way to China the wind rose to gale force. The hawser which made the ship's boat fast snapped, and the boat, with men in her, vanished in the raging sea. Duarte, considering it impossible for so small a boat to survive, determined to abandon her and to run

279

before the wind, which was the only chance of saving his ship. Francis begged him to wait, promised the return of the boat: "The daughter will return to her mother." In deference to his wishes the lateen sails were lowered and they tried to put the ship about. Duarte, however, refused to take the risk and ordered the sails to be hoisted again. Francis ran forward and held the main-yard so that it was impossible to hoist it without forcing him away. He ordered a man to the look-out. Nothing was to be seen but mountainous waves. For two hours then, says a member of the crew, the ship ran before the wind. At the end of that time Francis came out of his cabin, promised a Mass for the boat and two for the crew, and went to the gunwale, saying the boat would soon be back. Suddenly, through wind and waves, she appeared, reached the side of the ship, and lay there till the men were safely on board. Pinto adds a vivid touch to the narrative which is not found in the testimony of the three eye-witnesses nor in the Bull of Canonisation. After the men had climbed on board others were preparing to hoist the boat on deck. "Give a hand to Father Francis who is still in the boat," cried the rescued men. Nothing would persuade them that he had not been with them all the time, cheering, comforting and directing them till their safe return. With them in thought and prayer, he might well have seemed present to eyes and ears.

At the beginning of December the ship anchored in the sheltered bay of Sanchian. There they found the Santa Cruz, a ship belonging to Diogo Pereira, a friend of Francis's since the first visit to Malacca in 1545. Diogo was only waiting for a favourable wind to sail for Malacca, and Francis, who had expected to have to spend the winter at Sanchian, eagerly accepted the chance of a passage.

Hardly was he on board the Santa Cruz than the wind changed and they were able to sail.

During the voyage Francis questioned Diogo about China and heard that some Portuguese, imprisoned in Canton for three years for an attempt to enter China, had managed to smuggle a letter to Diogo. They declared that the only possibility of their own escape, and for permission to be gained to enter the country, was for the Viceroy to send an ambassador to the Emperor at Pekin. Francis listened eagerly, elaborated the plan, and settled all details. Pereira should be the ambassador, laden with gifts from the Viceroy, de Noronha. He himself would accompany the embassy, obtain from the Emperor permission to preach the Gospel, the repeal of the edict against foreigners, and the release of the tortured men in Canton. Undaunted by his failure to realise his dreams in Japan, he was now full of hopes. There was at least this justification for them. Japan was rent by civil war, Emperor and Shogun powerless. China was a vast empire, under a strong government and one ruler. He had no idea of its vastness, those hundreds of thousands of square miles which stretched from the Pacific Ocean to the northern frontiers of India, from the tropical coast of Tonkin to the steppes of Siberia.

Pereira cordially endorsed the Padre's plans. At once on arrival at Malacca he would order a large cargo of merchandise and himself pay all the expenses of the embassy. Francis's part was to obtain the Viceroy's consent and letters from him to the Emperor. Then a shadow darkened Francis's glorious vision of the future: "You will see that the devil will prevent everything." At last Diogo grew angry at the oft-repeated words of ill omen. "You will see," was the only answer to his arguments.

The weather was perfect as they sailed through the South China Sea. East, beyond the mountains of Borneo, lay the Moluccas, where Father Beira was working, and Seram, in whose stormy seas had been lost the crucifix that now hung again round Francis's neck, with a copy of his vows and Ignatius's signature. And, still to-day, the little crabs of the East Indies walk the sands with a sea-anemone in each claw as if in memory of the ancestor who had rescued the crucifix and laid it safely at the saint's feet. Near the Straits of Singapore another gale got up and Diogo feared his ship was lost. "Thank God, Señor Diogo," said Francis quietly in the worst of the storm, "for having been kinder to us than we deserve. Please heaven the ship that left Sanchian before us may be as lucky. Before long we shall see proofs of her disaster. As for your Santa Cruz, be at peace. She will moulder away where she was built." Then, with a smile, to the terrified pilot: "Be glad and of good courage. You will not die at sea but in your bed." All three prophecies were fulfilled. In Japan Francis on one occasion had turned to his companions with the unexpected words: "Pray for our brethren in Malacca, for the town is besieged and in sore straits." His second sight had been verified at Sanchian, where it was known that Malacca was indeed besieged by its old enemy, the Sultan of Bintang and his allies from Java and Sumatra. So now as the Santa Cruz crept up the straits, on the look-out for Achinese pirates, all were anxious as to what state of things they would find at Malacca. Francis again reassured them and promised those who, like him, wished to hurry on to India, that a ship was in Malacca waiting for them. "It was so," deposed the owner quaintly; "my vessel was kept there only by her anchor. I had only to hoist anchor and sails when suddenly a little boat brought me the Father's letter, saying he knew I was at Malacca and begging me to wait to take him on to India. At the same time I sighted his ship and waited gladly." A short note to the Fathers in India, warning them of his return, was written by Francis from the Straits of Singapore at the same time as the letter to the owner of the ship.

Malacca was a scene of desolation, though the siege had been raised after three and a half months. The native quarter and the Portuguese town had been burned. Only about a third of the Portuguese had been able to find shelter in the fort. Wells had been poisoned, and pestilence was raging. Still good Father Perez went on with his work, and his school, with four hundred scholars, was under the patronage of the captain.

Don Pedro met Francis, accompanied by his brother, Don Alvaro, who had come out to succeed him. Francis and Don Alvaro had already met at Mozambique where they had arrived together in 1541 and where Alvaro had been imprisoned by Martin de Sousa. Both brothers were enthusiastic in their approval of the Chinese plan. Diego gave Francis thirty thousand *cruzadoes* (a cruzado was worth about eight shillings) to invest in merchandise at Goa—a generosity rewarded by the cure of his child, who was epileptic. After a stay of only two days at Malacca Francis sailed on the Gallega, the ship which had brought out Gomez three and a half years before.

Father Perez had handed over a bundle of letters from India and Europe. Among the latter was one from Ignatius, now lost, of which we only know from Francis's answer, written a few days after his arrival in Cochin (January 24, 1552). In his letter Ignatius, usually so reserved, relaxed something of his self-control and, for a moment, revealed his heart to the beloved son on whom he had placed such a heavy burden. In his reply Francis poured out his joy at this intimate communication, and expressed the love which twelve years of absence and four years of silence had only deepened and strengthened.

"My true Father, I received a letter from your holy charity at Malacca when I returned from Japan. God our Lord knows how cheered was my soul to have news of a health and life so dear to me. Among many other holy words and comforts of your letter I read the last words: 'All thine, and I can never forget thee. Ignatio.' As I read these words with tears, so I write them with tears, as I remember past days and the great love that you had always and still have for me. I consider too how God our Lord delivered me from so many dangers and trials in Japan by the help of your holy prayers.

"Never shall I be able to describe what I owe to the Japanese, for God our Lord gave me, for their good, a deep knowledge of my infinite shortcomings. In truth I lived so little in myself that I did not know my own miserable state till I found myself in the midst of the trials and perils of Japan. God made me see clearly that I was in dire need of someone to care greatly for me. You see now what a burden you are laying on me by putting in my charge so many holy members of the Company out here—I who am so convinced, by God's mercy alone, of my own weakness. I had hoped, on the contrary, that you would have commended me to those of the Company, not them to me.

"Your holy charity writes to me of the great desire you have to see me again before ending this life. God our Lord knows what a deep impression these words of so great a love have made on my soul, and how many tears they cost me daily as I remember them. I have great joy in thinking that this may be possible, for nothing is impossible to holy obedience."

The letter continues with an account of the Japanese, advice that missionaries should be seen by the General at Rome before being sent to India, a description of China and the Chinese and his hope to go to China that year. There is too an urgent demand for a new rector: "If I were in your presence I should beg it of you throwing myself on my knees at your holy feet" (Cochin, January 29, 1552).

By the same ship went a letter to Simon Rodriguez—begging him to pick carefully the men for Japan: young enough to stand physical hardships but old enough to have gained experience—and the long account of the Japanese mission for the Fathers in Europe. This is the last of those annual budgets which are such a splendid prologue to the history of the eastern missions. This great letter of January 20 (from which many quotations have already been made), opens with a long description of the Japanese people and their customs and religion, then goes on to relate the work and journeys at Kagoshima, Hirado, Yamaguchi and Bungo, and Francis's future plans for the journey to China.

"I am already quite white-haired, but as regards bodily strength it seems to me that I was never better than at present. . . . As I arrived at Cochin just when the fleet was sailing, and as the visits of my friends have been so numerous that my letter has been continually interrupted, I have had to write in great haste, and things are not arranged in order. It is not very interesting, but believe that I mean well. There is so much to write about Japan that one cannot finish. I am afraid that what I have written will bore you; it will take so long to read. I console myself with the thought that those who are bored by it can escape by ceasing to read it!"

Among the many visits the Provincial had to receive and pay was one to the Viceroy, Don Affonso de Noronha, who was now in Cochin. An envoy from the daimio of Bungo had accompanied Francis, and he was now received by Don Affonso, who accepted the presents of the daimio, including a suit of Japanese armour. The Viceroy also approved the idea of appointing Diogo Pereira ambassador to China, and promised the necessary letters.

After an absence of nearly three years Francis was naturally overwhelmed with news and business. He wrote to Micer Paul at Goa: "I hoped for some comfort here after all my labours, and I find nothing but new painful labours, law-suits, quarrels with the people, all kinds of disedifying things. Little or no obedience, so far as I can see since I have been here. God be praised in all things" (February 4, 1552).

Two of the men he had sent to the Moluccas had been dismissed and sent back by Father Beira. A house at Cochin had been lent by the Brothers of the Misericord for a college. Gomez had taken the loan for a gift and begun building on an immense scale—result, disgust of the inhabitants and dispute with the Brotherhood. The very day after his arrival Francis, keys of the building in hand, declared that the aim of the Company was work for the salvation of souls, not the stirring up of strife, and renounced possession. The Brothers acknowledged his generosity by granting a lease to the Jesuits; but, like most compromises, this was to lead to more trouble in the future.

Father Anriquez, who was at Cochin, had nothing but

good to report of the Cape Comorin mission, where the Christians numbered forty thousand. He himself was able to preach and hear confessions in Tamil, and the fathers under him had resolved to speak only Tamil among themselves, so as to be able to rival his progress.

Lancilotti, who was also there, was able to tell Francis what had been happening at Goa and to prepare him for the state of things he would find there. The compromise which had been effected by Francis before his departure for Japan had resulted in Gomez's annexing all the authority, not only over the college, as was his right, but over the missionaries too. Micer Paul had been too gentle to assert himself, and Gomez, not content with his work at Goa, had accompanied the Viceroy, Jorge Cabral, to southern India, mixed himself up with the Rajah of Tanor in Ceylon, who for some time had been dallying with a pretence of conversion, changed rules and arrangements in the Comorin district, as well as dismissing the native students from the college at Goa.

When the appointment of Francis as Provincial had reached Goa, a delicate question had arisen. In his absence, was Gomez, as rector of the college, or Micer Paul, as superior of the Jesuit fathers, to act as vice-Provincial? The answer to the question was foreseen by all at Goa, and Lancilotti had written discreetly but frankly to Ignatius: "Antonio Gomez is a good man and a good enough preacher, but is judged by all to be absolutely incapable of governing. He will write you ardent and eloquent letters, but you have the spirit of God and will know how to read between the lines." Ignatius had responded by the appointment of a new rector, Melchior Nunez, who had arrived at Goa in the autumn of 1551. For some reason the letter of the General announcing his appointment was not forthcoming—only one from Simon Rodriguez. Gomez had then declared that, the Indies being now a province, Rodriguez no longer had authority there; and he had refused to resign. The difficulty had been temporarily shelved owing to Gomez's absence with the Viceroy, and in February, 1552, all the fathers who could manage it were to meet at Goa to elect a new rector.

Francis, hearing of all these complications, saw that his arrival now was specially providential, and left without delay for Goa, which was reached in the middle of February, 1552.

For the last time Francis approached Goa by sea. It was ten years since he had first seen its towers and walls, the cathedral and the viceregal palace rising from among the palms. Every time he had returned to it since, after absence on the Fishery Coast, Travancore, Malacca, or the Moluccas, it had been to meet trouble—often, as we have seen, to make it. Avarice, intrigue and vice marred the beauty of the city as the corruption of death mars the nobility of a face.

At the moment, however, Goa was suffering from an acute attack of religious fever. Ignatius had obtained from Pope Julius III an authorisation for the members of his order to distribute to the faithful the privileges and indulgences of the Roman Jubilee of 1550. Melchior Nunez had brought with him these privileges, never before obtainable in distant countries. On his arrival in the autumn of 1551 the Jubilee had been proclaimed, by him in the cathedral, in the college by Gaspar Barzee, who had returned from Ormuz in answer to Francis's letter summoning him to Japan. People crowded in from all the Portuguese forts in India. Every Friday evening in the college church was to be seen the edifying sight of cohorts of men flogging themselves before a great crucifix to the chant, "Christ became obedient for us unto death, even unto the death of the Cross."

The results of this revival of fervour were still felt when Francis landed and, according to his usual custom, went to pay his respects to the bishop before going to the college. At the gates of the Santa Fé were assembled about fifty fathers, brothers, and novices whose impatience Micer Paul found difficult to restrain. For most of them it was to be their first sight of the great missionary whose letters they had heard read and discussed, whose name was famous wherever there was a house or college of the Company. He must have seemed a legend rather than a man. Now at last they were to see him in the flesh. With the two Japanese samurai, with Bernard and Matthew, he arrived, looking as Texeira described him, the tall, thin figure, the "face gay and charming." With tenderness he embraced all—old friends like Micer Paul and Father Gaspar, all those others who had come since he had left Goa in Holy Week, 1549. There was only one absent from the welcoming group, Antonio Gomez.

Before he even ate or rested Francis went straight to the infirmary. A young brother lay on his deathbed, all hope given up by doctors and infirmarians. With dogged faith he had gone on whispering that if he were still alive when the Father came he would recover. Francis prayed over him, cheered him, and in a few days the young man was perfectly well again.

To the younger men who saw the Provincial for the first time it was like "a sound from heaven, as of a mighty wind coming, and it filled all the house where they were sitting." His presence filled hearts with fire as on the day of Pentecost the Holy Spirit had manifested Himself by tongues of flame. Among the younger newcomers were Texeira, to be one of the saint's earliest biographers, and Luis Frois, who over fifty years later was to find his memory still alive at Kagoshima. "Impossible to tell you what joy the arrival of the Father caused among ours and also among the people," Luis wrote home. "We desired it so deeply. We had such great need of him. Since he had been in the College great things are done for the glory of God and the honour of the Company." He ends lyrically by the passage: "The winter is over and past."

Melchior Nunez, too, waxed eloquent on paper: "You, my brothers, imagine what it is to see on earth the coming and going of a man whose conversation is already in heaven! . . . Oh, how this heart is consumed by the love of God! With what fire of love for his fellowmen does he burn! What zeal to succour dead and sickly souls! . . . What charm! Always laughing, his face cheerful and serene. He laughs always, yet never laughs—for his cheerfulness is all spiritual. The love and joy of his spirit shine in his face. So John the Baptist leapt in his mother's womb. But no, he does not laugh, for he is always recollected and not distracted." The good father's attempts to analyse that indefinable radiance and charm are somewhat involved, but none the less enthusiastic.

Father Quadros adds some corroborative details about the Saint's spiritual life: "I have reliable information about the union with God which this good servant retained in the midst of his unceasing labours, and I am truly amazed. When he was in Japan he was so much absorbed in prayer as he went that his shoes broke and he did not notice it. His legs knocked against pieces of wood and other obstacles, he was wounded and felt nothing. One of our brothers saw him walking in the garden one day, lost in

God. Suddenly he stopped, as if afraid of being seen, lifted his eyes to heaven, his hand to his breast, saying: 'Enough, Lord, enough!' I have heard from those who shared his room that he did not sleep more than three or four hours during the night; and during this short sleep they heard him murmur: 'O dear Jesus! O my Creator!' and other such words. . . . His recollection was not interrupted by conversations with men, even by the most familiar talks. Those who talked with him were so struck by his union with God that, for fear of disrespect, they dared not keep their eyes on him for long."

The divine light, indeed, was so brightly reflected on his face, as it had been on that of Moses when he came down from Mount Sinai, that it was sometimes too dazzling for mortal eyes. His brethren often feared to intrude on this union with God, which so marvellously remained unbroken through all the business and cares of these two months at Goa. Long ago in Italy he had dreamed of future toil and suffering and had been heard, in his sleep, to pray for more: *"Mas, Senor, mas!"* Now as he walked with God in the garden he was so overwhelmed with spiritual joy that mortal frame could bear no more, and he was forced to cry: *"Não mais, Senhor, não mais!"*

But for its churches Goa is now a city of ruins. Palm-trees grow in the market-place that Francis so often crossed on his begging expeditions. A mile from the centre of the town, along a palm-fringed road by the seashore a single wall, pierced by a pointed door, stands in a thicket, all that is left of the college of Santa Fé. Beyond it, through a waste of undergrowth, is the little hermitage chapel with white walls and tiled roof, which became for pilgrims the sanctuary of the *Não Mais,* the No More.

Beside it, on the left, is a deep, square well, cut out of the rock, with steps going down to it. There the saint used to kneel with his loba open at the breast as he vainly tried to cool the burning of his heart in the clear, cold water.

Francis's life—it cannot be repeated too often—was a continual prayer, a union with God unbroken by exterior occupations, troubles, or dangers. This—not his amazing energy, his miracles, his innumerable conversions, his overwhelming work and unending travels—is his true sanctity. This holiness, this love so shone in his face, flamed in his heart, that those who were with him caught something of its purity and fire, if it were only for a time. His brethren, his penitents, old and young, rich and poor, Portuguese, Paravas, Malays, Hindus, Japanese, all were touched by this radiance. Impossible and unnecessary to repeat and multiply quotations from those who gave evidence in the Processes of 1556 and 1616.

There is one testimony (1556) which is worth touching on, that of Catherine de Chaves, who was one of his penitents at Goa, and is the only woman, except Doña Isabella Casalino and her friend at Bologna, whose name occurs in his life. In her testimony she spoke of the wonderful spiritual help received from him in the confessional and the aura of holiness that surrounded him. His answer, when she once mentioned this to him, was brief, but no doubt the smile that accompanied them softened the dryness of the words: "Give thanks to God, my daughter, that your sins have been forgiven." It was to her, as he bade her farewell before he started for China that he spoke the prophetic words: "We shall not see each other again" —then added, to console her as she wept: "Come, be comforted. You shall see me again before you die." She saw him again when, in March, 1554, his corrupt body made its triumphal entry into Goa to be placed in the gorgeous silver shrine in which it now rests.

It is worthy of note that, except for his mother, there is no feminine influence in his life. He had no friendships with holy women or benefactresses such as are found in the lives of so many saints. Perhaps that incident in Rome, when his name had been associated with the scandal caused by one of his penitents, had given him a horror of intimacies fraught with danger. The old vicar of Meliapor has related for us those confidences about the almost miraculous preservation of the saint's chastity through the dangers of student days, and this purity remained untarnished to the end; even in this life it earned him the reward promised in the Beatitudes to the pure in heart.

Meantime at Goa, as always in Francis's life in the East, there was so much to do, so little time in which to do it. In April he would start for China, and an inner conviction assured him that he would not return. Barely two months remained to put all the affairs of the mission in order, and, most important of all, to settle the question of the rectorship, this time irrevocably.

In two cases had Francis been induced to reverse a decision. João Fernandez's entreaties to be left as a brother-coadjutor, instead of being ordained priest, had been granted, and God had abundantly blessed the change. But when Francis had allowed himself to be persuaded to leave Gomez as rector instead of insisting on his own appointment of Gaspar Barzee, this had been the cause of endless trouble and discontent. Only the prompt action of de Noronha on his arrival as viceroy had saved the college of Sante Fé from total extinction, for Gomez's plan of replacing natives by Portuguese had ended in only one student's being left in the college. It was now reinstated on the lines of the original foundation, as a training-school for native students for the priesthood. A few years after Francis's death the site became so malarial that the college was moved inland to Rachol, where it now stands. As the great seminary of Goa it is one of the few of Francis's works which are still flourishing to-day.

The Provincial had come back to a difficult task. Gomez, the popular preacher and social success, had powerful friends at Goa, among them the bishop, weaker and less wise as he grew older, and asking only for peace. But Francis had never flinched before difficulties. This time there was to be no going back. The axe was laid to the root of the tree. Gomez had been the only Jesuit in Goa to remain aloof from the welcome accorded to the Provincial. His was the sin of the angels, the spiritual fault which Francis, like Ignatius and the founder of every other religious order, held most dangerous—the disobedience which springs from pride. Francis's continual—and, no doubt Gomez thought, tiresome—reiteration of the words "humility, obedience, charity," had had no effect. The time of grace was over. Gomez was ordered to leave Goa and take charge of the mission in the little fort of Diu, at the entrance to the Gulf of Cambay, north of Bombay. The blow, though not unexpected, was worse than anything he had foreseen. He rushed round to the bishop, to Cosme Anes, to all his influential friends. Francis had gained his experience in the only way it can be gained, by past mistakes. He stood firm.

Gomez departed to Diu, and when Francis sailed for China he left with Barzee, as vice-Provincial, a sealed packet containing Gomez's dismissal from the Society. Antonio Gomez had failed, as Mansilhas had failed, in the first essential of the religious life. There was no place for them in the Company of Jesus. Rome appears to have known little of these intricacies. Gomez was said to have written to the General and to have been ordered by him to return to Rome with an explanation. The ship on which he sailed was lost, but the evil he had done did not perish with him.

The old rector had gone to Diu. The Provincial turned his attention to the one who had been sent out to replace him. "What are your qualifications for the post of rector?" he asked Melchoir Nunez. "Three years' study of philosophy and six years of theology," replied the doctor of Coimbra university. Francis fixed him with that sad look which penetrated to the depths of heart and soul, as it pierced the veil of the future. "Would to God you had studied theology for only three years," was his unexpected answer, "and had spent the other six in gaining experience." Barzee was appointed rector, while Nunez cheerfully accepted the order to work at Bassein. He was to be the first, since John of Montecorvino and Friar Arnold in the Middle Ages, to preach the Catholic Faith on Chinese soil, at Canton, three years later.

The superiors of the missions were all now appointed. Gonsalvez Rodriguez had succeeded Barzee at Ormuz; Gomez was at Diu, Nunez at Bassein, Eredia at Cochin, Anriquez at Comorin, Lancilotti at Coulam, Cypriano at Meliapor, Perez at Malacca, Beira in the Moluccas, Cosme de Torres at Yamaguchi.

Only two brothers could be spared for Japan. With them returned the ambassador from Bungo, who seems to have made singularly little stir at Goa, and the two samurai who had accompanied Francis to Bungo and who, he had hoped, would have embraced the religious life. The other two Japanese converts, Matthew and Bernard, were to go to Europe shortly, but Matthew died at Goa in April. Bernard left Cochin in charge of the brother to whom Francis was to confide his last budget to Europe. After a stay at Coimbra he went on to Rome, where he supplied the account of Francis's life and miracles incorporated by Ribadeneira in his "Life of St. Ignatius." He died at Lisbon in 1556 without having returned to the Indies or Japan.

The arrangements of the Provincial were practically complete. He had applied the pruning-knife as well as the axe. Not only many novices admitted by Gomez but also some sent out from Coimbra were dismissed. In his direction to Barzee he warns him most emphatically to accept no novice without careful inquiries and trial—better even to buy slaves to do servile work in the college than to admit subjects totally unfit for the religious life. He wrote letters of advice and instruction to Rodriguez at Ormuz ("preach morals, not literary subtleties"), to Nunez at Bassein (the old command: "make yourself loved by all"), to Cypriano at Meliapor. The last is a long and severe rebuke to that fiery old warrior for excess of zeal and quarrels with the old vicar, but in his own hand a postscript is added in Spanish, their common language: "If you knew with what love I write you these things you would remember me day and night. Perhaps even you would weep at the thought of my great love for you. If the hearts of men could be seen in this life, I believe, my brother Cypriano, that you would clearly see yourself in my soul. All yours without ever being able to forget you."

It is the ending of that letter of Ignatius which had so overjoyed Francis at Malacca and which was indelibly engraved on his heart, as those other words of Ignatius were, which sound again and again in Francis's speech and writings: "What shall it profit a man?"

The official appointment of Gaspar Barzee is dated April 6, 1552, and declares him superior "of all the Portuguese fathers and brothers of the Company of the Name of Jesus from the Cape of Good Hope to here, as well as of those who may be at Malacca, at the Moluccas, Japan, and all other regions."

Less than ten years ago, when Francis had landed at Goa, he was the only Jesuit in the East. Now, as the result of his labours he saw those of his brethren who had followed him stationed from Mozambique to Yamaguchi. His work was done. There remained only the crown— not of martyrdom, as he had hoped, but betrayal, insults, desertion, and a lonely death. "God be praised in all things."

The brother who was taking charge of Bernard was to carry letters to Europe, and Francis made up his last budget of four letters—two to Simon Rodriguez (April 7 and 8), one to Ignatius (April 9), and one to the King (April 15).

The letters to Simon recommend the bearer, tell him of the dismissal of some of those sent from Coimbra, repeat the hardships and occasions of sin to be encountered in Japan, suggest that Germans and Flemish would be the best able to stand the climate, and beg for news from Coimbra and Rome, whither Ignatius had summoned the original companions to discuss the draft of the Constitutions. "I have such a longing to see you, my brother, Master Simon, before ending this life that I never cease thinking how I can realise my desires. If the way to China is opened I feel that they will be realised."

The letter to the King, written "at the moment of leaving for China," reports the embassy of Diogo Pereira proposed for Pekin, and his own determination "to reprove this unknown and powerful king, and to tell him the truth —a very dangerous thing to do in our day, even among Christian kings and princes! How much more so then among the heathen." He had not feared to speak the truth very bluntly to John; but this, his last extant letter to him, closes with the hope that God will repay his good services "by eternal glory in the next life; and may He reunite us all there in His mercy. Amen."

In the letter to Ignatius, the last that he was to write to his "Father in the bowels of Christ," Francis announces his departure for China in six days. "This empire, situated opposite Japan, is very considerably larger, and possesses a great number of eminent and deeply learned men. As far as I have been able to find out, education and study are held in great honour there, and the most learned men hold the highest posts and have the greatest authority." There is a hint here of the means by which the Jesuits were to find favour at Pekin in the seventeenth century, building and fitting an observatory, and designing the plans for the Summer Palace.

After again repeating the qualities necessary for missionaries in the east and especially in Japan, and pressing for the despatch from Rome of a superior with experience and authority, he asks the General to commission his secretary to write and "give me news of all the Fathers who came from Paris to Rome with you [his own nine companions on that snowy journey from Paris to Venice] of all the other fathers, to let me know the progress of the Company, the number of colleges and houses, that of the professed fathers, persons of note admitted to the Company, those famous for knowledge and learning by whom its ranks are enriched. Let him give all information in great detail. The great consolation of such a letter will alleviate for us the great labours we endure on land and sea, in Japan and China. May God reunite us in the joy of the saints and even in this life, if it be for His glory. If this meeting is ordained for me, the virtue of obedience will smooth away all obstacles. Everyone agrees in telling me that one can easily travel on land from the empire of China to Jerusalem. If I find that this is so I will let you know the number of leagues between the two and how many months the journey will take. His memory has gone back to those happy days at Venice when the eyes and desires of the companions were turned to the Holy City. His fancy takes flight across half the world to the longed-for reunion which, in his inmost heart, he knows can take place only in that heavenly Salem where "death shall be no more, nor mourning nor crying nor any sorrow." So the last letter to Ignatius ends: "The least of your sons and the farthest exiled from your presence, Francisco de Xavier."

CHAPTER XXII

GOA, MALACCA, SANCHIAN
(APRIL 12, 1552–DECEMBER 3, 1552)

THE Vespers of the Tuesday in Holy Week were being chanted in the church of the college of Sante Fé. It was forty-six years since Francis Xavier had been born to the same chant from the church of Santa Maria de Javier. In two days he would be on board the royal ship commissioned by the Viceroy to take him to Malacca on the way to China.

For these last few days he had dispensed with the usual spiritual reading in refectory, and had questioned each of his brethren in turn about his youth, his vocation, his spiritual life and difficulties. Texeira, one of the youngest novices and a favourite of Francis's, was told to give the story of his short life. When he had done Francis turned to the others at table: "Did you hear how well my son Texeira spoke?"—precious words, which the boy of sixteen was to cherish all his life.

"For the love of God I implore you again and again, as often as I can, to practise humility," Francis had said to Gaspar Barzee; and not content with preaching it, he practised it himself by asking one of the other young novices to tell him of his faults. "They say, Father," was the naively blunt answer, "that you are a saint, but that you say Mass too fast." It was true that Francis hurried through the earlier part of the Mass in his eagerness to reach the Prayer of Consecration. That he did not hurry after that his servers could testify, for continually they found it necessary to try and rouse him from ecstasy by pulling at his chasuble, and often in vain.

The first four evenings of Holy Week he preached to his fellow Jesuits, sermons burning with that love, loyalty, and humility which for him were summarised in the four words: *"Societas Jesu, societas amoris."* There was no doubt in the minds of his hearers that they should see his living face, hear his voice, no more. "Act so that we may meet again in Paradise. Here all is finished." "I shall return no more to Goa alive, but my body will return." And, in answer to Cosme Anes's question when they should meet again: "In the Valley of Josaphat."

The ship was ready, laden with the presents for the Emperor of China and with the furnishings for a pontifical chapel brought by Barzee from Ormuz—brocades, velvets, silks and tapestry. Francis was taking with him to China Father Gago, Brother Alvaro Fereira, his Malabar servant Christopher, and Antonio, a young Chinese servant who had been at the college for eight years and was to act as interpreter.

"At the end of his last sermon he embraced each one of us with tears. . . . The evening of Holy Thursday, when the Body of our Lord had been ensepulchred with due solemnity, he left the chapel with his companions. You can well imagine, my dearest brothers, what we all felt at so sad a parting. Nevertheless consolation overcame sadness when we thought of the grandeur of the enterprise and the martyrdom which the Father was certain to encounter" (Luis Frois).

As at Lisbon, so at Goa it was the custom, when a ship

sailed, for friends to gather in church to pray for a good voyage and safe return. Only a few fathers accompanied the Provincial to the harbour. The rest remained in prayer before the Blessed Sacrament. For three days, however, the ship was delayed waiting for a favourable wind, a time spent by Francis in elaborating and repeating the instructions he had left with Barzee: "Remember that the glory of the Company consists not in making oneself famous in the eyes of the world but in pleasing God."

On Easter Day, April 17, 1552, the wind changed, the ship sailed. From Cochin a hurried letter went back to Barzee, asking for helpers to be sent to Father Anriquez, now single-handed since the death of a brother from Badagas' ill-treatment; asking also for money for Lancilotti, and giving final advice about finance. Between the Nicobar Islands and Sumatra there was the usual storm and danger of shipwreck but at the end of May the Straits of Malacca were entered in safety. As the city was approached the saint's face saddened: "My children, Malacca is in great distress." And: "Pray to God, for I fear that the captain will oppose our enterprise."

Plague was raging in Malacca. Thirty of the crew went down with it. Don Alvaro de Ataide, now "Captain General of the Sea" (chief admiral in the East Indies), was ill with fever, and Francis, knowing how essential was his favour for the success of the embassy, himself said Mass several times in the captain's house, and, when unable to go, sent Father Perez to the sick-bed.

As he had done at Mozambique, Francis worked tirelessly among the plague-stricken, carrying them himself to hospital, taking no risks against infection but going to and fro in his old loba and a wide straw hat to keep off the worst of the tropical sun. Soon hospital and Jesuit house overflowed; then Francis turned the hulls of dismantled ships on the shore into emergency hospitals.

About a week after the arrival from Goa a ship left for Japan. On her sailed the Bungo ambassador, the two samurai and Father Gago, whom Francis had designed as his own companion, but now, seeing the urgent need of Japan, sent to Yamaguchi to help Cosme de Torres and Fernandez. Diogo Pereira was away collecting pepper and other merchandise for the voyage to China. He heard at Singapore of the Father's arrival at Malacca with letters and presents from the Viceroy, so all promised success. But, as he was about to land from the Santa Cruz, a note from Francis was handed to him bidding him to be most careful not to breathe a word about the embassy to anyone. He had scarcely set foot on shore when Don Alvaro's men took possession of his ship with the curt explanation: "Requisition of war," and, to make it impossible for her to sail, they detached and took away the rudder. Don Alvaro then declared his determination at all costs to prevent Diogo from going as ambassador to China.

What had happened? Had the Captain General always meant to forbid the embassy? Was it anger that a mere merchant like Diogo should be appointed ambassador to the greatest empire in the East, appointed moreover without consulting him, the supreme authority west of Cape Comorin? The intrigues of the next weeks are impossible to disentangle, the motives still more so. It is certainly difficult to explain Alvaro's almost insane antipathy to Francis without the suggestion that he was the weapon used by the powers of evil in their last struggle with the saint. "You will see that the devil will prevent everything," the ill-omened words which had annoyed Diogo on the voyage from Sanchian, were now fulfilled. Pressure was brought to bear on Alvaro, by his brother and other friends of Francis's, but in vain. Don Pedro was so disgusted that, as a protest, he resigned the captaincy of the fort which he still held. His successor offered to use force to enable the Santa Cruz to sail. Alvaro's answer was to order out his troops.

Then Francis, who till now had remained in the background, asserted himself. No one but himself and the bishop of Goa knew of his appointment as Papal Nuncio to the East. The brief appointing him and signed by Paul III was in safe custody at Goa. Now that other means had failed he would use his legatine powers for the first time. He wrote a memorial stating the facts, and added that anyone who opposed a Papal Nuncio in the execution of his duty was *ipso facto* excommunicate. This memorial he sent by Perez to the vicar general, João Soarez, and he, armed with this and the viceregal letters sanctioning the embassy, went with Perez to the Captain.

Alvaro listened in silence to letters, memorial, and the vicar general's explanation that he would render himself excommunicate by preventing the departure of the Santa Cruz; then he leapt suddenly from his chair, spat on the ground, and grinding the spittle under his boot cried furiously: "That is how much I care for the king's orders!" He then poured a torrent of foul abuse on "this perverted hypocrite, this forger of papal letters," bawling so loud that every word was heard through the open windows in the street below.

The servants copied their master, the vulgar followed suit. Francis was mobbed and hustled whenever he showed himself in the streets. The crowd yelled filthy epithets after him. To every insult he made the unvarying answer: "God be praised!" Soon it was impossible for

him to go into the town. Diogo's friends who had put
money into the venture came to him in tears to say that
they were ruined. Only Diogo himself, with noble generosity, uttered no word of reproach, a silence which made
Francis reproach himself all the more bitterly.

Sometime late in June Alvaro relented enough to say
that the Santa Cruz might sail for China on condition that
Diogo remained in Malacca and that twenty-five of his
own men went on board. The embassy was finished.
There was no longer a chance of Francis's entering China
in its train. Into China, however, he was determined to
go, at whatever cost to himself, both to preach the Gospel
there and to rescue those miserable, tortured prisoners in
the dungeons of Canton. He would sail on the Santa Cruz
and accordingly Diogo made every arrangement for his
comfort. His men were ordered to consider the Father's
comfort in all ways, to supply him with all necessaries.
A cabin in the stern was prepared for him.

Francis's only consolation had been the nights spent in
the church of our Lady of the Mount, before the Blessed
Sacrament or the picture of our Lady. Now even this was
to be taken from him, for on June 25 he wrote to Diogo
that he was going on board the Santa Cruz in the harbour
to escape the tears and reproaches of those he had ruined.
"How much reason you have, Señor, to complain of me,
for I have ruined you and all your friends. . . . I beg
you, Señor, not to visit me lest you increase my unhappi-
ness, for my troubles would increase still more at the
thought that it is I who have ruined you. . . . I can do
nothing for you except to write to the king that it is I
who have so deeply wronged you, by begging you to go
to China as ambassador from the Viceroy in order to
render service to our Lord and to the king. If my inten-

tion did not excuse me I should die of grief, as I have told you. . . . Your sad and desolate friend, Francisco."

There was a delay in the departure of the Santa Cruz, and, as Francis was hiding his broken heart on board, a ship from the Moluccas came into the harbour with de Souza, the Captain of the Moluccas, and Father Beira, whom Francis had not seen since he had sent him out five years before. The meeting with him was the one gleam of brightness during these dark weeks. Beira had many tales of his own adventures to relate and good news from Ternate, for at last the power of Islam had been broken by the defeat of the persecuting sultans, and lapsed converts had returned to their duties in large numbers.

The two missionaries had but a short time together. Beira was on his way to India for more recruits, and the Santa Cruz was at last to sail. Francis landed for his farewell interviews. To Diogo Pereira he promised that, in spite of the present financial disaster, neither he nor his children should ever want. From Don Pedro he accepted three hundred *cruzadoes* owing to some merchants for the building of the Church at Yamaguchi; but he insisted that it should be only a loan, and in his letter to Barzee from Singapore (July 21) ordered its prompt repayment. Last of all he visited the Jesuit house, where he found Perez ill with plague and anxious to die in his arms. Francis reassured him that he had yet many years of work before him.

There was one strange little incident during this last visit to the Jesuits. Francis suddenly threw himself face downwards on the bed where he had been sitting, and remained without speech or movement. The others, amazed, stared at him in silent wonder. Was he asleep? Praying? Ill? Presently he rose with a tragic look and the words: "May God forgive you, Father!" The listeners afterwards ascertained that Simon Rodriguez, summoned to Rome by Ignatius, contrary to obedience was opposing his successor and was nearly dismissed from the Society by the General as Gomez had been by the Provincial.

Francis was on his way to the ship when the vicar-general came hurrying after him with a request that he should pay a farewell visit to the Captain in order to avoid scandal. A ridiculous request indeed, but probably the vicar-general was thinking of his own comfort during the next three years if Alvaro suspected him of favouring his enemies. "Don Alvaro will see me no more in this life," was the stern answer. "I shall await him before the judgement-seat of God, where he will have to give an account of what he has just done."

Francis had already rendered good for evil by saying Mass for Don Alvaro every morning; now, before the church which overlooks the harbour, he stood with extended arms and prayed aloud for his persecutor. Perhaps, through those open windows which had let loose his curses, the captain heard that prayer. It found him deaf to grace. When the saint's body was brought back he, almost alone in the city, paid it no honour, but continued his game of cards. He was sent back to Portugal, condemned to life imprisonment for having disobeyed the Viceroy's orders. He died a leper, but was said to have made his peace with God at the eleventh hour.

When Francis had finished his prayer for Don Alvaro he fell on his knees and remained for a little in silence. Rising he took off his shoes and shook the dust of Malacca from off them; then, in the midst of dead silence, he embarked. It was his final farewell to Portuguese soil, on which he had suffered so deeply. The town which had persecuted and insulted him alive, was to receive his dead body with processions, banners, candles, and hosannahs (March 22, 1553).

From Singapore he despatched six letters (July 21 and 22), two to Diogo, two to Barzee, one to Beira, and a note to a Japanese convert. The first letter to Barzee begins: "You cannot imagine how I was persecuted at Malacca. I will not describe these persecutions in detail, for I have told Father Francis Perez to write you all." He asks the bishop to notify the Captain of the excommunication he has incurred, and to confirm the possession of the papal brief, "so that another time the fathers of the Company of the Name of Jesus who are going to Japan or China may not be prevented." "I am on the way to the islands of Canton, deprived of all human help, hoping that some Moslem or heathen may land me in China. The craft I had to take me there has been retained by force by Don Alvaro. Alvaro Fereira comes with me, as well as Antonio, the Chinaman who was at Cochin. Both are ill with fever. They give me more work and worry than I can describe. Please God our Lord to return them to health."

In the letter to Diogo he mentions the invalids again, the bothers and trouble they give him. It is as if he felt himself nearly at the end of his forces, but: "Praised be God, for all things and always." He encloses an open letter to the King, recommending Diogo to him, condemns the vicar-general for his time-serving, advises Diogo to "approach God so that He may console you in these sad times," and frequently to visit the Jesuit fathers (July 22, 1552).

This is the last letter from Singapore. By the end of August the Santa Cruz anchored at Sanchian.

In the bay of Sanchian, sheltered from the open sea by two high, rocky promontories, some Portuguese ships and junks of Chinese traders lay at anchor. It was a convenient neutral ground where the traders of the West and East exchanged spices, pepper, woven stuffs from Europe, and Indian carpets, for Chinese silk, lacquer, porcelain, and cloisonné work. A few temporary huts of wood thatched with straw on one slope housed the Portuguese during the summer, and were destroyed when they left before the winter. A handful of Chinese lived miserably in one corner of the island wringing a bare livelihood from selling the produce of the barren soil and a few chickens. One of the huts was assigned to the Father, and he was helped to erect a rough chapel of thatch in which to say Mass. He had reached the end of an Odyssey which had circled half the globe and, but for the Americas, had included almost the whole of the known world. Now, like Ulysses on the rocky island of Ithaca, when the mists parted he was to come home.

"Go and set all on fire," had been the farewell of Ignatius, and fire is the symbol that springs inevitably to tongue or pen that speaks or writes of Francis Xavier, as it had to those of his brethren. The fire that had spread along the coasts of southern India, that had lit beacons in the Moluccas and Japan and was now the gates of China, was a consuming fire. It had burnt in him since the Feast of the Assumption at Montmartre and the Spiritual Exercises eighteen years ago, had left no time for rest and peace these ten years in the East, except those four months at Meliapor. Now the frail body, wasted by it, lived only by power of will and hope, and, these withdrawn, like the Moluccan bird of fire, was to sink to earth in death.

He had not been perfect. There had been failings of

hot temper, of enthusiasm, of imagination. His methods had been criticised even by his friends, who perhaps felt the loss of his bodily presence too acutely to realise its necessity elsewhere. Ignatius himself, in a letter written six months after the Saint's death, sent the longed-for recall to Europe, but added words that, for all their quietness, contain a hint of reproof: "If you have remained in the Indies, my advice is that you would do more good by sending others to work in China than you would have done yourself. In this way you will extend your influence to a larger number of countries, whereas in your own person, you would only have exerted it in one." There speaks the great organiser who controlled his sons and their work throughout the world from the house in Rome —like a spider motionless in the centre of its web, thought his enemies. But the General had no practical experience of mission work in the East. Perhaps, too, he underestimated the force of personality, that gift so irresistible and so dangerous, which Francis possessed in a supreme degree. It was his strength, but his weakness too, said his critics; so much depended on his presence, so much was apt to go wrong in his absence. Ignatius and Francis, founder of the Society of Jesus and its greatest son, were alike in nationality and nobility of birth, in entire renunciation of self, in their friendship; but in much else they were as the poles apart. Thank God, the saints are not all cast in one mould and "one star differeth from another star in glory."

Even on the desolate little island of Sanchian the Santo Padre found work. Mass said in the rude hut, he heard confessions, gave instructions and catechised. As he strolled along the shore with his breviary, his Office would be interrupted by one of the Portuguese merchants whom he had known before—Velho, who had been at Bungo last year, Jorge Alvarez, who had introduced Angero to him, and others. There were fifty or sixty negro and Arab slaves. He preached to them and baptised some of them. Velho relates one instance typical of him. One day to his horror Francis found a girl among this rabble, and repeated his Goan method: she must be married to her lover at once. A dowry was necessary, so off he went to Velho. He, half amused, half annoyed at being interrupted in the middle of a game of chess, handed over the key of his chest, telling the Father to take what money he needed. To his surprise when he got back to his hut he found his money intact. "What did you take, Father?" "Three hundred *cruzadoes*." "But nothing is missing, and I gave you the key so that you might help yourself to as much as you wanted." "I promise you, Velho, in the Name of God, you shall never want for anything in this world." The bride had a handsome dowry. The merchant was none the poorer for his generosity. He himself tells the story.

Francis mixed too with the Chinamen who landed to barter and bargain and had learnt a little Portuguese. He began by discussions on natural science and philosophy, Taoism, "the rule of right conduct," and Confucianism, an ethical system whose highest practice is the glorification of family and state. The few words they had in common must have limited such discussions in narrow bounds. He may have learnt a little more about that vast empire, four thousand years old, with its sixty million people, its ancient civilisation, its art and literature, now at their zenith under Shih Tsung, ninth emperor of the Ming dynasty. In 1521, the year before Shih Tsung had succeeded his grandfather, a Portuguese, Tomé Pirez, had

actually reached Pekin with letters from the King of
Portugal. He had not succeeded in entering it, and had
died in Canton, where the rest of his companions and the
crew of the ship had been starved or tortured to death in
the prisons. The Portuguese there now were suffering
worse than death. One of them, Manoel de Chaves, had
managed to escape with the help of a Cantonese merchant,
and was now on Sanchian, waiting to return to Malacca as
soon as a vessel sailed. From him Francis could learn
further details of the horrors awaiting any foreign devil
caught trying to enter the forbidden land. The Portuguese begged the Padre to put out of his head such a
mad idea as that of attempting to land. They felt too
that unpleasant consequences might recoil on themselves
from his inevitable capture.

The weeks passed. The Portuguese began to prepare
for departure. For a fortnight Francis had been ill with
fever and shivering fits, but he had managed to say Mass
most mornings. He was better now, and wrote letters to
go on the first ship to leave—two to Father Perez at
Malacca (one a duplicate), one to Diogo Pereira, and one
to Gaspar Barzee.

He orders Perez under obedience to leave Malacca,
where no good work can be done under Alvaro da Gama,
tells of his talks with the Chinese merchants and the hope
that one may land him at Canton. He mentions some of
the "many and great dangers" of the enterprise and the
possibility of loss of trust in God, "a danger much greater
than any evil that all God's enemies can raise against us,
for without God's leave and permission the devils and
those who serve them can in no way hurt us. Also to
encourage us there is the saying of our Lord: 'He who
loves his life in this world shall lose it, and he who loses

it for God shall find it.' Which agrees with those other words of Christ our Lord: 'He who puts his hand to the plough and looks back is not worthy of the kingdom of God.' When we consider such spiritual dangers, so much worse than bodily ones, it seems to us safer and surer to endure bodily dangers than to be conquered before God by spiritual dangers. So, no matter how, I am determined to land in China" (October 22, 1552).

Between the lines of this letter one seems to catch a glimpse of the shadow which had fallen on him in the Moluccas and had grown so deep on the voyage to Japan. "One must prevent oneself from showing the slightest fear," he had written then, and had added about the approach of death: "In that hour temptations will increase, there will be troubles and dangers of body and soul such as we have not felt." The knight-errant of Christ had one last battle still to fight before he could lay aside his armour and let his wounds be healed.

In his letter to Diogo of the same date he says: "Every day I am expecting a merchant to take me to Canton. We have already agreed that he shall take me there for twenty *picos*" (a Chinese weight). "If it chances, which God forbid, that this merchant does not come to fetch me and I do not get into China this year, I do not know what I shall do, if I shall go to India, or to Siam to accompany the embassy of the King of Siam next year. If I return to India I leave without any hope that during the time of Don Alvaro da Gama anything worthy to be remembered will be done in China."

The letter to Barzee (October 25) merely repeats parting instructions and spiritual advice and makes arrangements about missionaries. There is a postscript: "This letter was written in such haste that I do not know how it goes. Before I leave for China I will write at greater length by another channel."

October ended, the month when in Italy was born Matthew Ricci, the Jesuit who was to enter Pekin under the last of the Ming emperors, the first to preach Christianity there for over three centuries. Francis had had to postpone the coming of his merchant. The "chief captain" (of the largest ship, perhaps) had begged him not to make the attempt till all the Portuguese ships had sailed, in case the mandarins were so enraged at finding him on shore that they would order an attack on the Portuguese ships. The frank self-interest of the captain was understandable. His calm, cold-blooded acceptance of the Father's martyrdom reflects little credit on him.

From the Portuguese standpoint it was indeed the act of a madman. Brother Fereira, who had been almost continually ill, did not show the spiritual qualities to fit him for the Society, so Francis was sending him back by the next ship, with a suggestion in his letter to Barzee that Fereira might make a good friar. Antonio, on whom Francis had been relying as an interpreter, found that, during his eight years at Goa he had so far forgotten his native language, or at any rate the variety spoken at Canton, that he was useless in this way. To him, however, we owe the only authentic account of Francis's last days, which he related two years after the Father's death to Texeira and repeated later to Father Valignano. Another interpreter who had volunteered had then refused to face the practical certainty of capture. Yet Francis proposed to go alone with the two servants, Antonio and Christopher—none of them speaking Chinese—to be deposited at the gates of Canton with his few books and belongings and so abandoned by the merchant who was to put him ashore. "From there," he had written, "I shall go straight to the Governor's house and tell him that we have come to present ourselves to the King of China, to show him the letter we have brought from the Lord Bishop and tell him that we are sent by His Highness to preach the law of God."

Madness indeed, but divine madness. No doubt the ship-owners heaved a deep sigh of relief when the captain told them he had achieved the postponement of the lunatic venture till after they had gone. They were Portuguese traders, out for the riches they could make by barter. They could hardly be expected to understand the mind of a Basque nobleman, still less that of a saint. They had in their veins none of that wild restless spirit which had always made Basques pioneers, pirates, explorers, missionaries. Less than a generation ago Elcano, the Basque admiral, had been the first to sail round the world. It was three Azpilcuetas, cousins of Francis's, who were to found the missions in Brazil and Mongolia and to organise that in Mexico. From the days of those vivid dreams in Italy, perhaps before, Francis had always felt it his own vocation to carry the Gospel into unknown lands, to blaze the trail for others to follow and open up. Like those of his sea-faring people his eyes had been always on the far horizon, his desires beyond it. Over the bay of Sanchian, soon to be empty but for the Santa Cruz, over the steep promontories, the sweep of the Canton river, the vision of his mind went out, over plains whose vast stretches were broken by pagodas rising like rocks from the sea, through the blurring veil of grey rain it reached to the imperial city, more than a thousand miles away in its great walls that stood square to the four quarters of heaven.

On November 12 Francis wrote four letters, two to

Perez and two to Diogo, for despatch by the last ship on which Pereira was going. He tells Perez that he is expecting the Chinaman to fetch him and the two servants in eight days' time. "We run great risk of being captured. We are comforted by the thought that it is better to be a prisoner for the love of God than to be free because one has fled from the sufferings of Christ."

The letters to Diogo are full of praise and affection; if the Gospel is preached in China it will be thanks to him. "If I get into China I fancy you will probably find me in one of two places—a prisoner in the dungeons of Canton or at the royal palace in Pekin."

The next day he writes to Gaspar Barzee, the last of those wonderful letters which for twelve years have poured from his pen. This is an emphatic direction for the publication of the papal brief announcing his appointment as Nuncio to the East, and for the proclamation of Don Alvaro's excommunication, so that it should no longer be in his power to prevent missionaries from travelling to new countries. "Be certain of one thing and do not doubt it, that it is excessively displeasing to the devil that members of the Company of the Name of Jesus should penetrate into China. . . . I should never finish if I were to write you the obstacles which have been opposed to me and are daily opposed. But be sure also of something else: that with the help, favour and grace of God our Lord I shall confound the devil on this issue; and it will be greatly to the glory of God to confound such great pride as the devil's with so vile a thing as I am. . . . Be not negligent in the execution of my orders because you believe me already dead, as others have. If it please God I shall not die, though the time is long past when I had more desire to live than I have now."

The ship left with the letters. The Chinese junks were gone. In the deserted hut of Alvarez Francis waited for the Chinaman from Canton. It was bitterly cold. Provisions were scarce. Often Antonio had to go to the cluster of huts belonging to the crew of the Santa Cruz and beg a crust of bread for his master. Francis waited as the days passed. Every morning he said Mass. Soon even that consolation would be taken from him. He dared not take the sacred vessels with him. They were to go back on the Santa Cruz to Diogo, who had charge too of the rich vestments in which Yoshitaka had thought Francis "looked like a god."

November 19, the day appointed for the arrival of the Cantonese merchant, came and went. There was no sign of him, nor on the following three days. It was evident that he would not come. The devil had blocked that channel too. Then suddenly the worn-out body, which had been kept going only by that indomitable spirit and hope, gave way. On Monday, November 21, as he finished saying Mass, Francis began to feel ill, and the evening of the next day he was persuaded by Antonio to go on board the Santa Cruz. She was at anchor, rolling violently in a strong north wind. Francis found it impossible to remain on board. He was presented with a pair of warm stockings and a handful of almonds (strange food for a desperately sick man) and put ashore. He was found lying on the shore, "burning like a live coal" with fever, and was taken across the bay to another hut. He was bled, fainted; the next day the same thing happened, and all the while the fever grew worse, till he became delirious (Thursday and Friday).

"His eyes on heaven, his face beautiful to look at and full of joy, he spoke with a clear voice as if he were preaching, in different languages which he understood and I did not." After eight years at Goa Antonio knew Portuguese, probably a little Castilian and certainly some Latin, so the language he did not understand was surely Basque —"my own language," as Francis had called it, the tongue in which he had learnt his prayers from his mother.

On this Friday evening, as on other Fridays this year, the face of the miraculous Christ in the chapel of San Miguel at Javier was wet with a bloody sweat, as if, in the agony of His devoted servant, the Master's own Agony were renewed.

"He was absolutely stripped of all human help, lying in a hut open to the cold and the wind without any comfort but that which came from God. . . . That lasted three days, during which he knew no one and ate nothing."

On Thursday, December 1, consciousness and speech returned, and Antonio heard him murmur prayers and ejaculations continually: "Most Holy Trinity, Father, Son and Holy Ghost! Jesus, Son of David have mercy on me! Virgin Mother of God, remember me!"

On Friday he looked at the Malabar with a gaze of sadness and pity. *"Ay, triste de ti!"* (Alas, I grieve for you) he repeated. A few months later the young man was killed while living in sin.

That evening Antonio, seeing the end approaching, placed a crucifix in the cold hand and, alone with the dying man, watched all night.

We do not know what visions are reflected in mind and heart when physical consciousness flies at the approach of death. It has been said that in this moment a man's life is before him as it will be at the particular judgment. Behind those dark eyes, fixed unseeing on the crucifix, behind those unhearing ears, how many scenes and faces must have flashed and faded: Japan, with the blossom rosy as the snow of Roncesvalles at dawn; the scented forests of the Moluccas, gay with the chatter of scarlet parrots and the jewelled beauty of butterflies; the Ghats, hugely black against the sunrise; white houses of Lisbon along the Tagus; the silent waterways of Venice; the surge and babble of the Paris streets; the still coldness as the Christmas stars shone on Javier. And bells, always bells; the tinkle of tiny ones on temple eaves, of the little one in his own hand as he called through the streets of Goa and Ternate; the church bells at Malacca, Goa, Rome, Paris, Pamplona; little bells on the feet of dancers; the silver of the sacring bell. And again and again, like the deep note of a passing-bell, the voice of Ignatius of Loyola: "What shall it profit a man, Master Francis, if he gain the whole world and suffer the loss of his own soul?"

The eastern sky was paling before dawn. There was no movement nor sound, only a little change in the still face. Antonio lit a candle and wedged it between the powerless fingers. The icy wind blew it out. The fluttering breath grew slower, then ceased.

EPILOGUE

"WHEN the blessed Father was dead," said Antonio: "his face remained so beautiful, of such a rose-red colour that he seemed alive, as I hope he is in the kingdom of heaven." The body was buried the same day, Saturday, December 3, 1552, by Antonio, two negro slaves and a stray Portuguese; it was too cold for the others to leave their huts. Two sacks of quicklime were poured round it, but two and a half months later, when the Santa Cruz was leaving it, it was found incorrupt, and so remained during the voyage to Malacca, where it was temporarily buried. It arrived at Goa March 15, 1554, the Friday in Passion Week, and was accorded a royal reception by the entire population from the Viceroy down. It still lies in the church of the Bom Jesus in an ornate reliquary of silver, and is exposed for veneration every ten years.

MAP

OF THE CHIEF PLACES MENTIONED
IN THIS BOOK

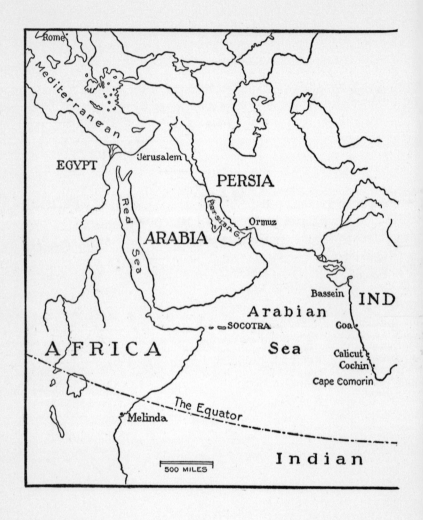

Rome

Mediterranean

EGYPT

Jerusalem

PERSIA

Red Sea

Persian G.

Ormuz

ARABIA

Bassein

IND

Arabian

SOCOTRA

Goa

AFRICA

Sea

Calicut

Cochin

Cape Comorin

The Equator

Melinda

Indian

500 MILES

ASIA

JAPAN

Tokio

Pekin.

Kioto.

Yamaguchi

Osaka

Inland Sea

HIRADO

Str. of Bungo

CHINA

Kagoshima

KIUSIU

TIBET

Pacific

Changchow

FORMOSA

Canton.

Ocean

Macao

SANCHIAN

Calcutta

TONKIN

IA

BURMA

Mckong R.

South China Sea

PHILIPPINES

Madras

ANDAMAN

Meliapor

ISLANDS

G. of

Negapatam

Siam

CEYLON

NICOBAR

ISLES OF THE

Kandy

ISLANDS

MOORS

TERNATE

HALMAHERA

NEW

Pekan

GUINEA

Malacca

BORNEO

SERAM

Singapore

CELEBES

Amboina

Mucassan

Ocean

Malay. Archipelago

JAVA

AUSTR

ALIA

SOME BOOKS CONSULTED

Monumenta Xaveriana (1900).

S. Francois Xavier, A. Brou, S.J. (2 volumes, 1922).

S. Francois Xavier, A. Bellesort (1920).

Lettres de S. Francois Xavier (translated by E. Thibaut, S.J., 4 volumes, 1922).

St. Francis Xavier, G. Schurhammer, S.J. (translated by F. Eble, 1928).

S. Francois Xavier, sa Vie et ses Lettres, P. L. Cros, S.J. (2 volumes, 1900).

S. Francois Xavier, son pays, sa famille et sa vie, P. L. Cros, S.J. (1891).

Vie de S. Francois Xavier, D. Bouhours, S.J. (translated by Dryden, 1682).

The Admirable Life of St. Francis Xavier, O. Torsellini, S.J. (translated by T. F., 1632).

Life of St. Francis Xavier, H. J. Coleridge, S.J. (2 volumes, 1872).

Life of St. Francis Xavier, M. T. Kelly (1918).

St. Francis Xavier, E. A. Stewart (1917).

"St. Francis Xavier," C. G. Martindale, S.J. (from *In God's Army,* 1915).

"The Failure of St. Francis Xavier," Archbishop Goodier, S.J. (from *Saints for Sinners,* 1930).

San Francisco Javier, Francisco Escalada, S.J. (1917).

Autobiographie de S. Ignace de Loyola (translated by E. Thibaut, S.J., 1924).

A Short Life of St. Ignatius Loyola, A. Astrain, S. J. (translated by R. Hull, S.J., 1928).

St. Ignatius, C. Hollis (1931).

Spiritual Exercises of St. Ignatius, J. Rickaby, S.J. (1923).

S. Ignace, Maître d'Oraison, A. Brou, S.J. (1925).

Historia de la Compana de Jesus en la Asistencia de Espana, A. Astrian, S.J. (2 volumes, 1902).

Storia della Compagna de Gesú in Italia, P. Tacchi Venturi, S.J. (1910).

History of the Popes, L. Ranke (1889).

History of Europe, Bede Jarrett, O.P. (1929).

History of France, W. Smith (1865).

Universities of Europe in the Middle Ages, H. Rashdall (2 volumes, 1895).

The Renaissance, Walter Pater (1910).

The Renaissance in Italy, J. A. Symonds (1897).

Spain, its greatness and decay, H. Hume (1895).

Queens of old Spain, H. Hume (1896).

An Hour of Spain, "Azorin" (1931).

The Moors in Spain, S. Lane-Poole (1895).

Turkey, S. Lane-Poole (1891).

The Saracens, A. Gilman (1891).

A Book of the Basques, R. Gallop (1931).

Historia del Crucifijo de San Francisco Javier, llamado el Crucufijo del Cangerjo, Francisco Escalada, S.J. (1917).

The Lusiads, Luiz da Camoens (translated by W. Mickle, 1877).

The Rise of Portuguese Power in India, R. S. Whiteway (1899).

India, Alberini (edited E. Sachau, 1910).

Further India, H. Clifford (1904).

The Malay Archipelago, A. R. Russell (1890).

The Soul of a People, H. Fielding (1899).

A Brief History of Eastern Asia, I. C. Hannah (1900).

A Prisoner in Japan, D. Donnelly, S.J. 1928).

The Cross in Japan, C. M. Cadell (1904).

Flowers and Gardens of Japan, E. and F. du Cane (1908).

Sayonara, "John Paris" (1924).

Banzai, "John Paris" (1925).

Memorials of the Empire of Japan in the XVI. and XVII. Centuries, edited by T. Rundall (1850).